NOBEL LECTURES IN PEACE

1981–1990

NOBEL LECTURES

Including Presentation Speeches
And Laureates' Biographies

PHYSICS

CHEMISTRY

PHYSIOLOGY OR MEDICINE

LITERATURE

PEACE

ECONOMIC SCIENCES

NOBEL LECTURES

INCLUDING PRESENTATION AND ACCEPTANCE SPEECHES AND LAUREATES' BIOGRAPHIES

PEACE

1981–1990

EDITOR-IN-CHARGE

TORE FRÄNGSMYR

Uppsala University, Sweden

EDITOR

IRWIN ABRAMS

Antioch University, USA

World Scientific
Singapore • New Jersey • London • Hong Kong

Published for the Nobel Foundation in 1997 by

World Scientific Publishing Co. Pte. Ltd.

P O Box 128, Farrer Road, Singapore 912805

USA office: Suite 1B, 1060 Main Street, River Edge, NJ 07661

UK office: 57 Shelton Street, Covent Garden, London WC2H 9HE

992223

NOBEL LECTURES IN PEACE (1981–1990)

ISBN 981-02-1180-5
ISBN 981-02-1181-3 (pbk)

Printed in Singapore by Uto-Print

FOREWORD

In their foreword to the series of Nobel prize lectures following the earlier series covering the period up to 1970, the chairman of the board of the Nobel Foundation, Lars Gyllensten, and the executive director, Stig Ramel, wrote that it was

> "with great satisfaction that the Nobel Foundation has given World Scientific Publishing Company the right to bring the series up to date beginning with the Prize lectures in Economics in 2 volumes 1969–1990. Thereafter the lectures in all the other prize fields will follow.
>
> The Nobel Foundation is very pleased that the intellectual and spiritual message to the world laid down in the laureates' lectures, thanks to the efforts of World Scientific, will reach new readers all over the world."

The Norwegian Nobel Committee has noted with pleasure that the turn has come to the Nobel Peace Prize lectures. It is to be hoped that the message conveyed in these lectures, eloquently expressed by the many outstanding laureates, will serve as an inspiration to all those, individuals and institutions, who in different ways and all over the globe are striving for the great cause of reconciliation, fraternity and peace.

Francis Sejersted
Chairman of the Norwegian Nobel Committee

INTRODUCTION

These volumes present for the first time a collection of the Nobel Peace Prize addresses and lectures from 1971 to 1990, authorised by the Nobel Foundation in Stockholm and edited with the assistance of the Norwegian Nobel Institute in Oslo.[1] This follows the authorised publication in 1971 of the volumes covering the years from the beginning in 1901 to 1970.[2]

The texts are based upon the Nobel Foundation's annual publication, *Les Prix Nobel*, which prints the speeches and other basic information concerning the Nobel prizes presented the previous 10 December. On this day, the anniversary of Alfred Nobel's death, the prizes in every category are presented each year, the Peace Prize in Oslo and all the others in Stockholm.

Each entry in these volumes is preceded by a brief explanatory introduction to the following texts, as printed in the original English or in English translation: the official announcement of the prize, generally released to the press in October; the presentation address by the chair or another member of the Committee; the acceptance speech by the laureate, usually, but not always, printed in *Les Prix Nobel*; and the Nobel lecture by the laureate. Also included are endnotes to the preceding documents, kept to a minimum; biographical and descriptive information about the laureates; and a selective bibliography.

The official announcements were not printed in *Les Prix Nobel* before 1993 and appear here for the first time in an authorised collection of Nobel documents. Since each announcement must be approved by the Norwegian Nobel Committee, it represents the only official document we have in presenting the Committee's reasons for the choice. The speech of presentation may refer to the Committee's rationale as well, but it does not have to be approved by the Committee in advance, and it may represent the particular interpretation or emphasis which this Committee representative wishes to give.

The biographical or descriptive information about each prize winner printed in *Les Prix Nobel* is generally submitted by the laureates themselves. There is no prescribed format, and the variety in print ranges from a brief listing to the valuable autobiographical statement by Andrei Sakharov. In these volumes this information has been reprinted as updated.

Finally, to make these volumes more useful, there is to be found for each entry a brief list of reading suggestions, generally restricted to publications in English. For fuller information about the Peace Prize, its origins and how it has been administered by the Norwegian Nobel Committee, and for extensive bibliographies, the reader is referred to the editor's authoritative reference work which is referred to below.[3]

In the years covered by these volumes, all but two of the prize ceremonies in Oslo took place in the festival hall of the university, the aula, whose walls are covered by the murals of Edvard Munch, which evoke the spirit of Norway. In 1978 the award ceremony for Prime Minister Menachem Begin of Israel was held at the Akershus castle-fortress for security reasons, while the 1990 award ceremony for President Mikhail Gorbachev of the Soviet Union was moved to Oslo's city hall before it was learned that he would send a Soviet diplomat to represent him. Gorbachev did give his Nobel lecture in the city hall in the following June, and the December ceremonies have been held there every year since then. Not only is the spacious hall able to accommodate a greater number of attenders, but security can be tighter and there are more facilities for press photographers and reporters in the balconies encircling the seating area.

The ceremony itself is simpler than in Stockholm and usually finishes in about ninety minutes. In the presence of the royal family, the cultural and political leaders of the country, the foreign diplomats and other invited guests, the chair or another representative of the Norwegian Nobel Committee makes the speech of presentation and then gives the tokens of the award, the Nobel gold medal and the diploma, to the prize winner. Appropriate musical selections are played by an orchestral ensemble. Some acceptance speeches have been very moving; others have been mostly brief expressions of thanks.

The laureate speaks more at length in the required Nobel Prize lecture. This is to take place within six months of the presentation, according to the statutes of the Nobel Foundation, but in these years, except on two occasions, the lectures were delivered a day or two after the award ceremony. In 1988 Secretary-General Pérez de Cuéllar accepted the award for the United Nations Peacekeeping Forces on December 10 but had to return a month later to give the address, while Gorbachev could come to give his lecture only in June 1991, some six months after the prize had been presented to his representative. Since 1992 the lectures have been delivered as part of the award ceremony.

The speech of presentation is always delivered in Norwegian, but it is printed in English translation in *Les Prix Nobel*. Formerly the translations were passed out to the audience, as was done for the laureate speeches in languages other than English. In the years 1971–1990 only the speeches by Willy Brandt and Pérez Esquivel were printed in *Les Prix Nobel* without English translation, and they have been especially translated for these volumes. At the award ceremonies today members of the audience can listen to translations on their headsets while the speeches are being delivered.

In the early evening of 10 December there is usually a torchlight procession honouring the laureate, which ends at the Grand Hotel, where the prize winners are lodged. Then the Norwegian Nobel Committee hosts a formal banquet there for the laureate, which is a high point of the Oslo winter social season. In earlier years the after-dinner speeches were printed in *Les Prix Nobel*.

In the years 1971–1990 there were 23 prizes awarded, 19 to individuals and four to institutions. Once, in 1972, there was no award, and the postponed 1976 award was announced and presented in 1977. A variety of peacemaking was represented. Prizes went to eight statesmen: Brandt (1971), Henry

Kissinger (1973), Eisaku Sato (1974), Begin and Anwar al-Sadat (1978), García Robles (1982), Arias Sánchez (1987) and Gorbachev (1990). One statesman, Le Duc Tho of North Vietnam, declined to accept the prize (1973).

There were eight human rights prizes: Seán Mac Bride (1974), Andrei Sakharov (1975), Amnesty International (1977), Pérez Esquivel (1980), Lech Wałesa (1983), Desmond Tutu (1984), Elie Wiesel (1986) and the Dalai Lama (1989). Four prizes for the organised peace movement went to Betty Williams and Mairead Corrigan (1976), Alva Myrdal (1982) and International Physicians for the Prevention of Nuclear War (IPPNW, 1985). Prizes for humanitarian work were granted to Mother Teresa (1979) and to the Office of the United Nations High Commissioner for Refugees (1981). This Office and the United Nations Peacekeeping Forces were the two prize winning institutions linked to that international organisation.

It must be admitted that these prize winners cannot all be made to fit so snugly into such categories. For example, Mac Bride was not only prominent in the cause of human rights, but a leader in the organised peace movement as president of the International Peace Bureau. Before Alva Myrdal made her contributions to that movement, she had participated in the disarmament effort both as a cabinet minister and Sweden's representative to United Nations discussions. The Dalai Lama of Tibet is a force for peace as a world religious leader with a powerful message of peace and compassion, but also as the defender of the human rights of his people.

Nineteen of the 23 laureates came to Oslo for the ceremonies, a higher percentage than in earlier periods, testifying to the growing prestige of the prize, but also to the greater facility of air travel. Of the four absentees, political reasons kept Kissinger and Sadat away, while Sakharov was prevented from coming by the Soviet government, and Wałesa feared that if he left Poland, his government would not allow him to return. Sadat, Sakharov and Wałesa, however, sent their lectures to be read for them. In our first volume, covering the years 1971–1980, ten lectures are to be found, while in the second, including the years 1981–1990, there are twelve, with two by the co-presidents of IPPNW.

According to the Nobel Foundation statutes, the prize winner is "to give a public lecture on a subject connected with the work for which the prize has been awarded". This injunction gives the laureate a great deal of latitude, and the reader will find much variety in the ways the peace laureates have sought to meet their obligation. The subjects range from a description of a treaty or a discussion of the work of an organisation to efforts to grapple with the most fundamental problems of peace. The lectures represent a great diversity on the different roads to peace, and also in the personalities of leading travelers on those roads and in the ways each has chosen to interpret the particular path he or she has taken.

It must not be forgotten that these statements were written first of all to be heard, not for a book. Nor were the prize winners chosen for their oratory. They were honoured for their deeds, not for their words. Yet there is eloquence here and high inspiration. No one can miss the sense of commitment which moves most of these speakers and the depth of their sincerity. Altogether the contributions collected here represent an unrivalled documentation of the many ways in which some of the noblest spirits of our time have worked on the most crucial problem facing humanity today, the restraining of violence and the building of peace based upon human solidarity.

Irwin Abrams
Antioch University

Notes

1. In particular, I wish to thank Anne C. Kjelling, Head Librarian of the Institute.
2. The lectures for the years from the first award of 1901 through 1970 are to be found in the exemplary volumes edited by Frederick S. Haberman, *Nobel Lectures. Peace*, 3 vols. (Amsterdam, London & New York: Elsevier Publ. Co., 1972). These were also authorised by the Nobel Foundation. The format is similar to the present volumes, but there are extensive footnotes, a feature considered less needed for the present volumes, as well as biographical essays by the editor, replacing the information submitted for *Les Prix Nobel* by the laureates themselves.
3. Irwin Abrams, *The Nobel Peace Prize and the Laureates. An Illustrated Biographical History, 1901–1987* (Boston: G.K. Hall & Co., 1988). The third printing in 1990 includes the 1989 prize winner. This work is being revised and updated for publication in 1997. See also Irwin Abrams, ed., *The Words of Peace. Selections from the Speeches of the Winners of the Nobel Peace Prize*, revised, expanded edition (New York: Newmarket Press, 1995). Another collection of Nobel peace lectures has been published by UNESCO in its Cultures of Peace series: *Peace! An Anthology by the Nobel Peace Prize Laureates*, edited by Marek Thee (Paris: UNESCO, 1995).

For biographical reference works on the Nobel Prizes in all categories, see *Nobel Prize Winners. An H.W. Wilson Biographical Dictionary*, edited by T. Wassoon (New York: H.W. Wilson Co, 1987); *Nobel Prize Winners. Supplement 1987–1991*, edited by Paula McGuire (New York: H.W. Wilson Co., 1992); and *The Who's Who of Nobel Prize Winners, 1901–1990*, edited by B.S. Schlessinger and J.H. Schlessinger, 2nd edition (Phoenix, AZ: Onyx Press, 1991).

CONTENTS

Peace 1981

**UNITED NATIONS HIGH
COMMISSIONER FOR REFUGEES
(UNHCR)**

INTRODUCTION

The October announcement referred to the earlier 1954 prize for the United Nations Office of the High Commissioner for Refugees (UNHCR), which had been awarded in 1955 when refugees were principally a European concern. Now the problem had become global, "a veritable flood of human catastrophe and suffering", and the work of the UNHCR was of even greater importance.

In his presentation speech, Professor John Sanness, Chairman of the Committee, stresses the tradition of Norwegian concern for refugees, which goes back to Fridtjof Nansen (1861–1930), the famous Norwegian whose humanitarian work as High Commissioner for Refugees of the League of Nations had been acknowledged by the Committee with the 1922 prize. After Nansen's death, the League had established in 1931 the Nansen International Office for Refugees in his honour. For its efforts to aid refugees from Hitler's Germany, the Nansen Office was awarded the prize for 1938 by the Committee, which continued the series with the 1954 and 1981 prizes for the UNHCR.

These prizes, Sanness explains, have not just been for what the UHHCR had achieved, but to emphasise the need for this work to continue. Moreover, motivating such awards has been the Norwegian Committee's "vision of a world community in which the respect for man and human rights, on which all refugee work must inevitably be based, would succeed in achieving universal recognition and validity".

After sketching the history of the refugee problem and the international attempts to deal with it, culminating in the work of the UNHCR, Sanness declares that the UNHCR "is a bridge linking the world community conceived as a community of states and the world community conceived as a community of men and women".

In accepting the diploma and the medal, Poul Hartling, the UN High Commissioner for Refugees, formerly Premier of Denmark and now at mid-term in this office which he is to leave in 1985, declares, "We receive the Peace Prize in Alfred Nobel's spirit. Just as the event today stimulates and encourages us, we hope that it will make people and nations understand that refugees are fellow human beings...". Peace and freedom can only exist, he says, when their needs are met.

The next day Hartling delivers his Nobel lecture. Beginning with a tribute to Nansen, he goes on to repeat some of the same themes and historical detail which Sanness presented. He notes that the UNHCR is still not a permanent body and its life must be extended periodically by the UN General Assembly. The fact that the UNHCR has existed for three decades is nothing to be proud of — "rather, it is a sad reflection of our times; without persecution, without violations of human rights, without armed conflicts, there would be no need for UNHCR".

Hartling tells of specific achievements of the UNHCR in repatriation, resettlement, and rehabilitation of refugees, yet he observes that whereas in 1954 "there were some 2.2 million refugees in the world, today there are some 10 million. But during the same period many millions have ceased to be refugees. Thus we must not despair".

Speaking directly to the refugees of the world, he assures them that "this Nobel Peace Prize bears witness to the fact that your voices are being heard!... Today the world is focusing on your plight and today it renews its commitment to help". Appropriately, Hartling has entitled his lecture, "From Tragedy to Hope".

The lecture is not accompanied in *Les Prix Nobel* with the customary description which other institutional laureates ordinarily submit. However, the speeches of Sanness and Hartling both contain an abundance of factual information. A note referring to the years since 1981 will be found below in the usual place.

ANNOUNCEMENT

The Norwegian Nobel Committee has awarded the Nobel Peace Prize for 1981 to the Office of the United Nations High Commissioner for Refugees.

The prize for 1954, too, was awarded to this institution, in appreciation of its work in bringing relief and aid to the countless refugees and displaced persons to be found in Europe during the immediate post-war years.

Today, in many parts of the world, we witness tremendous and increasing numbers of refugees, estimated at between fourteen and eighteen million in all.

In recent years we have, among other tragedies, watched the mass exodus of people fleeing by land and sea from Vietnam. Today, we have, in addition, two million refugees from Afghanistan and an equal number from Ethiopia. But the problem of refugees is one we encounter in every part of the world. We are face to face with a veritable flood of human catastrophe and suffering, both physical and psychological.

The Office of the High Commissioner for Refugees has, in the opinion of the Committee, carried out work of major importance to assist refugees, despite the many political difficulties with which it has had to contend. This work is supported and supplemented by the large-scale contributions made by other international organisations, state-sponsored as well as private. In particular, the Committee would emphasise the assistance given by organisations and public authorities in those developing countries of Asia and Africa that have borne the strain of receiving and accommodating huge streams of refugees.

The establishment of the Office of the High Commissioner for Refugees was based on respect for human rights. It is on this basis that we must seek to find the answers to the refugee problems of our age, both on the national and international plane. Refugees who dare not return to their native land must be given the opportunity to start a fresh life in their host country. Still more important in the long run is the work of ensuring that people are not compelled to save their lives by escaping from their native land, with no prospect of ever returning. The stream of refugees, moreover, creates serious problems in relations between states, and for this reason the activities of the Office of the High Commissioner serve the interest of humanity and peace as well.

PRESENTATION

Speech by JOHN SANNESS, Chairman of the Norwegian Nobel Committee

Your Majesty, Your Royal Highnesses, Your Excellencies, Ladies and Gentlemen:

The Norwegian Nobel Committee has awarded the Peace Prize for 1981 to the Office of the United Nations High Commissioner for Refugees.

I take it that no one regards the award for the prize as exclusively — or primarily — a gesture of thanks for work well and truly carried out in the past.

Never have so many millions of people been driven from their native lands as the case is today. The great majority of these are to be found in other continents than the one to which our own country belongs.

They are people from countries situated far away, countries of which we know very little. If we wanted to, we could so easily close the portals of our senses and the road to our hearts. One particular group of refugees on which the attention of the world was focused some years ago, as a result of newspaper reportage, pictures, and TV programmes, comprises the so-called Boat People[1] escaping across the sea in the waters off South-East Asia.

We read with satisfaction that our sea captains gave orders to heave-to whenever these wretched people were encountered in their leaky craft, take them on board, and transport them to some harbour. They did not choose the easy way out — closing their eyes and sailing past.

They acted according to the moral law of the sea: you are not allowed to sail past men, women, and children in peril on the sea, abandoning them to the perils of wind and wave, to hunger and thirst, to pirates and sharks.

On the occasion of this prize award the question we ought to put to ourselves is as follows: Is one law valid at sea, another law — or no law at all — in operation on land for all of us?

The award of the prize this year is one of the very few occasions on which one and the same organisation will be receiving the Nobel Peace Prize for the second time. The first time this occurred was in 1955. But on both occasions the Norwegian Nobel Committee made its decision in accord with a tradition that has roots going far back in time. Before the Second World War, in 1938, the Nobel Peace Prize was awarded to the Nansen Office, which had been established by the League of Nations.

This office bore the name of the Norwegian Fridtjof Nansen, the bold polar explorer, scientist, statesman, and humanitarian — a man who looms large in the history of his own country.

After the First World War he decided to devote his life and his energy first and foremost to international humanitarian aid for people in distress or suffering privation, in the first place refugees and people who had been driven from various countries. For this work he was awarded the Nobel Peace Prize in 1922. For countless homeless people, people deprived of legal rights, the so-called Nansen Passport provided a key that would open the door to a new life in a new country.

A strong wave of public opinion here in Norway supported Nansen in his new work — in admiration, in pride, and in a spirit of true humanitarianism.

In making its awards the Norwegian Nobel Committee is never swayed by the hope of maximum popularity and general approval. It must never act under pressure from public opinion or from any form of political pressure. It is independent of all authorities, and its duty is to arrive at its decision in accordance with its best judgment and conviction.

Nevertheless, in making its award for 1981, as in 1955 and as in 1938, the Committee has done so in the certainty that in this instance it enjoyed the support of a tradition in our people which can truly be called a living tradition.

A tradition of this kind, however, among our people and in other countries, is a flame which must be kept alive if it is not to die down. When a flood of refugees has ebbed away, it is tempting to slacken in one's efforts to provide aid and relief. The next flood arises, making the same demands on our conscience and on our willingness to make sacrifices. It is easy to be seized by feelings of helplessness and fatalism. What, we may ask, is the use of all this? Let us cultivate our own garden. And the prosaic questions arise: Can we afford it? Have we room? But even if there is plenty of room in our hearts, there may be a shortage of housing and of employment. Only on a broad international basis can effective refugee aid be organised.

It is precisely in situations of this kind that the Norwegian Nobel Committee has endeavoured to direct the attention of the world to the problem of refugees — in 1938, in 1955, and now today in 1981.

Fridtjof Nansen's humanitarian work aimed to relieve the harrowing human tragedies that resulted from the First World War, and the violent upheavals that followed in its wake. His work benefited a great many groups of refugees, not least Russians and Armenians.

During the decade that ensued the Nansen Office made a substantial contribution to the solution or alleviation of the problems facing these refugees. This work was continued throughout the 1930s. New categories of refugees arose, but gradually interest in their problem lapsed.

After 1933, however, a new and frightening series of problems arose, this time involving first and foremost the stream of political and Jewish refugees fleeing from National Socialist Germany.

There is hardly a single country in Europe, our own included, in which we are able today with the best conscience in the world to review our conduct during these years, when a new stream of refugees knocked at our doors. Fear of competition in the labour market mingled with reluctance and hostility of various kinds towards these new strangers.

Faced with this situation, the Norwegian Nobel Committee considered it right and proper to rouse feelings of conscience and responsibility by awarding the Peace Prize to the Nansen Office, which was now faced with fresh tasks. Today we can only state, in the light of what then happened, that this was in the eleventh hour, in the twilight of world peace.

When the Second World War came to an end in 1945, Europe was strewn with human flotsam and jetsam — millions of prisoners of war, slave labourers, displaced, homeless people, many of them living in camps or wandering desperately around.

The task of caring for these so-called displaced persons was one that fell to the Allied military authorities and to the United Nations Relief and Rehabilitation Administration.

It was no easy matter to separate the refugees from the mass of displaced persons; and we know today that many refugees, against their will and without further investigation, were forcibly returned to the country in which they had lived, there to face an extremely uncertain future.

For the years that followed, right up to the time of the establishment of the Office of the United Nations High Commissioner for Refugees in 1951, we are today in a position to state that major refugee problems were solved thanks to the work of governments, international organisations such as the provisional IRO (International Refugee Organisation), and voluntary organisations. Millions of refugees and displaced persons found a home and work in European and overseas countries. The same relief work also covered the new stream of postwar refugees in Europe fleeing from East to West. For refugees outside Europe special relief organisations were set up — for Arab refugees from Palestine and for refugees in Korea.

When the Office of the High Commissioner for Refugees was set up in 1951, a great many governments expressed their reluctance and doubts. In their opinion the work of caring for refugees could now be left to governments and voluntary organisations. These, they confidently believed, could cope with the problems.

The Office of the High Commissioner for Refugees was almost still-born: a large majority voted in favour of the proposal in the United Nations General Assembly that the Office should be established with a view to functioning for three years. During these years it was in receipt of a very limited contribution from the United Nations budget — between US$600,000 and US$700,000 — and it was expressly forbidden to solicit governments and organisations for voluntary contributions unless this had been sanctioned in advance by the General Assembly.

In 1953 the General Assembly voted to extend the life of the Office of the High Commissioner to January 1, 1959. Its future, however, was still uncertain. During these years refugee problems in Europe were numerically not so overwhelming as to convince everyone of the need for an institution under the auspices of the United Nations.

This was the position when the Norwegian Nobel Committee in 1955 decided to give the prize to the Office of the United Nations High Commissioner for Refugees. It was not awarded in gratitude for work carried out: it was given with a view to emphasising that the work must be continued, so that one would be ready to meet new refugee problems on the basis of the principles of humanitarianism and international justice on which the Office was built.

Hardly a year after this award of the prize, Europe was the scene of an as yet unforeseen flood of refugees, as two hundred thousand Hungarians escaped across the border in October 1956 and the following months.

At the same time a major refugee problem was developing on the African continent, as a result of the war in Algeria. The tasks taken on by the High Commissioner's Office are a direct forerunner of the new situation that arose in the course of the 1960s and 1979s, and in which we are involved at present. The refugee problem was no longer first and foremost a European problem, but had become a global problem, and appropriately the year 1960 was proclaimed World Refugee Year.

Today, a quarter of a century after the event, looking back at the prize award in 1955 we can safely say that the women and men who at that time comprised the Norwegian Nobel Committee were not devoid of foresight and realism. But it was no easy task in 1955 to find general acceptance for this view.

The High Commissioner, Poul Hartling, who is present in the University Festival Hall here today in order to receive Nobel's Peace Prize on behalf of the Office of the United Nations High Commissioner for Refugees, expressed himself as follows when the Committee in October informed him of their decision: "I am happy and honoured to receive the prize on behalf of all refugees. For us in the Office of the United Nations High Commissioner for Refugees, this means that the voices of the world's many millions of refugees have been heard and understood". In 1955 the then High Commissioner[2] expressed himself in similar terms. In both cases they presented a correct picture of the Committee's purpose in making these awards.

A question that was discussed in the Committee in 1955, and which was then raised in the public and critical debate on this decision, was whether it was right to award the prize to an organisation that carried out the duties with which it had been entrusted as a result of a resolution passed in the General Assembly of the United Nations. It was dependent on the aid granted by governments willing to support this work — and not all of them were — and it received advice from these governments. Frequently — and to an increasing extent during the decades after 1955 — it was forced to resort to diplomacy and make itself inconspicuous, on occasions where others could assert their opinions. The status of the Office of the High Commissioner provided great opportunities, but also entailed limitations.

It would not have been difficult in 1955 to pick good candidates for a prize awarded in order to direct world attention to the fate of refugees and to the work of assisting them. There were statesmen and politicians who had made bold moves in order to help refugees generally or to assist particular groups of refugees. There had been heads of state who had shown generosity and hospitality. There were the many voluntary organisations that had carried on over many years self-denying, energetic, and patient relief work.

But prompting the Committee's choice, and the reasons it gave at the time, a definite line of thought can be glimpsed. It harboured a vision of a world community in which the respect for man and human rights, on which all refugee work must inevitably be based, would succeed in achieving universal recognition and validity. A utopia, a great many people might say, in 1981 just as much as in 1955. But this attitude also runs as a leitmotif throughout the practical and realistic political work undertaken to solve urgent tasks more quickly and more efficiently. And in both its visionary and realistic form this attitude is linked, as a symbol and an instrument, to the United Nations.

In discussions on the urgent and difficult refugee problems that arose in the distant 1930s, in this country as well as in other countries, experts in international law maintained that the right to asylum was not a refugee's right to asylum but the right of the individual nation to provide asylum and refuse extradition to the country from which the person concerned had fled. To what extent and in what way a government wished to exercise its right of asylum depended on legislation, political climate, and the fundamental ideals of one's own country. According to international law it was under no obligation to practise universal rules.

In the interwar years, too, governments entered into agreements and undertook obligations in this sphere. But after the Second World War the attempt was made to achieve a breakthrough, and this resulted in the drafting of a Convention related to the Status of Refugees. It was drawn up in connection with the establishment of the Office of the United Nations High Commissioner for Refugees in 1951, and came into force in 1954.

It established the right to asylum as a right enjoyed by the refugee in the land in which he was staying: no refugee could be handed over to a country in which his life or freedom was in danger on the grounds of his race, his religion, his nationality, his social group, or his political opinions. The Convention also establishes his rights as well as his obligations in the land that grants him asylum. It goes a step further by establishing in addition his social and economic rights, which will enable him to build a new and independent existence and to be integrated as an individual on equal terms with others in the community in which he is now living.

New provisions have subsequently been added to the Convention. By no means all governments have subscribed to the Convention or felt themselves bound by its provisions. But their number is growing markedly, among all the nations of the world outside Europe and North America. In a convention which in 1969 was adopted by the Organisation of African States on "special aspects of the refugee problem in Africa" it was firmly established that the Convention of 1951 is "the basic and universal document where the status of refugees is concerned".

The two Peace Prizes which, in the course of a quarter of a century, have been awarded to the Office of the High Commissioner are therefore not merely a recognition of far-reaching work carried out by the Office in full agreement with governments and in collaboration with many other international and national organisations, both government-controlled and voluntary. These awards were justified by the resolution of the General Assembly of the United Nations governing the High Commissioner's Office and by the Convention on the rights of refugees. They represent both a symbol and a practical instrument in the long-term work carried out to ensure that the fundamental principles for this refugee work will achieve universal recognition and validity. This was the line of thought that inspired the Committee of 1955, and the Committee in 1981 has been no stranger to this approach.

Today a total of ten million refugees has been registered for the whole world. We know that in reality the number is greatly in excess of this. Conservative estimates put it at fourteen to eighteen millions. Only at one point of time were the figures higher — before the ten million refugees in Bangladesh were able to return when their country achieved independence in 1972. Other major refugee problems, too, have been solved wholly or partly during the last two decades. Here the High Commissioner's Office has participated, often playing a vital role. But one flood of refugees has replaced another, and the number is on the increase. The majority are no longer to be found in Europe, but in Asia, Africa and Latin America. Half the registered refugees are in Africa, but in Asia a new overwhelming refugee problem has arisen as a result of the war in Afghanistan. Well over two million Afghans have sought refuge in Pakistan — a developing country which, without the assistance of international organisations, is not in a position to tackle the problem involved in caring for these refugees. As yet we can see no solution to the problem that their future entails.

According to the terms defining the work of the High Commissioner's Office as its commencement in 1951, its primary task was to provide economic and social help. The so-called stateless refugees still remaining in Europe were to be given the legal and diplomatic protection which the governments in the countries from which they had fled could not or would not give them. The High Commissioner's Office, in fact, assumed the protective role which is normally the lot of governments in relation to their citizens. The most important task was now to find a final solution to the refugee problem: this would involve either the refugees voluntarily returning to the land from which they came, or their being fully integrated with the population of the country to which they had fled, or that they would be allowed to emigrate overseas. All this demanded a great deal of diplomatic cooperation with, and urgent appeals to, a great many governments.

It is imposible in the time at my disposal to enumerate all the categories and groups of refugees which exist in the world in this year of 1981, and not even in the Nobel lecture of the High Commissioner tomorrow will there be room for them all. The list is a very long one. This is also true of the states which have received refugees and helped to solve their problems, and the same is true of the list of countries in which conditions have been such that people have fled beyond their borders. As far as a great many of these groups are concerned, the work of the High Commissioner's Office is of a traditional nature. But the very magnitude of the floods of refugees has necessitated a fundamental revision of the working methods of the High Commissioner's Office and an extension of its sphere of activity. When hundreds of thousands, or even a million, people come pouring across the borders, the first urgent task is to provide the aid needed in order to safeguard their lives and health. We have all read accounts and seen pictures of families in desperate flight, and of the camps where they have suffered from shortage of water, food, shelter, and the most elementary medical care. Most refugees have made their way to poor countries incapable with their own resources of rescuing them and caring for them. It is here that the aid given by international organisations is directed; this must be done rapidly, often with improvised means, and the difficulties involved are so great that this work inevitably lays itself open to criticism. It has been the task of the High Commissioner's Office and voluntary organisations to be prepared to face constantly new situations, and to ensure that the experience gathered from one crisis is not irretrievably lost before the next one crops up.

This involves not least people fleeing from war and chaos in their homeland. These may be wars that constitute various stages in the discontinuance of colonial rule, or wars between newly created states. They may be civil wars or wars of secession in which ethnic groups are frequently opposed to one another. Or again, there may be conditions of anarchy in which large sections of the population are bereft of all security and safeguards for life and property. These conditions will often result in widespread famine, and occasionally it may be difficult to establish which catastrophes are the work of the natural elements and which are the work of man.

The great bulk of refugees hope to be able to return to their land of origin. Refugees fleeing from countries struggling or at war with colonial powers have returned once independence has been achieved. This was true of the refugees from the war in Algeria, which was to comprise a turning-point in the activities of the High Commissioner's Office. In the 1970s yet more hundreds of thousands have returned to the one-time Portuguese colonies. This has also been the case in Zimbabwe after the cessation of white colonial rule. In Bangladesh, too, repatriation was the obvious solution after secessionary wars. This ensued, too, after the civil war or secessionary war in Sudan had been concluded with an amicable compromise settlement. In this case the return of the refugees also involved what has been called "internal refugees" — people who have fled from their homes and sought refuge in remote areas within the boundaries of their native land. The aid that had been made available for the refugees was continued in order to assist them to return and rebuild their lives after resettlement.

The decision on the part of refugees to return home may, of course, be an expression of the resignation and desperation provoked by their life as refugees. This may be true of refugees today returning to Ethiopia or to Laos and Cambodia. In such cases the important task is to assist them materially, and, if possible, to protect them against persecution. But the High Commissioner's Office has maintained the fundamental principle that no refugee must be repatriated against his or her will, or under any form of coercion whatever, and in cases where this has taken place it has been in direct violation of the wishes of the High Commissioner's Office.

There are also refugees who have little or no hope of ever being able to return to the land from which they came — or at any rate not unless this were made possible as a result of a war conducted against the government in their land of origin. This applies in Africa, e.g., to refugees from Rwanda and Burundi. In such cases the expulsion of ethnic groups, rather than flight, may be involved. Many of these and other refugees in Africa have been assisted to start a new life in the adjoining countries to which they have fled. Often, but by no means always, refugees have been received with hospitality on the other side of the border by a population belonging to the same ethnic group. In other respects, too, there are grounds for expressing our profound gratitude for the hospitality that a large number of African states have shown. Many of these refugees have been given grants of land to cultivate, and Tanzania has set an excellent example by giving over 30,000 refugees full citizen rights.

The opportunities for permanent settlement in the host country are far more limited in South and Southeast Asia, where there is a shortage of land and extreme population density. The settling of ten million refugees from Bangladesh in the Indian border areas was never a feasible proposition. Special historical reasons made it possible for 700,000 refugees from Vietnam, Laos, and Cambodia to be granted asylum in western countries, in the first place in the United States, but also in France and a number of other countries. In the 1980s, however, there will be limits to the number of refugees from Asia and Africa who can be received and integrated in the industrial countries. Economic crises and unemployment have created a situation very different from the one obtaining in the 1950s and 1960s. This also applies to refugees who are more difficult to integrate than is the case with refugees in postwar Europe.

Dealing as it does with a great many governments, whose cooperation is desirable, in many cases as well governments in the countries from which the refugees come, the High Commissioner's Office has had to make use of diplomatic channels. It has been in a position to offer what might be called "its good offices" as arbitrator and go-between in relations between governments with different interests to safeguard. But throughout this activity consideration for the refugees themselves and their fate has been inevitably the one and only guiding principle.

We may well entertain a vision of a world without refugees — a world in which men and women are never in jeopardy on account of their religion, their nationality, their political views, or their membership of any group, of a world in which people need never flee from war and civil strife. But this is not the sort of world in which we live. We can so easily be seized by despair or cynicism, by the wish to cultivate our own garden and to be sufficient unto ourselves.

In the years that lie ahead, too, we shall encounter men and women on the run. It is beyond the capacity of mankind to predict where and when new refugee problems will arise. But we possess the fundamental ideas on human rights and a sense of fellow feeling that goes beyond countries and continents, religions, cultures, and racial borders. We live in a world community of states, as reflected in the United Nations. But we are living, too, in the world community of men and women — many of them men and women who are stateless.

The Office of the United Nations High Commissioner for Refugees is a bridge linking the world community conceived as a community of states and the world community conceived as a community of men and women. We have a duty to the refugees, and this is a duty to ourselves and the very basis of our own existence.

We thank the Office of the United Nations High Commissioner for Refugees for all it has done for countless refugees, and we should like to express the hope that in the troubled times that may lie ahead the High Commissioner's Office will carry the flaming torch that Fridtjof Nansen once lit in our country and in other countries, and that the Office will turn to us again and again and challenge us to do our duty.

THE UNITED NATIONS HIGH COMMISSIONER FOR REGUGEES (UNHCR)

UNHCR was established by the United Nations General Assembly on 1 January 1951, for a three-year period and has been renewed since for successive five-year periods. An integral part of the United Nations, the High Commissioner follows policy directives from the General Assembly and the Economic and Social Council. The current High Commissioner is Ms Sadako Ogata of Japan.

UNHCR has provided international protection for refugees by maintaining their right of asylmn and seeking to prevent any forced return to the country from which they have fled. UNHCR works for voluntary repatriation and when this is not possible, integration within the first country of asylum or resettlement elsewhere.

In 1955, when UNHCR won its first Nobel Peace Prize, the number of refugees worldwide was about 2.2 million, more than half of them in Europe. Ten years ago there were 11 million. By the beginning of 1995, while the refugee population had reached 14.5 million, the total number of people of concern to UNHCR had risen to some 28 million. Humanitarian emergencies have increased in both scale and complexity. Although UNHCR's mandate is to protect and assist refugees, the agency has been called on increasingly to assist a broader range of people living in refugee-like situations. In 1995 they included 5.4 million "internally displaced persons" (those who have been displaced within the borders of their own countries, usually because of civil or ethnic conflicts); 4 million returnees (refugees who have recently returned to their homelands and are assisted by UNHCR); and 3.5 million others of concern (people who are in a refugee-like situation but who have not been formally recognised as refugees).

With the end of the Cold War, many refugees were repatriated to countries in Africa and Asia where conflicts which had been fueled by that struggle came to an end. This produced a new problem, however, the need to assist returnees who had spent over a decade away to reintegrate into home communities whose social and economic infrastructure in many cases had been destroyed. Despite the success of the Namibia operation, of the 45,000 former refugees who returned to Namibia in 1989, for example, 90 per cent of them were unemployed one year later, and by 1991 the figure was still 75 per cent. It was clear that just meeting the goal of repatriation was not enough, and in such cases the General Assembly has directed UNHCR to provide humanitarian assistance and promote social reintegration.

In recent years UNHCR has faced growing challenges. In addition to the need for such assistance for returning refugees, the number of new refugees has continued to rise. Most difficult of all for UNHCR have been an accelerating series of crises which have included the flight of 1.8 million Iraqi Kurds to the Islamic Republic of Iran and the border between Turkey and Iraq, major population displacements in the Transcaucasus, the Horn of Africa and parts of Western Africa, the massive exodus of over 2 million refugees from Rwanda and the war in former Yugoslavia, which alone has produced nearly 4 million refugees, displaced persons and others of concern to UNHCR.

In response to the most severe refugee crises in history, UNHCR has continued to develop its emergency response capacity and to pursue preventive and solution-oriented approaches. In so doing, it has collaborated increasingly closely with political, peacekeeping and development initiatives, with other organs of the United Nations, with intergovernmental and regional bodies and with a wide range of non-governmental organisations.

FROM TRAGEDY TO HOPE

11 December, 1981
by
Mr. Poul Hartling

Throughout the history of mankind people have been uprooted against their will. Time and again, lives and values, built from generation to generation, have been shattered without warning. Time and again, people in fear, individuals or whole groups, persecuted on account of their profound convictions, have had to make a most dramatic decision: to take the uncertain, even perilous road to exile, from home, community and homeland, from friends and often family, rather than bear the intolerable burdens of injustice and oppression.

But, throughout history, mankind has also reacted to such upheavals and brought succour to the uprooted. Be it through individual gestures or concerted action and solidarity, they have been offered help and shelter and the chance to become dignified and free citizens again. Through the ages the giving of sanctuary has become one of the noblest traditions of human nature and communities, institutions, cities and nations have generously opened their doors to refugees and — a fact which should be stressed — many refugees have, in their turn, been valuable assets to those who have taken them in.

It was only in the twentieth century, however, after the cataclysm of the First World War and the fall of empires, that governments came to realise the need to treat the refugee problem as an issue which, in nature and importance, went far beyond their national frontiers, and was a responsibility of what has come to be known as the "international community".

A man of great renown and exceptional talents was needed to set the international machinery in motion — such a man was Fridtjof Nansen, the eminent Norwegian. In 1921, the young League of Nations appointed him High Commissioner for Refugees. At that time, when a universal definition of what is meant by the word refugee was still a long way off, he was to serve as High Commissioner for Russian refugees. Fridtjof Nansen headed the new body and brought life and inspiration to it. In 1922, a resounding tribute was paid to him when he was awarded the Nobel Peace Prize. Little by little, Nansen's efforts were extended to include other categories of refugees, more particularly the Armenians in 1926. One of his key ideas was to create a passport for refugees. The Nansen Passport was much more than a purely functional document: it restored safety, dignity and hope to its holder and gave him back some of his lost identity. After 1930, the year of Fridtjof Nansen's death, the League of Nations entrusted the protection of refugees to the Nansen

International Office for Refugees, better known simply as the "Nansen Office". Today, the spirit and memory of Nansen is still alive and is given practical effect when, once a year, the Nansen Medal is awarded for outstanding services to the cause of refugees.

While the Nansen Office was pursuing its endeavours, and was, in turn, awarded the prestigious Nobel Peace Prize in 1938, the Second World War was already looming on the horizon — a war that would annihilate millions of human beings, overwhelm entire countries and open the floodgates to new and tragic mass exoduses of the uprooted.

It is a strange truth, however, that man constantly strives to restore what man himself undoes. Thus, even in the darkest hours of the Second World War, refugees and displaced persons were not forgotten at the international level. As early as 1943, 44 nations gathered in Washington to sign the Charter of a new international body which was to be called the United Nations Relief and Rehabilitation Administration. One of its prime tasks would be to help the uprooted and to repatriate them after the War whenever circumstances permitted.

With the end of the War in 1945, UNRRA started to tackle the task of voluntary repatriation. That same year, when despair was gradually being replaced by the hope of a better society for the future, saw the adoption on 24 October of the San Francisco Charter leading to the creation of the United Nations. The United Nations was born with the noble objectives of maintaining international peace and security, developing friendly relations among nations based on the principle of equal rights and self-determination, and enhancing international cooperation in solving economic, social, cultural and humanitarian problems.

The Relief and Rehabilitation Administration completed its task in 1947 and, through its efforts, seven million persons returned to their homes. Thus, after years of anxiety in the ruins of war followed the emotional moment of return to life in peace.

Unfortunately, there were many other refugees or displaced persons who could not, or did not, wish to return to their countries; at the same time new refugee problems were emerging. A further major international effort was required, and in 1947 another temporary body, the International Refugees Organisation, was set up by the United Nations. Within a limited period of time the IRO organised the resettlement of more than 1.5 million refugees in new host countries, often overseas.

Despite the success of the IRO, however, it could not solve all the refugee problems of the post-war period, and in December 1949, while the IRO was still pursuing its activities, the General Assembly of the United Nations[3] decided in principle to establish the Office of the United Nations High Commissioner for Refugees. UNHCR actually came into existence on 1 January 1951 after the adoption of its Statute by the General Assembly in December 1950.[4] UNHCR was founded on respect for human rights. How ironic then that the very violation of these human values has made of UNHCR a virtually permanent feature of the international community. Initially, UNHCR was established for a period of three years after which the General Assembly was to decide whether it should be prolonged. Three weeks from now, however, UNHCR, which is still not a permanent body, will have been in existence for 31 years. It forms part of the handful of organisations which, year after year, observe their anniversaries with a certain feeling of regret. Vision and foresight marked the foundation of UNHCR as a body to deal with refugee problems on a non-political and purely humanitarian basis — a fact that the United Nations can take pride in. But the fact that UNHCR has now existed for three decades is nothing to be proud of — rather, it is a sad reflection of our times: without persecution, without violations of human rights, without armed conflicts there would be no need for UNHCR.

It is worth dwelling momentarily on the actual definition of a refugee as contained in the Statute of UNHCR. A refugee is any person who "owing to well-founded fear of being persecuted for reasons of race, religion, nationality or political opinion, is outside the country of his nationality and is unable or, owing to such fear or for reasons other than personal convenience, is unwilling to avail himself of the protection of that country...". So, a refugee is someone who is a victim of intolerance, someone forced to break — often abruptly — his links with the past, with friends or even with family, with his environment, someone forced to cross an international border in search of safety, often taking practically nothing with him. What does a refugee who has lost everything, whose view of the world is temporarily clouded by despair, hope for? First, for physical safety. Looking back, he feels apprehension mixed with the turmoil and confusion of his departure.

By crossing the border, he hopes to find a safe haven. Little by little, his ambitions go further: he hopes to put an end to his undesirable status, to see the future other than with scepticism, to rebuild his life with the material and moral attributes that will restore him to a place in society.

In the United Nations the arduous and vital task of analysing and endeavouring to eliminate the causes of exodus and flight lies with political fora. Whereas one may sometimes deplore the inability of governments members of the United Nations to tackle the causes creating refugees, one may take pride in the ability and readiness of governments to support the humanitarian bodies, such as UNHCR, dealing with the symptoms of the problems. Governments recognised long ago that, irrespective of the causes of the conflagration or of the accident, the victim must be helped until he is back on his feet.

How to go about it? First, by offering him asylum. On 10 December 1948, 33 years ago yesterday to be precise, the General Assembly of the United Nations unanimously adopted the Universal Declaration of Human Rights. It is when these rights are violated that people are in danger and forced to flee. Article 14(1) of the Declaration embodies a key concept: "Everyone has the right to seek and to enjoy in other countries asylum from persecution".

Secondly and closely interrelated is the principle of non-refoulement, that is to say, that a refugee must not be forcibly returned to his country or to any other country where he has well-founded reasons to fear persecution. Here we come to the primary function of UNHCR: international protection, which is designed to ensure that refugees enjoy a number of fundamental rights. Today, the idea has become firmly rooted that a refugee — who must, of course, comply with the laws and observe the public order of the host country — is entitled to certain recognised rights. Asylum and non-refoulement are the cornerstones of the system of protection. The forcible return of a single refugee to his country is — as a principle — as preoccupying and as disquieting as the return of a large group.

The concept of non-refoulement appears in two universally binding instruments: the 1951 Geneva Convention relating to the Status of Refugees, supplemented by the 1967 Protocol. These instruments, to which 90 countries from every continent have acceded to date, lay down minimum standards for the treatment of refugees which should enable them, as far as possible, to lead a normal and independent life.

There are also conventions relating either to refugees or to asylum that form part of a more regional approach to these problems, such as the Organisation of African Unity's 1969 Convention governing the Specific Aspects of the Problem of Refugees in Africa, and regional legal instruments in Latin America and Europe.

To increase the number of accessions to international instruments, to make sure that national legislation fully reflects their clauses and, above all, to ensure that these provisions and a number of universally recognised values are effectively applied to refugees throughout the world — that is the substance of UNHCR's task regarding legal protection. It is a strenuous effort at all times. Sometimes rapid interventions are required to save a person from unbearable hardship, persecution, or even death.

It is quite remarkable that the definition of a refugee, formulated in 1950 in an essentially European context and marked by the traumatic experience of the Second World War and the period of the Cold War, should still apply today to situations which, of course, could not have been foreseen 30 years ago.

Notwithstanding, the General Assembly has been obliged, by successive resolutions, to extend UNHCR's area of competence. Indeed, UNHCR has had to keep pace with history in the making. The foundations were solid and remain unchanged, but the edifice itself has been shaped by time and circumstances. And the world has changed dramatically since the United Nations came into existence. More than a hundred new countries have become independent, sometimes at the cost of violent struggles. Developments — or lack of developments — in power relations throughout the world have given rise to tensions, disturbances and national or international conflicts. Under the impact of all these events, in the whirlwind of suffering that they have engendered, the number of refugees or displaced persons has been great — far too great. Was it then possible to make use of UNHCR, the body created by the community of nations under other circumstances? Indeed it was. UNHCR evolved and adapted to new situations. The operations for voluntary repatriation and now also rehabilitation of refugees in their countries of origin provide examples of new tasks that were added to UNHCR's traditional list.

The most gratifying event for the great majority of refugees is precisely the possibility of returning home, to their own country, following a change in circumstances, for example, the end of a conflict, the restoration of peace and human rights, the achievement of national independence. The long-cherished dream comes true: with deep emotion, the refugees again cross the border — but this time in full daylight — to go back — to rebuild their homes in their own environment.

The Statute of the High Commissioner, which requires him to seek permanent solutions — today we prefer to say durable solutions — to the refugee problem, provides for such voluntary repatriation. But it has to be organised — it can often mean wide-ranging operations — and in many cases the repatriated refugees have to be helped to put down roots again, because they sometimes return to empty, even destroyed homes, with as little as they had when they left.

The General Assembly of the United Nations, the Secretary-General and the governments concerned have on many occasions turned to UNHCR, requesting the Office to organise the repatriation and initial rehabilitation of the returnees. Thus UNHCR, in the wake of national or international treaties can, and often does, through its humanitarian action, participate in the arrangements for consolidating a newly-acquired peace. UNHCR is also sometimes asked to extend its assistance to groups of persons who have been displaced within their national frontiers during conflicts and — at the same time as those repatriated — also return to their homes when peace has come. Example of large-scale UNHCR operations for the repatriation and return of refugees and displaced persons are plentiful. A rapid overview of these operations in chronological order will take us from one country and continent to another. It will be a reassuring exercise for it will show that all over the world — although new refugee problems continually arise — solutions to existing problems continue to be found. Many of the examples demonstrate that rapid solutions to refugee problems strengthen the forces for peace and, conversely, that failure to provide such solutions can lead to the shattering of peace.

The first of such large-scale repatriation operations in which UNHCR was involved took place in 1962 with the return of some 250,000 Algerians, who had fled to Morocco and Tunisia during the strife in their country. In 1972, some 10 million refugees returned home to their newly-independent state, Bangladesh, after months in relief camps in India. That same year, UNHCR helped to bring back some 150,000 Sudanese refugees from four adjoining countries and set up an operation for their rehabilitation. In 1973, UNHCR was instrumental in organising a two-way movement of large numbers of people between Bangladesh and Pakistan — one of history's largest airlift population exchanges. Then — beginning in 1974 — came the news of the independence of the territories in Africa formerly under Portuguese administration. Hundreds of thousands of refugees returned to their homes in Guinea-Bissau, Mozambique and Angola; these were moments of history and emotion. In 1975, the General Assembly[5] requested the High Commissioner "to intensify his efforts on behalf of refugees in Africa, notably those returning to their countries following independence...".

In 1978, following an agreement between the two countries, UNHCR was asked to facilitate the repatriation and initial rehabilitation in their country of origin of 200,000 people from Burma who had taken refuge in Bangladesh. The repatriation of 150,000 Zairian refugees living in Angola also commenced in 1978. Conversely, in 1979, UNHCR helped to ensure the return home of approximately 50,000 Angolans in Zaire. In the same year, 100,000 refugees from Nicaragua who were living in Costa Rica and Honduras were repatriated. In 1979 and 1980, refugees returned to Equatorial Guinea, Kampuchea and Uganda and received basic assistance. Today the return of refugees to the Lao People's Democratic Republic, although still limited in numbers, is under way and negotiations are taking place in Bangkok and Phnom Penh to ensure the safe voluntary return and integration of further groups of Kampucheans. In the Horn of Africa the return movement of Ethiopia has begun, and plans are being worked out to extend the present repatriation programme. The most recent repatriation operation brought to a successful conclusion has been the one which has seen 650,000 refugees and internally displaced persons go back to their homes in independent Zimbabwe. Finally, UNHCR has just embarked on a programme for the return and initial readaptation of citizens from Chad who were uprooted during the troubles in their country.

This list shows important events in which governments joined forces under the umbrella of UNHCR, as the strictly non-political international body, to carry out some of the largest population movements in history and thus achieve the most desirable solution to numerous refugee problems. It demonstrates that the process of peace building can be dynamic when there are institutions through which the consensus of nations can be expressed.

Repatriation is not, unfortunately, the automatic result of all efforts made to help refugees. In some cases they have to settle for long periods — or perhaps forever — in the countries in which they were first received, also called the countries of first asylum. The task to assist them in such circumstances can be overwhelming, since the countries that are geographically or geopolitically situated in the "front line" for refugees are frequently developing countries — some of them belonging to the group of the least developed. More often than not they take in refugees with magnanimity and generosity, but they have to contend with their own economic and social problems and, in the beginning, the presence of refugees can be a heavy burden on them. This is particulary true in some countries where many factors may hinder the early integration of refugees or make it difficult, even illusory: lack of arable land, water or pasture in the countryside;

lack of job opportunities in the towns; lack of an infrastructure capable of absorbing these new groups when already burdened by a very difficult situation; psychological, social and political problems. Refugees in need, wherever they are, can generate tension with the local population that is also poor or, at the very least, fears competition for limited resources. In many ways, the mere presence of refugees may give rise to suspicion, unrest and agitation with numerous repercussions; and the situation may become even more disturbing when the refugees have nothing, are deprived of support and are apprehensive about their future. Will they be helped? Will they be heard? This is where concerted national and international efforts can make for less anxiety, bring stability to a situation fraught with danger and prevent minor or major conflicts from breaking out. It is in such situations that UNHCR can help to encourage a decisive display of international solidarity. Programmes — sometimes of considerable magnitude — will be worked out, financed and implemented in order to provide refugees with relief to meet their immediate need for housing, food, health, or long-term settlement leading to self-sufficiency, the ultimate aim of all UNHCR programmes.

Whenever refugees cannot return freely to their own countries or stay in the country of first asylum, UNHCR has a role to play in resettling them in third countries. It is a delicate operation because in some sense it consolidates their uprooting. But, here again, forces unite to try to ensure the success of the operation: governments, non-governmental organisations, individuals, all will play their role, endeavouring to work in harmony and help their fellow man in need. Thus, in September 1973, as a result of events in Chile, UNHCR found itself charged with an urgent resettlement operation. A few years later, the Office could look back on an operation which had found solutions for more than 25,000 refugees. But, while that chapter was being closed, a new drama requiring speedy solutions unfolded in South East Asia. Again the international community rose to the occasion. As of today, 700,000 Indo-Chinese refugees — including 400,000 "boat people" whose odyssey still moves the world — have been resettled over the last five years. Many of them have been reunited with members of their family, thus ending the ordeal of separation.

However, in spite of the many achievements we shall not forget the many refugees who still await a solution.

I have met refugees in Pakistan, their tents erected in the rough deserts in an imposing setting at the foot of bare mountains, who are longing to return to their own country; the authorities tell us that there are more than two million of them.

I have met "boat people" in the camps in South East Asia, very often suffering from the shock of arduous or horrifying journeys, anxious to rebuild their future as soon as possible, in calm and confidence; some 50,000 in six different countries still await a solution. "Boat people" continue to arrive but fortunately there is the possibility that the number of departures organised from Vietnam can be increased, which should reduce the number of those who risk the journey by sea.

I have met refugees in countries and regions with scant and limited resources, refugees for whom relief and emergency assistance operations continue over the years: approximately 40,000 in Djibouti, hundreds of thousands in Somalia and many thousands in similar conditions in the Sudan.

In Central America, I have met refugees trying to understand their plight, proclaiming their right to survive, waiting for a positive outcome to their situation.

These refugees have their suffering, their daily struggle, in common. But each one views his problem through his own sensibilities, his own aspirations, his own background. In numbers, the refugee problem is ten million people: what this really means, is ten million problems. Statistics are only reference points for reality. We can summarise ten million lives in a short sentence but, eventually, we must deal with the individual human problem. In the final analysis it is a matter for the individual to safeguard his personality, his dignity and his future.

The first United Nations High Commissioner for Refugees, Mr. van Heuven Goedhart, said the following on the occasion of the award of the Nobel Peace Prize to UNHCR in 1954: "... Peace is more than just absence of war. It is rather a state in which no people of any country, in fact no group of people of any kind live in fear or in need...". Today, more than ten million refugees live in fear or in need. On our road towards a better future for mankind we certainly cannot ignore the tragic presence of those millions for whom peace does not exist. Whenever we solve one single problem we have contributed to peace for the individual. Whenever we bring peace to the individual we are making our world a slightly better place in which to live.

Today, while clashes in the world and violations of human rights continue, while calamities still infest the earth, we are meeting here for the best of all causes: the cause of peace. In 1954, when UNHCR first had the great honour of receiving the Nobel Peace Prize, the life of the Office had just been extended by the General Assembly of the United Nations for the first time. It then had a staff of some 100 people working mainly in Europe or for European refugees in the Middle East and the Far East, with a budget of little less than US$5 million. Fifteen countries had acceded to the 1951 Convention. It was consolidating the basis for its role of protection and assistance and was seeking durable solutions to the problems. Today, when the great honour of the Nobel Peace Prize is conferred upon us once again, it is distressing to see how much the refugee problem has grown. Problems have indeed grown, but so have solutions. In 1954, there were some 2.2 million refugees in the world, today there are some 10 million. But, during the same period many millions have ceased to be refugees. Thus, we must not despair. Problems that appeared insoluble have indeed proved to be otherwise.

It is on behalf of my Office that I came here to receive this Nobel Peace Prize, a symbol that has long enjoyed universal recognition. Allow me therefore to pay tribute to my colleagues, with a special word of praise for those who have worked, or are working, outside Headquarters — in the field — in daily contact with the refugees, frequently in very difficult conditions.

I would also like to pay homage to my predecessors in the post of High Commissioner for Refugees for the immense work they accomplished, constantly adapting the Office to its responsibilities and its new tasks.

For the honour conferred on UNHCR we are beholden to a large number of governments and peoples. My thoughts turn to the many countries in the Third World which, while dealing with their own problems, generously open their doors to groups — sometimes very large groups — of uprooted people, giving them land and assistance as well as the human warmth which is one fundamental need of the refugees. I think of the economically developed countries and their sustained and energetic efforts, often on a very large scale, towards the planning, financing and implementation of assistance programmes that have constantly grown larger. May these countries continue to provide a response that is equal to the challenge. I think of those countries that display a vital understanding of our role in protection, support UNHCR and enable the voices of the refugees to be heard in national and international fora, the countries that, each in its own way, promote a cause that is just. I cannot enumerate them all. I would simply say that Norway stands out as a model in this respect: it is a spirited spokesman for the rights of refugees wherever they are; it participates in programmes all over the world; it welcomes refugees to its soil and offers them a future.

I would also like to stress how much UNHCR and refugees owe to other international organisations and, in particular, to non-governmental organisations which, through an increasingly comprehensive network around the world, assist refugees with a willingness, competence and dedication often — and rightly so — described in the most eloquent terms. In this field, we are shown the way by the prominent role played for years by a Norwegian agency, namely the Norwegian Refugees Council.

Finally, I should like to pay tribute to those thousands of men and women throughout the world, some in high — others in humble — places, who with devotion and perseverance give their time, energy and action to the cause of the world's refugees.

Today, the voices of millions of refugees in the world are being heard. Voices seeking belief in man, in human dignity, in basic human rights. Voices praying for justice, freedom and peace, pleading for love and generosity. Voices calling on the governments of the world to use reason rather than force.

Permit me to address myself directly to the refugees of the world — wherever they are — and say: Yes, this Nobel Peace Prize bears witness to the fact that your voices are being heard! If we have allowed ourselves to stop for a moment to rejoice in the memory of the achievements of the past, we realise that the challenges of the present are no cause for joy. They need to be addressed and met with urgency and determination. But today the world is focusing on your plight and today it renews its commitment to help. This gives us reason to send you a message of hope for the future.

From this platform of peace, I would like to appeal to all those in whose hands the future of mankind lies, to use their power not to destroy or kill, not to create suffering in a grasping search for selfish objectives, but to help alleviate the plight of the needy; to aim at justice and freedom for the individual.

And I appeal to each and everyone. Let us never cease to feel compassion for those in want. Let us never tire of helping the victims of injustice and oppression. He who puts his faith in the restoration of human dignity cannot be wrong.

ENDNOTES

1. After the surrender of South Vietnam and the uniting of the country by North Vietnam in 1976, many "boat people" fled the country, seeking to reach Hong Kong by sea in whatever kind of craft they could find.
2. Dr. Geritt Jan van Heuven Goedhart (1901–1956).
3. Resolution 319 (IV).
4. Resolution 428 (V).
5. Resolution 3454 (XXX).

SELECTED BIBLIOGRAPHY

By UNHCR:
Refugees. A monthly journal published by UNHCR.

Other Sources:

Loescher, G. *Beyond Charity: International Cooperation and the Global Refugee Crisis.* New York & Oxford: Oxford University Press, 1993. (An excellent concise examination of the historical origins and present consequences of the refugee crisis, with a plea for comprehensive political actions to deal with it.)

Holborn, Louise W. *Refugees, a Problem of Our Time: The Work of the United Nations High Commissioner for Regugees, 1951–1972.* 2 vols. Metuchen, N.J.: Scarecrow Press, 1985.

Kismaric, Carole. *Forced Out. The Agony of the Refugee in Our Time.* New York: Random House, 1989. (Well illustrated, highly recommended.)

Marrus, Michael R. *The Unwanted European Refugees in the Twentieth Century.* New York: Oxford University Press, 1985. (Excellent survey.)

United Nations Yearbook. (This annual publication includes a summary of the work of UNHCR.)

The State of the World's Refugees 1993. The Challenge of Protection. New York: Penguin Books, 1993.

The State of the World's Refugees 1995. In Search of Solutions. Oxford: Oxford University Press, 1995.

Peace 1982

ALVA MYRDAL and ALFONSO GARCÍA ROBLES

INTRODUCTION

In its October announcement the Committee referred to Alfred Nobel's specific mention in his will of disarmament as a path to peace and named two champions of that cause, Alva Myrdal of Sweden and Alfonso García Robles of Mexico, for the prize. The Committee declared that each had worked for disarmament both in international negotiations and through appeals to public opinion.

Chairman Egil Aarvik of the Committee amplifies these themes in his presentation address, praising the efforts of the two laureates for their "magnificent work in the disarmament negotiations of the United Nations". Aarvik also lauds Myrdal, now almost eighty-one years old, for a whole lifetime of contributions to social betterment. He acclaims García Robles in particular for his leading role in achieving the 1967 Treaty of Tlatelolco, which declared Latin America a denuclearised zone.

Aarvik speaks of the difficulties in the way of disarmament, having in mind no doubt the disappointing second special session on disarmament of the UN General Assembly which took place earlier in the year. He notes, however, that the laureates are among those who believe that "giving up is not human", citing the very words which Myrdal expressed in accepting the Einstein Prize in 1980. The Nobel Peace Prize of 1982, Aarvik concludes, is intended not only to recognise the efforts of the two laureates to find "constructive solutions" to the difficult problems of arms control, but to support the popular movement of public opinion for peace and disarmament.

In her acceptance, Myrdal speaks her thanks briefly, saving her energy for the next day's lecture. García Robles emphasises the necessity of nuclear disarmament for the survival of the human race. He refers to the joint Manifesto of 1955 in which the famous scientist Albert Einstein and the renowned philosopher Bertrand Russell gave such a warning to the world and of subsequent resolutions by the UN General Assembly echoing this grim thought. García Robles proposes that the Nobel Committee use efforts for disarmament as a decisive criterion in awarding future Peace Prizes. Recognising the growing interest in awarding the Peace Prize to champions of human rights, he suggests that funds be found to create a separate prize to be awarded by the Norwegian Nobel Committee for achievements in that field.

Myrdal's Nobel lecture draws upon her recently revised book, *The Game of Disarmament*, in which she blamed the leaders of the two superpowers for the arms race. In her address she declares that they are guilty of "a clearly irredeemable misconception: that the use of war, violence, can lead to victory".

Moreover, they have kept building nuclear weapons even though since 1960 each has had enough to deal a decisive blow to the other. She cites the report that General Maxwell Taylor, President John F. Kennedy's military adviser, advised him that 100 to 200 intercontinental missiles on each side would serve as sufficient deterrent. She says that she is growing weary of pointing this out, but "I shall go on repeating the truth until the politicians get into their heads, that *when one has sufficient, one does not need more*".

She takes hope from the current movement for a nuclear freeze, but she is concerned that the acceptance of war and the spread of arms have produced a cult of violence which permeates the mass media and affects everyday life. She is also concerned that progress in technology, which could be used for the good, is likely to concentrate power in evil hands.

In conclusion, like García Robles in his acceptance speech, Myrdal makes a suggestion to the Committee, noting that it would be consistent with a clause in Nobel's will to give prizes to organisers of peace congresses, thus strengthening the popular movement for peace.

The lecture of García Robles, presented on the same day as Myrdal's, is very different. He gives a scholarly exposition of the Treaty of Tlatelolco, tracing its evolution, analysing its provisions, demonstrating its influence on the resolutions of the UN General Assembly, and suggesting that it presents an exemplary method of achieving the establishment of a nuclear-free area of the world. It is also a model for the negotiation of a multilateral treaty for any purpose, showing, as he declares, the crucial importance of the preparatory efforts. In a footnote on page 62 García Robles tells, with modesty, something of his own role.

ANNOUNCEMENT

The Norwegian Nobel Committee has decided to award the Peace Prize for 1982 to two persons who for many years have played a central role in the United Nations' disarmament negotiations, namely, Alva Myrdal of Sweden and Alfonso García Robles of Mexico.

In the disarmament negotiations in Geneva and in many other international bodies, as well as in her writings, Alva Myrdal has made public opinion all over the world aware of the problems of armaments, and helped to arouse a general sense of responsibility for the development these involve.

García Robles has played a prominent part in the work of disarmament within the United Nations Organisation, both in Geneva and in UNO's special disarmament sessions. In common with Alva Myrdal he has helped to open the eyes of the world to the threat mankind faces in continued nuclear armament. He was the driving force behind the agreement to declare Latin America a denuclearised zone, which was concluded in 1967.

Alfred Nobel's will and testament states that the Peace Prize shall be awarded to the person or persons who have made a special contribution to peace, disarmament and the brotherhood of mankind. In the opinion of the Nobel Committee this year's laureates fulfil these conditions.

In today's world the work to promote peace, disarmament and the brotherhood of mankind is carried on in various ways, and this year's award focuses on two of them. There is the patient and meticulous work undertaken in international negotiations on mutual disarmament, and there is also the work of the numerous peace movements with their greater emphasis on influencing the climate of public opinion and the appeal to the emotions. Both these approaches are important, and, in the opinion of the Committee, this year's prizewinners are worthy representatives of both.

The Committee is also convinced that it expresses the spirit of the two laureates in the hope that the award of the prize to Alva Myrdal and García Robles may be interpreted as a stimulus to the climate of peace that has emerged in recent years, first and foremost in the Western world, gradually surmounting boundaries and frontiers of so many kinds. If this climate of opinion is only allowed to gain in strength and vigour, surmounting still more boundaries, it might well provide our best hope that realistic and factual negotiations, culminating in mutual disarmament, may one day be crowned with success.

PRESENTATION

Speech by EGIL AARVIK, Chairman of the Norwegian Nobel Committee

Your Majesty, Your Royal Highnesses, Your Excellencies, Ladies and Gentlemen,

People occasionally ask whether the task of nominating Peace Prize winners may not prove a difficult one.

It is certainly not difficult to understand the reasoning prompting this sort of question. Naturally a Peace Prize committee, too, is bound to feel a sense of affliction at the setbacks suffered by the cause of peace. Great is our disappointment every time national boundaries are violated, and naked force of arms unleashed. One knows the feeling of despair at the news that innocent people are being killed and old enmity rekindled.

The world in which we live is not at peace. Tensions and unresolved disputes are dominant features of our age. Despite disarmament conferences and other verbal endeavours to promote peace, the armaments race continues. Military budgets merely mount up, and have today reached a level of close on 65 billion dollars annually. Nuclear armaments are the cause of deepest concern. With these weapons the killing power of the superpowers appears to have reached its maximum potential — the extermination of the human race. There are, in short, ample grounds for pessimism in our time.

But, as one of this year's laureates has declared: "Giving up is not human!" And it is, in fact, from the ranks of people imbued precisely with such ideas that the Norwegian Nobel Committee has this year made its choice.

Alva Myrdal and Alfonso García Robles have, in the opinion of the Committee, proved outstanding candidates for two reasons. In the first place owing to their magnificent work in the disarmament negotiations of the United Nations, where they have both played crucial roles and won international recognition; and secondly because, too, they have made such a notable contribution to the task of informing world opinion on the problems of armaments and of arousing the acceptance by the general public of their joint responsibility for the train of events.

In awarding Nobel's Peace Prize to these two the Committee wishes to focus attention on what — despite the many gloomy prospects — nevertheless constitutes a bright spot. There are people who are not satisfied merely to draw attention to alarming trends, but who also devote their energy and their ability to turning the tide. Pessimism and anxiety for the future have failed to unnerve a few hardy souls, who are endeavouring to convey the message that the fate of mankind has by no means been finally sealed, and that the nuclear holocaust is not the only possible outcome of the conflicts and disputes we face.

The climate of public opinion for peace and disarmament initiated in the Western world is on the march, and is now thrusting its way across many national boundaries. The idea of calling a halt to the nuclear armaments race is no longer quite so impossible. Leading politicians on both sides of the Atlantic have grasped its sense of deep commitment, and are giving it their support. It may well be a sign of the times that during the recent elections to Congress and the Senate in the USA there was a substantial majority in a number of states in favour of freezing nuclear armaments at their present level.

The leaders of public opinions for peace and disarmament in the West know to their chagrin what a poor hearing they command in the East. But even here, too, they are not without their allies, of which maybe the most important is the common fear of total extermination in a nuclear war, a fear which we may assume is felt just as forcibly over there as in our part of the world. After all, overriding all conflicting interests there exists a common interest in survival.

Nevertheless, under no circumstances would it be human to give up. And this is precisely the keynote of the message we have received from this year's Peace Prize winners.

Alva Myrdal's commitment to the service of disarmament has long since established her international reputation. The many awards and other marks of high honour she has received testify to her standing in the international community.

Her commitment, moreover, reveals a tremendous span, both in terms of time and spheres of interest. As far back as the 1930s she played a prominent part in developing the modern Swedish welfare state. She was a staunch champion of women's liberation and equal rights. She has proved a brilliant diplomat, and was the first woman to be appointed head of a department in the United Nations.

On an occasion like this it is only right and proper that a *Norwegian* Nobel Committee should recall her fearless and notable work on behalf of Norway during the Second World War. For this she was deservedly awarded His Majesty King Haakon VII's Freedom Cross.

Alva Myrdal belongs to the world community: but she is ideologically firmly rooted in Nordic constitutional principles and in our democratic ideals. These were the ideals that motivated her when she acted as head of delegation during the disarmament negotiations in Geneva. Nor is that all: in other UN contexts, too, she has been a staunch spokesman of peace and disarmament.

As a researcher and disarmament expert, with a wide knowledge of the problems of world politics, she has commanded attention in the international forum, and not least in her literary work her influence has been profound.

It is no doubt typical of great personalities that it is easy both to agree and disagree with them. Alva Myrdal is hardly an exception to this rule: but on one point all will agree — her name has become a rallying point for men and women who still cling to the belief that in the last resort mind is bound to triumph over matter.

Today, in her eighty-first year, she can look back on a life which must of necessity have been not only rich but also dramatic. It must have alternated between hope and disappointment, and almost certainly, too, between encouragement and discouragement.

So much the greater on such occasions the joy of witnessing the fruits of one's labour, heralding the consummation of the dream conceived in the finest moment of life. In this connection it might be fitting to recall Bjørnstjerne Bjørnson's words:

"All that your hopes have illumined,
all that your fears have bedewed — now grows apace".

For obvious reasons Alfonso García Robles is less well known in the Nordic countries. But, as we all know, a considerable part of the world is situated outside the North. And in international disarmament work García Robles bears a name that is truly illustrious. He was the driving force behind the agreement, signed in Mexico City in 1967, that declared Latin America a denuclearised zone. And in view of the fact that the wording of this treaty is so markedly the work of García Robles, it gives us at the same time a very fair description of the man and his way of thinking.

The outstanding feature of this agreement — the first of its kind in the world — is a realistic view of the destructive power inherent in nuclear arms. The starting point for the agreement that was reached is a clear recognition that nuclear arms are in essence not defensive weapons, but weapons of self-destruction. They are — to quote the words of the agreement — an attack on the integrity of the human race, and could in the final resort even render the world uninhabitable.

It has rightly been maintained that the first essential condition required for the solution of political problems is the moral courage to look these problems in the face. Frequently this is precisely what is lacking, and this is maybe particularly applicable to the problem of nuclear arms. It is such a temptation to shut one's eyes. It is as though the process of comprehension was obstructed. We are not in a position to pursue our own reasoning to its logical conclusion. At some point or other we recoil, lacking the courage to know what we actually know. The truth concerning the situation that has been created by modern nuclear weapons is so horrifying that in a way it numbs our ability to comprehend it.

The American social economist and author Professor John Kenneth Galbraith has expressed this in the following words:

"The truth that men seek there to evade is that this small planet cannot survive a nuclear exchange ... . Asked if we want life for our children and grandchildren, we affirm that we do. Asked about nuclear war, the greatest threat to that life, we regularly dismiss it from mind. Man has learned to live with the thought of his own mortality. And he now has accommodated to the thought that all may die, that his children and grandchildren will not exist. It's a capacity for accommodation at which we can only marvel. I suspect that our minds accept the

thought but do not embrace the reality. The act of imagination is too
great or too awful. Our minds can extend to a war in some distant
jungle and set in motion the actions that reject it. But not yet to the
nuclear holocaust. A commitment to this reality is now the supreme
test of our politics".

It is in the light of this that we should consider the agreement that declared
Latin America a denuclearised zone. Alfonso García Robles has rightly been
called the father of the Mexico Agreement. It is his ideas and his realistic
assessment that are reflected in the wording. He is one of those people who
possess the courage to face the truth of the situation created by nuclear arms.
And it is precisely for this reason, too, that the successful negotiation of the
agreement redounds so very much to his credit.

Once the horrific truth about nuclear arms is recognised, the question of
nuclear armament likewise acquires a fresh dimension. It is no longer a
question of being for or against national defense or an international system of
security. The development of nuclear arms has taken us well beyond this
stage in the argument. As everyone knows, there are today divided opinions
on the justification of military defense. Many of us believe — in the light of what
history has taught us — that a credible defense of freedom, independence, and
humanity must, in fact, be regarded as the defense of peace. Others adopt a
more or less consistent pacifist attitude.

What the Mexico Agreement, however, so clearly demonstrates is that we can
no longer continue our argument on this level. The matter has acquired a fresh
perspective: we must seek a way out, so that mankind can survive. This is the real
disarmament problem facing us today.

This has provided a platform on which all mankind will have to come
together, irrespective of political views or strategic considerations. The alternative
is a continued nuclear build-up and the proliferation of nuclear arms, which
can only lead ultimately to a catastrophe.

Man was once told: "Blessed are the peacemakers, for they shall inherit the
earth". Today we know that if the peacemakers fail in their efforts, there will be
no one left to inherit the earth, an earth, moreover, no one would consider it
worthwhile inheriting!

Putting this truth across has been, and still is, the prime concern of this
year's Peace Prize winners. What they have clearly shown us, too, is that the
work of promoting peace and disarmament must be carried on at several levels.
It is vital to spread information on the issue involved, so that a growing body of
public opinion capable of exerting pressure can be built up. But this is not the
only object, as Alva Myrdal has explained:

"We must dare to believe that in their heart of hearts men desire peace
on earth, but we shall never achieve this merely by coining slogans
such as 'We Want Peace!'. Our aim must be backed by intense efforts
to find constructive proposals. The challenge facing peace workers is
not to be found in a single universal question-and-answer, but in

peaceful solutions to a host of conflicts, and in the exertion to achieve peace on many different levels".

This is precisely what the two Peace Prize winners have confirmed in their endeavours. They know — better than most people — what means "to make intense efforts to find constructive proposals". They have sought no facile short cuts, because they know how vital it is that negotiations on disarmament should be conducted on the basis of down-to-earth realism and on the assumption of give-and-take between the great powers.

And it is precisely in this connection — when we mention the concept of give-and-take — that we get some notion of how complicated and exhaustive the problem of disarmament is. It is not sufficient merely to demonstrate a desire for peace; nor is it sufficient simply to declare that nuclear arms must be done away with. There is no difficulty in getting a wide measure of agreement on aims of this kind.

Difficulty arises when these aims are to be realised through the medium of practical political decisions; and this too is a problem we must have the courage to face up to.

We have watched with growing impatience how difficult it is for the nuclear powers to reach agreement on even the most modest measures of disarmament; and we may well ask why it has not been possible to make any progress with all the negotiations that have been conducted. Maybe the ideological differences are too great? Maybe it is impossible to break through the barrier of mutual mistrust, which unfortunately has received far too much nourishment? Is it once again fear that dominates and dictates the premises on which global political decisions are made?

It is not easy to give a simple answer. Maybe this, too, is a fact we shall have to take into account.

But what we can all see is that a power struggle and intense rivalry are being waged between the great powers. In this struggle there are several parties who believe that they are compelled to safeguard vital interests, and who are genuinely afraid of jeopardising the security of their country. For this reason they feel compelled, one and all, to take military precautions. It is not difficult to understand an attitude of this kind.

But there is also a great deal to suggest that the big powers are caught in what has been called the symbiotic trap, in which the parties concerned are mutually motivating one another to arm. This is how the trap works: In the East information is received to suggest that the West has plans for further rearmament. And for this reason the East is compelled to arm — out of consideration for its own security. In the West similar information is received on new types of weapon being developed in the East, and so the West is forced to react — they dare not do otherwise. With each side placing the blame on the other an excuse is found for justifying the arms race.

The persons principally responsible for the present development are as a result of this bound to be subject to tremendous pressure. In these circumstances it would be difficult to arrive at solutions which all parties concerned would consider worthwhile and which they feel would ensure their safety. Very careful assessment is necessary in order to arrive at solutions of this kind, the main problem being to arrive at a platform on which all interested parties can, despite their differences, come together.

The question now is whether the fresh situation that has been created by the nuclear powers might not be capable of providing a platform of this kind, since no one can any longer be in any doubt that today a joint interest, overshadowing all else, exists for all the nations of the world — viz. to put a stop to the nuclear arms race. This is the problem, overshadowing all others, to which we must turn our gaze, and in our endeavours to reach this goal all our efforts must and can be coordinated.

It is in the light of this that we can observe two clear lines emerging in the work of disarmament. We have the meticulous work, demanding a great deal of patience and time, that is carried on through international negotiations for mutual disarmament. And it should be emphasised that it is along this line that lasting and real results can be achieved. But we have in addition the work of the various peace movements, consciously committed to creating a body of public opinion, and it must also be emphasised that if this body of opinion is allowed to grow in strength and health, reaching out across still more national boundaries, it could constitute a decisive factor in ensuring the success of international negotiations.

The way ahead may appear long and difficult, and it certainly makes great demands both on the imagination and the patience — and maybe above all on the unflinching honesty which dares to look truth in the face, and still has the courage to continue.

In awarding this year's Peace Prize to Alva Myrdal and García Robles the Norwegian Nobel Committee wishes to express its recognition of the intense endeavours undertaken by two people to find constructive solutions to difficult international disarmament negotiations.

At the same time the Committee is anxious — and in this connection we believe we are speaking in the spirit of the prizewinners — that the Peace Prize this year should be interpreted as well as a helping hand to that body of public opinion for the promotion of peace and disarmament to which they themselves have proved such a valuable inspiration.

Alva Myrdal

ALVA MYRDAL

Alva Myrdal was born in Uppsala in 1902, graduated from University in 1924, and married Gunnar Myrdal the same year. Together with her husband she made a major contribution in the 1930s to the work of promoting social welfare. They were joint authors of a book entitled *The Population Problem in Crisis*, and she was also actively engaged in the discussion on housing and school problems. She was a prominent member of the Social Democrat Party in Sweden, and in 1943 was appointed to that party's committee with the task of drafting a post-war programme. Also in that year she was appointed to the Government Commission on International Post-War Aid and Reconstruction.

After the Second World War she devoted more and more of her time and energy to international questions. In 1949–1950 she headed UNO's section dealing with welfare policy, and in 1950–1955 she was chairman of UNESCO's social science section. In 1955 she was appointed Swedish ambassador to India, and in 1962 was nominated Sweden's representative to the Geneva disarmament conference. In that year she became a member of Parliament and in 1967 a member of the Cabinet, entrusted with the special task of promoting disarmament. For a number of years she has represented her country in UNO's political committee, in which questions of disarmament have been dealt with.

During the negotiations in Geneva she played an extremely active role, emerging as the leader of the group of non-aligned nations which endeavoured to bring pressure to bear on the two super powers to show greater concern for concrete disarmament measures. Her experiences from the years spent in Geneva found an outlet in her book *The Game of Disarmament*, in which she expresses her disappointment at the reluctance of the USA and the USSR to disarm.

In her work for disarmament Alva Myrdal has combined profound commitment with great professional insight. With the support of experts she has familiarised herself with the scientific and technical aspects of the arms race. Her understanding of the need to base the work of disarmament on professional insight also found an outlet in her active participartion in the establishment of the Stockholm International Peace Research Institute, SIPRI. Through her many articles and books Alva Myrdal has exercised a very significant influence on the current disarmament debate.

Alva Myrdal continued to work for peace as long as she was able. During her last two years, however, she was hospitalised, and she died in February 1986 in Stockholm at the age of eighty-four.

ACCEPTANCE

ALVA MYRDAL

Your Majesty, Your Royal Highnesses, Mr. Chairman,

I wish to assure you that the brevity of my speech is in no way a measure of the depth of my gratitude.

I would like to express special thanks to the Chairman of the Nobel Committee for a bold acknowledgement of the principles which must support all efforts to attain peace and disarmament.

My main purpose today is to express my warmly felt thanks to the Norwegian Nobel Committee for granting me this year's Nobel Prize for the cause of peace.

I also extend my thanks to the large groups of people who have, due to a new awareness, brought forth a strong popular movement for peace. Now sounds the cry "Down with nuclear weapons!"

My gratitude also goes to those great numbers of experts and authors in many countries who have destroyed false misconceptions and provided us with powerful arguments for a cessation of this competition in overarmament.

All mankind is now learning that these nuclear weapons can only serve to destroy, never become beneficial.

And thus we can hope that men will understand that the interest of all are the same, that hope lies in cooperation. We can then perhaps keep PEACE.

DISARMAMENT, TECHNOLOGY AND THE GROWTH IN VIOLENCE

Nobel Lecture, 11 December 1982
by
ALVA MYRDAL

Mr. Chairman, Honoured guests:

In the first place it is my obvious and at the same time most pleasant duty to express my gratitude for the honour that has been accorded me by the award of the 1982 Nobel Peace Prize.

May I then mention that I shall deal not only with the general subject of *disarmament*, but I shall also direct the attention to the connection between armament problems and the headlong on-rush of *technology* and the growth in *violence*. We must never forget the trampling down of human dignity and rights, the increase in acts of violence and the use of torture. All of this testifies to an incredible persistence in contempt for the suffering of individual men and women.

But I would also like to express my very special thanks to the Nobel Committee for hitting on the idea of dividing the prize between Dr. García Robles and myself. This indicates that we have not received the prize only as personal tributes to ourselves, but that the entire movement which aims at promoting peace and reducing the use of violence has been given a great encouragement. This was emphasised, too, by the chairman of the Norwegian Nobel Committee, Egil Aarvik. The whole popular movement of protest, which at present is and has to be directed mainly against the use of the extreme weapon of terror, the atom bomb, has acquired a recognised legitimacy. This is bound to influence the attitudes and decisions not least of leading politicians and military chiefs in the superpowers.

I am intentionally not using the phrase "striving for *peace*" too frequently. The longing for peace is rooted in the hearts of all men. But the striving, which at present has become so insistent, cannot lay claim to such an ambition as leading the way to eternal peace, or solving all disputes among nations. The economic and political roots of the conflicts are too strong. Nor can it pretend to create a lasting state of harmonious understanding between men. Our immediate goal must be more modest: aimed at preventing what, in the present situation, is the greatest threat to the very survival of mankind, the threat of nuclear weapons.

I should in the beginning like to emphasise also that I am particularly gratified that on this occasion the award goes to two citizens of nations which are both *denuclearised* and *non-allied*. The mass media calls attention to this fact all too seldom, as they are so one-sidedly concerned with the rivalry between the two superpower blocs. There are, after all, so many other countries in the world, and most have refused to serve as hostages to the superpowers.

Maybe I should add — and I hope this does not sound boastful — that we are two delegates who have shown at the disarmament negotiations and in the United Nations that rhetoric is by no means enough. We have tried to speak for greater emphasis on analysis, and constructivity.

More must be done in *concrete* terms in order to promote the cause of disarmament. García Robles has ingeniously constructed and tenaciously sought to follow up the Tlatelolco agreement, with a view to making the whole of Latin America a denuclearised zone. He has actually succeeded so far as to get the nuclear weapon powers to enter into binding agreements to refrain from attacking with nuclear arms nations that have joined a zone free from nuclear weapons.

I for my part, with some colleagues of mine, have presented many concrete and elaborated proposals. Sometimes we have had some success, though more rarely on major questions. But I have, for example, managed to get the Swedish government budget to pay the costs of SIPRI (Swedish International Peace Research Institute) as well as the less known seismological Hagfors station. That enables us to monitor independently, and systematically even the smallest subterranean nuclear tests, using the most modern equipment, and to publish the results internationally, unhampered by any political considerations. This work has more recently been followed by efforts to build up an international network for open verification of nuclear test explosions.

These efforts of our two countries are mentioned as examples of the opportunities that exist for objectively refuting so many of the attempts by the nuclear weapon powers to conceal or give false explanations of actual facts. Or at least their attempts to delay the truth breaking through. The smaller nations can in fact exercise greater influence on disarmament negotiations than they have hitherto done. But then we must exert ourselves to break through the wall of silence which, unfortunately, the great powers have erected to ward off the small powers' influence in the international debate.

It is of the greatest importance that people and governments in many more countries than ours should realise that *it is more dangerous to have access to nuclear arms than not to possess them.* Without nuclear arms we run less risk of being drawn into the orbit of the great powers, with their hyper-dangerous weapons. And after all, there is no defense against them.

The world generally speaking is now drifting on a more and more devastating course towards the absurd target of extermination — or rather, to be more exact — of the northern hemisphere's towns, fields, and the people who have developed our civilisation.

The distressing situation of our era, which recalls the fate that overtook Rome, is rising from a clearly irredeemable misconception, viz. that the use of weapons, *violence,* can lead to *victory.*

How would it be possible, even at immense expense, to inaugurate a new and happy existence for the world on the ruins of one that would be at least half-destroyed? The misconception that *a victory can be worth its price*, has in the nuclear age become a total illusion.

There is no doubt that what the superpowers are now planning, and in which they are investing billions, is precisely the preparation for *waging war.* New super-technological weapons systems committed to the service of new strategies are now quite openly aimed at the waging of war, and at an imagined "victory".

The new generations of intercontinental missiles do not change the basis for, but just continue the same old strategy, for example the United States MX (which will not be ready for deployment before 1986, if ever) or its counterparts, the SS-17, SS-18 and SS-19, which are already in place. They do not alter the fact that both superpowers have possessed a decisive basic capacity since about 1960, viz. to deal a decisive blow at one another's mainlands. At that time, a so-called "balance of terror" may be said to have existed. As I and so many others have pointed out, the two great powers already at that time had "sufficient" capacity to deter one another from launching a nuclear strike.

Soon after Kennedy had been elected President, General Taylor in 1960 advised him that between 100 and 200 long-range missiles would be sufficient; and various experts ever since have made similar assessments. One or two scientific writers have even gone so far as to say that one missile on each side would be enough (e.g. McGeorge Bundy and Herbert York).[1] As the arms race proceeded, however, the experts have as a rule stayed at the conclusion that the target for a sufficient deterrent would involve something like 400 missiles, capable of reaching from one continent to the other. All developments over and above this have simply meant one more step in the direction of increased instability. They have been unnecessary, and at what a cost!

A great amount has been talked and written about what constitutes a sufficient balance and what really is meant by the concepts of "balance" and "deterrence". And despite the fact that the experts have disclosed what is the simple truth, misconceptions arise and are proliferated: the idea that *more* is needed when one already has *more than sufficient.*

After having read reams and personally written so much on this subject on numerous occasions, without obtaining a hearing, I am actually starting to find it a trifle wearying. But the truth must be brought home and emphasised again and again. This I have done most recently in the revised preface to the third edition of my book *The Game of Disarmament* which had so far only been available in English. Today, of all days, it is appearing in a Swedish translation, in an issue of the periodical *Tiden.*

That the argument is mainly carried out with the long-range intercontinental missiles in view, does not mean that other nuclear arms are not subject to the same reasoning. I shall go on repeating the truth until the politicians get it into their heads, that *when one has sufficient, one does not need more.*

The conclusion of where the rivalry of the two superpowers is leading us is terrifyingly realistic. Just now the ongoing process is moving from deterrence to the capacity for waging actual war. This has been described in a flood of new books, particularly in America. Here I would like to give just one quotation; it is from the highly respected, and by no means dangerously radical, daily paper *The Washington Post* of April 13, 1982:

> "A point was reached long ago at which both the United States and the Soviet Union had such monstrous arsenals that further accretions became senseless. These have been 37 years of lunacy, of idiots racing against imbeciles, of civilised nations staggering blindly toward a finishing line of unspeakable peril.
>
> The immediate necessity is to call a truce, to stop the further buildup of nuclear weapons by either side".

I agree with the many who consider *freezing* all sorts of weapons systems a first step in a realistic disarmament policy. If only the authorities could be made to realise that the forces leading them on in the armament race are just insane. I have lately come to understand this all the more clearly since being in contact with the international campaign among medical doctors against nuclear arms, both in Boston and Stockholm. They now encompass a membership of 38,000, being specialists from both East and West. At the present moment they are, in fact, holding a meeting in Stockholm.[2]

Physicians have now clearly explained how human beings react to the threat of nuclear weapons. On the one hand by just closing their eyes, and this, in fact, has long been the reaction of the "ordinary man". Or, on the other hand, by a kind of nationalistic paranoia. As the experts so bluntly put it: persecution mania. There is a constant magnifying of the enemy, exaggerating the threat he poses, persuading people that he is "the absolute enemy", ready to gobble them up. And so the reasoning goes, more armaments are required. But this is insane when we know that both superpowers already have so much more than "enough".

The medical specialists have also clearly demonstrated how completely insufficient our resources are for giving medical care to the wounded, even in highly developed countries, in the event of a strike with nuclear weapons.

The persecution mania supported by what already Eisenhower called the military-industrial complex is what now motivates leading politicians to indulge in an unlimited arms race. It is brought forth from the nationalism that flares up during any conflict of interests between states. But it goes far beyond the boundaries of any natural patriotism, which is based on love of one's own country and its cultural traditions. We have recently seen examples of that kind of distorted nationalism in the conflict between Great Britain and Argentina.

A mighty protest movement, speaking the language of common sense in more and more countries, has now arisen to confront all these forces that are engaged in the armament race and the militarisation of the world. For the moment this movement has won most remarkable strength in countries like the Netherlands and Norway, but more recently in West Germany and the

United States as well. It also lives in the hearts of the people in the East, although there it has so much greater difficulty in making itself heard.

In this new popular movement of protest against nuclear weapons women and, more and more churches and professional organisations are playing a leading role. I have unfortunately not the time to describe at greater length this flood of mighty protests against the acceptance of nuclear weapons. But in all sincerity, I personally believe that those who are leaders with political power over the world will be forced some day, sooner or later, to give way to common sense and the will of the people.

Violence and technology
War is murder. And the military preparations now being made for a potential major confrontation are aimed at collective murder. In a nuclear age the victims would be numbered by the millions.

This naked truth must be faced.

The age in which we live can only be characterised as one of barbarism. Our civilisation is in the process not only of being militarised, but also being brutalised.

There are two main features which mark this senseless trend. Let me briefly — just as everything in my lecture must necessarily be abbreviated and simplified — refer to them as *rivalry* and *violence*. Rivalry for the power to exploit the headlong on-rush of technology militates against cooperation. The result is increased violence, with more and more sophisticated weapons being used. This is precisely what sets out our age as one of barbarism and brutalisation. But the moment of truth should now have arrived.

I know that these are strong words. I know, too, that there are good forces at work, trying to check this ill-starred development.

May I at this juncture make a personal confession? I have always regarded global development as a struggle between the forces of good and evil. Not to be simplified as a struggle between Jesus and Satan, since I do not consider that the process is restricted to our own sphere of culture. Rather perhaps to be symbolised in the most general terms as a struggle between Ormuzd, the good, and Ahriman, the evil. My personal philosophy of life is one of *ethics*.

It seems to me as if the evil forces have now concentrated more and more power in their hands, Dare we believe that the leaders of the world's great nations will wake up, will see the precipice towards which they are heading and *change direction*?

The driving force in the development of our civilisation, at least since the Renaissance, has evidently been the progress of technology. But technology is two-edged. It can always be exploited either by good forces or by evil forces. And we human beings do not seem to have succeeded to make a choice quite consciously, nor how to *steer the considerable consequences*.

The credit side of this necessarily double-entry form of bookkeeping has naturally to record the tremendous progress that has helped to overcome so much misery and raise millions of people to a comfortable living standard.

The inventions and the great discoveries have opened up whole continents to reciprocal communication and interchange, *provided we are willing.* The scientific innovations, not least in the field of medicine, and a great deal more must, of course, be placed to the credit of technology.

But on the other hand, the triumphs of the evil forces are visible in numerous areas. I shall confine myself here to what I really know something about, and which is also the most ominous development: the growing role played by armaments. First and foremost arms are tools in the service of rival nations, pointing at the possibility of a future *war.* War and preparations for war have acquired a kind of legitimacy. The tremendous proliferation of arms, through their production and export, have now made them available more or less to all and sundry, right down to handguns and stilettoes. The cult of violence has by now so permeated the relations between human individuals that we are compelled to witness an increase in everyday violence, violence in the streets and in the homes. *These are the models we set for our young people.* It does not just happen. It is disclosed by science that practically one-half of trained intellectual resources are being mobilised for murderous purposes. During the post-war years we have been in a position to observe a development ranging from the simple Hiroshima bomb to all sorts of advanced technological devices. As an example I could select the invisible STEALTH aircraft, or the increasingly razor-sharp competition being played out in the oceans of the world, ASW (Anti-Submarine Warfare).

I have indicated how armaments promote — though admittedly not cause — collective military violence. But we should never forget the interconnections with the fact that the aforementioned personal violence, the crimes of violence committed in our cities, are to a large extent a result of the spread of arms.

How great is not the importance of weapons being so easily available? This should be studied. How often and with what weapons are killing and murder committed, in society and within families, which actually appears to be the commonest scene of violent crime? Where do these arms come from, these Saturday night specials that constitute the instrument of threats in bank robberies, or the hand grenades used by terrorists? How can their sales and their import be permitted?

The very fact that war, despite the ordinances issued by the United Nations, should receive more and more of a kind of "sanction" as a natural exercise of force by various nations, in my opinion plays a more ominous role in maintaining what I have called the weaponry and violence cult of our age.

Militarisation proceeds not only through acts of war and the purchase of arms. It is also promoted — primarily, of course, where young men are concerned — by military training, defense manuals etc. Exercises and war games erode the basic ethical values contained in the command "thou shalt not kill". We tolerate, in fact, more and more the exact opposite of what both religious creeds and the international law on more humane warfare are endavouring to instil in us.

It is frightening that in recent years such an increase has occurred in acts of terrorism, which have even reached peaceful countries such as ours. And as a "remedy", more and more security forces are established to protect the lives of individual men and women. The life of a politician is becoming increasingly hazardous. Where is the end of this spiral of force and counter-force?

Many countries persecute their own citizens and intern them in prisons or concentration camps. *Oppression* is becoming more and more a part of the systems. Lech Wałesa's sufferings may stand as a symbol for the way in which human rights are being trampled down, in one country after another.[3]

A cultural factor promoting violence which nowadays undoubtedly is highly effective is the *mass media*. And particularly everything that enters our minds through pictorial media. A wide range of investigations on this subject have been made and published in many countries. Some programmes tend to have a more momentary effect, while others confirm more permanent effects of indoctrination.

The violence shown in the mass media also has a differentiated effect, since violence committed by the "good guys" is imprinted more deeply in our apperceptions than violence committed by the "bad guys".

We also know that children and young people are more liable to accept a brutal pattern of action. This inability to filter or select the impressions that make their mark on us also has consequences in an international context: the morals and customs of the Western world are taught to the Third World through the medium of film and news exports, which are paralleled by the export of arms, and which at any rate hardly work in the opposite direction.

These are signs that there is something very sick in our society.

Finally, I should like briefly to return for a moment to the subject of *technology and peace*. I do this mainly in order to submit a practical proposal. And in this connection I should like to mention Nobel, a man who maybe better than anyone symbolises the two-edged nature of technology.

Nobel was a genuine friend of peace. He even went so far as to believe that he had invented a tool of destruction, dynamite, which would make war so senseless that it would become impossible. *He was wrong.*

But, in common with the forces of technology generally, his and other people's inventions can be used in the service of both good and evil. Nitroglycerine is a good example, which he himself cited. It is capable of soothing the pains of cardiac cramp, as he experienced, in common with myself. It can be used to blow up harbours as well as human beings. Nobel himself built up a great war industry.

In that man's breast, as is so often the case with human beings, dwelt two souls. Psychology is beginning, however, to draw aside the veil and reveal the labyrinths which are part of our personalities.

I should like to quote a passage from Nobel's will and testament, which I believe has gone unobserved and which is of direct practical value. Nobel states, *inter alia*, that the purpose of the fund is to support "the holding and promotion of peace congresses".

As far as I know, no peace congresses have been held in the nearly 100 years of the will's existence. I should like to suggest a change of policy for coming years, welcoming organisers of "peace congresses" as Nobel Prize candidates. Such conferences might provide excellent occasions for submitting important questions to a dynamic, intellectually factual analysis and debate. The mighty popular movement against the arms race which is now gaining strength, will facilitate and at the same time require a stimulus of this kind — to serve the building of our future.

ALFONSO GARCÍA ROBLES

Alfonso García Robles was born in Zamora in Mexico in 1911. After studying law he entered his country's foreign service in 1939. From 1962 to 1964 he held the post of Ambassador to Brazil, and from 1964 to 1970 was State Secretary in the Ministry of Foreign Affairs. From 1971 to 1975 he was Mexico's permanent representative in the United Nations; in 1975–76 he was Foreign Minister, and since 1977 he has been the Permanent Representative of Mexico to the Committee on Disarmament which has its headquarters in Geneva.

García Robles played a crucial role both in launching and implementing the agreement on a denuclearised zone in Latin America, which was concluded in Tlatelolco on March 12, 1967. He has in fact been called the father of the Tlatelolco Agreement. This, proposed by Adolfo López Mateos, President of Mexico at the time, was the outcome *inter alia* of the Cuba crisis. The idea was that a ban on nuclear arms would ensure that this part of the world would not be involved in any conflict between rival great powers. Negotiations were conducted by García Robles, and his enterprise and diplomatic skill deserve a large measure of credit for the fact that the agreement was successfully concluded after some years of negotiation. The final goal, however, has still to be reached, as countries such as Brazil and Argentina have signed the agreement but as yet not implemented it.

García Robles has also played a central role in UNO's work to promote general disarmament. He has represented his country during the negotiations in Geneva, but his name is primarily associated with the special UNO disarmament session. The first special session of this kind was held in 1978, and García Robles was one of the representatives entrusted with the task of coordinating the various views and proposals in a joint document. He was largely responsible for the successful adoption of what is known as the "Final Document" of that session of the Assembly. Though UNO's next special session in 1982 failed to repeat this success, García Robles received support for his idea of a world disarmament campaign.

García Robles continued his work in Geneva with the UN Conference of Disarmament until his retirement. He wrote a total of eighteen books on international affairs.

He died in September 1991 in Mexico City at the age of eighty.

ACCEPTANCE

ALFONSO GARCÍA ROBLES

Your Majesty, Your Royal Highnesses, Mr. President, Ladies and Gentlemen,

It is indeed a special privilege to have been distinguished with the Nobel Peace Prize for 1982.

Such a high honor carries for me on this occasion particular significance both for the exceptional qualities of the person with whom I share the prize — Alva Myrdal, my old friend and partner of so many battles fought in the forums of multilateral diplomacy, which have emphasised once again the identity of purpose of Mexico and Sweden in the fields of peace and of disarmament — and for the reasons specifically mentioned by the members of the Nobel Committee in their explanatory statement to the effect that they have decided to award the Peace Prize for 1982 "to two persons who for many years have played a central role in the United Nations' disarmament negotiations" and who have helped "to open the eyes of the world to the threat mankind faces in continued nuclear armament".

To correctly appraise that threat it will suffice to recall that the United Nations General Assembly unanimously declared in 1978, at its first special session devoted to disarmament, that it is "the very survival of mankind" which finds itself threatened by "the existence of nuclear weapons and the continuing arms race".

Similar reasons, no doubt, moved Albert Einstein and Bertrand Russell to state in their historic Manifesto of 1955, speaking "not as members of this or that nation, continent, or creed, but as human beings, members of the species Man, whose continued existence is in doubt", that we have "to learn to think in a new way".

In fact, every time that in the past a new weapon was invented, people would say — and, as is well known, Nobel himself originally shared this belief — that it was so terrible that it would never be used. Nevertheless it was, and even though it was terrible, it did not make the human race disappear. But, as so rightly stated by that eminent philosopher of history who was Arnold Toynbee "now we have something that could really extinguish life on our planet. Mankind has not found itself in a similar situation since the end of the palaeolithic age … . In fact, the threat to mankind's survival has been much greater since 1945 than it was during the first million years of history". There is no doubt that — and I again use here the authoritative concepts of Einstein and Russell expressed almost thirty years ago and which obviously are even more valid today — "it is feared that if many H-bombs are used there will be universal death — sudden only for a minority, but for the majority a slow torture of disease and disintegration".

The foregoing considerations, of unimpeachable authority, have led me to think something which I would not dare mention had I not already received the Nobel Peace Prize, inasmuch as otherwise I would risk being accused of acting *pro domo* or, in other words, for personal reasons: the advisability that when awarding the prize in the future, the highest priority be given to the contribution which the candidates, be they individuals or non-governmental organisations, have made to disarmament.

To justify this suggestion it would be enough to bear in mind that, as the General Assembly of the United Nations rightfully proclaimed — and it did so by consensus — if it continues to be true that security is "an inseparable element of peace", at present "the increase in weapons, especially nuclear weapons, far from helping to strengthen international security, on the contrary weakens it", inasmuch as "the accumulation of weapons, particularly nuclear weapons, today constitutes much more a threat than a protection for the future of mankind". Thus, it is evident that the time has come "to seek security in disarmament".

I am convinced that a man with the foresight of Alfred Nobel would have so provided if he were to draw up his will in our days, when it can rightly be said that there is an organic relation between peace and disarmament. Naturally, that should not mean disregard to the numerous contributions which can be made indirectly to peace in the broad field of human rights, beginning with the right of self-determination of peoples whose obervance requires also respect for the basic principle of non-intervention. A practical solution could perhaps be one involving a procedure similar to that which resulted in the creation of the prize of economics in 1968 thanks to a donation from the Bank of Sweden and which is awarded by the Royal Academy of Sciences of Sweden, which awards the prizes of physics and chemistry. If another Maecenas were now to be found who might provide the necessary funds, a new prize devoted to human rights could be established and awarded annually by the same Nobel Committee of Norway which awards the Nobel Peace Prize.

I trust that this suggestion, which I deem constructive, be interpreted as it is meant: a modest contribution to show my sincere appreciation for the honor which has been conferred on me by the Nobel Committee. Were it to become a reality, the intervals between the Nobel Peace Prizes awarded for achievements in the fields of disarmament would never again be as extended as has unfortunately been the case during the second half of the current century.

The fact that lately some circles, not less powerful by their small size, have been actively promoting certain theories, as dangerous as they are illusory, of a "limited", "winnable" or "protracted" nuclear war, as well as their obsession of "nuclear superiority", make it advisable to bear always in mind that the immediate goal of all States, as was expressly declared in the Final Document of the Special Assembly of 1978, "is that of the elimination of the danger of a nuclear war".

In order to contribute to the achievement of this pressing objective, the United Nations has just launched last June, during the second special session of the General Assembly devoted to disarmament, a "World Disarmament Campaign", which, under the auspices of the Organisation and coordinated by it, will have the task of "mobilising world public opinion on behalf of disarmament".

If disarmament, as I have taken the liberty to suggest, were in the future to become the decisive criterion for the evaluation by the Nobel Committee of the activities for peace, it would constitute, just as the Campaign which I have mentioned, another invaluable element to convince all nuclear powers, including those which have been more reluctant up to now, of the necessity to respect the "vital interests" of all peoples and to become fully aware of the profound truth of the following conclusion which the United Nations approved by unanimity four years ago:

> "Mankind is confronted with a choice: we must halt the arms race and proceed to disarmament or face annihilation".

THE LATIN AMERICAN NUCLEAR-WEAPON FREE ZONE

Nobel Lecture, 11 December 1982
by
ALFONSO GARCÍA ROBLES

In seems advisable to point out from the outset that the Latin American nuclear-weapon-free zone has the privilege of being the only one in existence which covers densely inhabited territories. Outside it only in Antarctica, the Outer Space and the sea bed are similar prohibitions in force, based on treaties concluded in 1959, 1967 and 1971, respectively.

The official title of the treaty which established the Latin American zone and defined its statute is the "Treaty for the Prohibition of Nuclear Weapons in Latin America", but it is usually referred to as the "Treaty of Tlatelolco", employing the Aztec name for the district of the Mexican capital where the Ministry of Foreign Affairs of Mexico is located and where the treaty itself was opened to signature almost sixteen years ago, on February 14, 1967.

The modest purpose of this lecture is to provide a synoptic view both of the genesis and the provisions of the treaty.

I. *Genesis of the Treaty of Tlatelolco*
The first international document in the history of the events directly related to the genesis of the Treaty of Tlatelolco was the Joint Declaration of 29 April 1963. In this declaration the Presidents of Bolivia, Brazil, Chile, Ecuador and Mexico announced that their governments were willing to sign a Latin American multilateral agreement by which they would undertake not "to manufacture, store, or test nuclear weapons or devices for launching nuclear weapons".

Seven months later, the United Nations General Assembly, taking as a basis a draft resolution submitted by eleven Latin American countries (the five previously mentioned, plus Costa Rica, El Salvador, Haiti, Honduras, Panama and Uruguay), approved on 27 November 1963 resolution 1911 (XVIII). In this resolution *inter alia* the General Assembly welcomed the initiative of the five Presidents for the military denuclearisation of Latin America; expressed the hope that the States of the region would initiate studies "concerning the measures that should be agreed upon with a view to achieving the aims" of the Joint Declaration, and requested the Secretary-General of the United Nations to extend to the States of Latin America, at their request, "such technical facilities as they may require in order to achieve the aims set forth in the present resolution".

Almost one year elapsed between the adoption of this General Assembly resolution and the next step worth mentioning in a review of the antecedents of the treaty. This interval was not wasted, however. The Mexican Government put it to good use with active diplomatic consultations which resulted in the convening of a Latin American conference known as the "Preliminary Session on the Denuclearisation of Latin America" (or REUPRAL, its Spanish acronym). Meeting in Mexico City from 23 to 27 November 1964, REUPRAL adopted a measure which was later to prove decisive for the success of the Latin American enterprise — the creation of an *ad hoc* organ, the "Preparatory Commission for the Denuclearisation of Latin America" (known also by its Spanish acronym, COPREDAL). The Preparatory Commission was specifically instructed (in the same resolution whereby it was established) "to prepare a preliminary draft of a multilateral treaty for the denuclearisation of Latin America, and to this end, to conduct any prior studies and take any prior steps that it deems necessary".[*]

COPREDAL had its first session in Mexico City from 15 to 22 March 1965. In this session, the Commission adopted its rules of procedure and set up four subsidiary organs: a Coordination Committee and three working groups. Subsequently the Commission would create another subsidiary organ — the "Negotiating Committee".

The Preparatory Commission held a total of four sessions, the last of which took place just under two years after its creation, from 31 January to 14 February 1967. Contrary to what has generally happened with other disarmament treaties and conventions, the draft articles for the future treaty dealing with verification, inspection, and control were the first to be completed at the second session of the Commission (23 August–2 September 1965). At that time a full declaration of principles was also drafted to serve as a basis for the Preamble of the draft treaty.

During its third session, COPREDAL received from its Coordinating Committee a working paper which contained the complete text of a preliminary draft for the treaty that the Commission had received the mandate to prepare. This draft, together with other proposals submitted by member states, provided the basis for the deliberations of the session. Their result was the unanimous approval of a document entitled "Proposals for the Preparation of the Treaty for the Denuclearisation of Latin America" which played as prominent a role in the history of the treaty as that of the Dumbarton Oaks proposals in the history of the United Nations.[4] These "Proposals" included all provisions which might prove necessary for the treaty as a whole, although in some cases COPREDAL, not having been able to find solutions satisfactory to all, had been obliged to present to the Governments two parallel alternatives.

---

*The author of this study presided over the "Preliminary Session on the Denuclearisation of Latin America" (REUPRAL) held in 1964, as well as over the four sessions of the "Preparatory Commission for the Denuclearisation of Latin America" (COPREDAL), held from 1965 to 1967, which made possible the elaboration and approval of the Treaty for the Prohibition of Nuclear Weapons in Latin America known as the Treaty of Tlatelolco. He was also Chairman of the "Preliminary Meeting" (REOPANAL), contemplated in Article 28 (3) of the Treaty and of the two parts of the first session of the General Conference of the Agency for the Prohibition of Nuclear Weapons in Latin America (OPANAL) which took place in 1969 and 1970, respectively.

From those few pending questions which the Commission would be called upon to solve at its fourth session, the most important one was the entry into force of the treaty. This issue provoked what was probably the greatest discussion in COPREDAL's proceedings. Because of this problem and due to the positive precedent established by COPREDAL's solution to the problem, it is worth examining the proceedings in somewhat greater detail.

When the Preparatory Commission considered this subject in April 1966, two distinct views became apparent. According to the first view, the treaty should come into force, between states which would ratify it, on the date of deposit of their respective instruments of ratification, in keeping with standard practice. The representative Latin American body to be established by the treaty should begin to function as soon as eleven instruments of ratification were deposited, as this number constituted a majority of the twenty-one members of the Preparatory Commission. Those states supporting the alternative view argued that the treaty, although signed and ratified by all member states of the Preparatory Commission, should enter into force only upon completion of four requirements, essentially those defined in Article 28 of the treaty. These four requirements may be summarised as follows: the signature and ratification of the Treaty of Tlatelolco and its Additional Protocols I and II by all states to which they were opened, and the conclusion of bilateral or multilateral agreements concerning the application of the Safeguards System of the International Atomic Energy Agency by each party to the treaty.

As a result of these differing views COPREDAL was obliged to present, in its proposals, two parallel texts. These texts stated respectively the provisions that the treaty would contain, according to whether one accepted the first or the second thesis. To solve the problem, the Coordinating Committee, in its report of 28 December 1966, suggested the adoption of a conciliatory formula, which could receive the approval of all member states of the Commission without detriment to their respective positions on the alternative texts. It was this formula, with some modifications, which was finally adopted and incorporated into Article 28 of the treaty. In keeping with it, the treaty would go into effect for all states that had ratified it upon completion of the four requirements specified in paragraph 1 of Article 28. That notwithstanding, the second paragraph of the Article states:

> "All signatory states shall have the imprescriptible right to waive, wholly or in part, the requirements laid down in the preceding paragraph. They may do so by means of a declaration which shall be annexed to their respective instrument of ratification and which may be formulated at the time of deposit of the instrument or subsequently. For those states which exercise this right, this Treaty shall enter into force upon deposit of the declaration, or as soon as those requirements have been met which have not been expressly waived".

Moreover, the third paragraph of the same Article stipulates:

> "As soon as this Treaty has entered into force in accordance with the provisions of paragraph 2 for eleven states, the Depositary Government shall convene a preliminary meeting of those states in order that the Agency may be set up and commence its work".

As one can see, an eclectic system was adopted, which, while respecting the viewpoints of all signatory states, prevented nonetheless any particular state from precluding the enactment of the treaty for those which would voluntarily wish to accept the statute of military denuclearisation defined therein.

The Treaty of Tlatelolco has thus contributed effectively to dispel the myth that for the establishment of a nuclear-weapon-free zone it would be an essential requirement that all states of the region concerned should become, from the very outset, parties to the treaty establishing the zone. The system adopted in the Latin American instrument proves that, although no state can obligate another to join such a zone, neither can one prevent others wishing to do so from adhering to a regime of total absence of nuclear weapons within their own territories.

Once the question of the entry into force of the treaty had been settled, at the fourth session of COPREDAL, the Preparatory Commission proceeded to settle, without major difficulties, the few other pending problems. On 12 February 1967, the Treaty for the Prohibition of Nuclear Weapons in Latin America was unanimously approved and two days later, at the solemn closing ceremony of the Commission's proceedings, it was opened to signature and subscribed to by the representatives of fourteen of its twenty-one members. As of August 1982, fifteen years later, the number of signatory states stands at twenty-five, of which twenty-two are already parties to the treaty.

Additional Protocol I which is open to the four States — United Kingdom, Netherlands, United States, and France — which are internationally responsible for territories lying within the limits of the geographical zone established in the treaty, has been signed by all those states and ratified by the United Kingdom, the Netherlands and the United States. With regard to France it seems that the ratification process is at present well advanced.

The five nuclear weapon states — the United Kingdom, the United States, France, China and the Soviet Union — are already parties to Additional Protocol II which is destined for them.

As provided for in paragraph 3 of Article 28 previously quoted, as soon as the treaty entered into force for eleven states, the Depositary Government convened a "preliminary meeting" of those states in order to set up the Agency for the Prohibition of Nuclear Weapons in Latin America known by its Spanish acronym OPANAL. This preliminary meeting (REOPANAL) took place in late June 1969 and carried out successfully all the preparatory work necessary for the first session of the General Conference of OPANAL. The latter was inaugurated on 2 September 1969 in the presence of U Thant, the then Secretary-General of the United Nations, and Sigvard Eklund, the Director-General of the International Atomic Energy Agency (IAEA). After seven working days the General Conference gave its approval to a series of basic juridical and administrative documents which provided the foundations for the Latin American Agency created by the treaty. To date the General Conference has held seven regular sessions and two special sessions in accordance with the provisions of Article 9.

II. *Analytical Summary of the Treaty of Tlatelolco*
As a complement to the above brief survey of the preparatory work leading to the conclusion of the Tlatelolco Treaty, the following paragraphs are intended to give a general idea of its contents and to carry out a brief analytical summary of some of its main provisions.

The treaty comprises a preamble, thirty-one articles, one transitional article and two additional protocols.

The preamble defines the fundamental aims pursued by the states which drafted the treaty by stating their conviction that:

> "The military denuclearisation of Latin America — being understood to mean the undertaking entered into internationally in this Treaty to keep their territories forever free from nuclear weapons — will constitute a measure which will spare their peoples from the squandering of their limited resources on nuclear armaments and will protect them against possible nuclear attacks on their territories, and will also constitute a significant contribution towards preventing the proliferation of nuclear weapons and a powerful factor for general and complete disarmament".

It is also worth noting that the Final Document approved by the first special session of the UN General Assembly devoted to disarmament, which met May–June 1978, contains several declaratory statements of a striking similarity to those included in the sixteen-year-old preamble of the Treaty of Tlatelolco. The Latin American states, for instance, declared themselves convinced:

> "That the incalculable destructive power of nuclear weapons has made it imperative that the legal prohibition of war should be strictly observed in practice if the survival of civilisation and of mankind itself is to be assured,
>
> That nuclear weapons, whose terrible effects are suffered, indiscriminately and inexorably, by military forces and civilian population alike, constitute, through the persistence of the radioactivity they release, an attack on the integrity of the human species and ultimately may even render the whole earth uninhabitable".

The United Nations, for its part, has proclaimed:

> "Mankind today is confronted with an unprecedented threat of self-extinction arising from the massive and competitive accumulation of

the most destructive weapons ever produced. Existing arsenals of nuclear weapons alone are more than sufficient to destroy all life on earth ...

Unless its avenues are closed, the continued arms race means a growing threat to international peace and security and even to the very survival of mankind ...

Removing the threat of a world war — a nuclear war — is the most acute and urgent task of the present day. Mankind is confronted with a choice: we must halt the arms race and proceed to disarmament or face annihilation".

As to the articles of the treaty, their contents may be described briefly as follows:

Article 1 defines the obligations of the parties. The following four articles (2–5) provide definitions of some terms employed in the treaty: contracting parties, territory, zone of application and nuclear weapons. Article 6 deals with the "meeting of signatories", while Articles 7–11 establish the structure and procedures of the "Agency for the Prohibition of Nuclear Weapons in Latin America" (OPANAL) created by the treaty, and state the functions and powers of its principal organs: the General Conference, the Council and the Secretariat. The five succeeding articles (12–16) and paragraphs 2 and 3 of Article 18 describe the functioning of the "control system", also established by the treaty. Article 17 contains general provisions on the peaceful use of nuclear energy and Article 18 deals with peaceful nuclear explosions.

Article 19 examines the relations of OPANAL with other international organisations, whereas Article 20 outlines the measures that the General Conference shall take in cases of serious violations of the treaty, such measures mainly involving simultaneous transmission of reports to the Security Council and the General Assembly of the United Nations. Article 21 safeguards the rights and obligations of the parties under the Charter of the United Nations and, in the case of states members of the Organisation of American States, under existing regional treaties. Article 23 makes it binding for the contracting parties to notify the Secretariat of OPANAL of any international agreement concluded by any of them on matters with which the treaty is concerned.

The settlement of controversies concerning the interpretation or application of the treaty is covered by Article 24. Articles 22, 25–27 and 29–31 contain what is generally known as "final clauses" dealing with questions such as privileges and immunities, signature, ratification and deposit, reservations (which the treaty does not admit), amendments, duration and denunciation, and authentic texts and registration. The transitional article specifies that "denunciation of the declaration referred to in Article 28, paragraph 2, shall be subject to the same procedures as the denunciation" of the treaty, except that it will take effect on the date of delivery of the respective notification and not three months later as provided in Article 30, paragraph 2, for denunciation of the treaty. In paragraph 2 of Article 26, the Government of Mexico is designated the "Depositary Government" of the treaty whereas Article 7, paragraph 4, stipulates that the headquarters of OPANAL "shall be in Mexico City". Finally, Article 28 reflects in its text the compromise formula which, as already explained, overcame the most serious obstacle which confronted COPREDAL: the entry into force of the treaty.

The two *Additional Protocols* to the treaty have identical preambles. Their texts recall UN Resolution 1911 (XVIII) and state the conviction that the treaty "represents an important step towards ensuring the non-proliferation of nuclear weapons". The texts also point out that the treaty "is not an end in itself but, rather, a means of achieving general and complete disarmament at a later stage", and finally express the desire to contribute "towards ending the armaments race". The operative parts of the protocols are naturally different from one another, although they have identical duration (the same as that of the treaty) and entry into force for the states which ratify each Protocol (the date of the deposit of the respective instruments of ratification).

Under Article 1 of *Additional Protocol I*, those extra-continental states which, *de jure* or *de facto*, are internationally responsible for territories lying within the limits of the geographical zone established by the treaty would, upon becoming parties to the protocol, agree "to undertake to apply the statute of denuclearisation in respect to warlike purposes as defined in Articles 1, 3, 5 and 13 of the Treaty" to such territories.

One aspect which should be borne in mind is that this protocol does not give those states the right to participate in the General Conference or in the Council of the Latin American Agency. But neither does it impose on those states any of the obligations relating to the system of control established in Article 14 (providing for semi-annual reports), in Article 15 (providing for special reports), and in Article 16 (providing for special inspections). In addition, the prohibition of reservations included in the treaty's Article 27 is not applicable to the protocol. Thus, in the protocol the necessary balance has been preserved between rights and obligations: although the rights are less extensive, the obligations are also fewer.

With regard to *Additional Protocol II*, the obligations assumed by the nuclear powers parties to the protocol are stated in its Articles 1 through 3 in the following terms:

— Respecting "in all its express aims and provisions" the "statute of denuclearisation of Latin America in respect of warlike purposes, as defined, delimited and set forth" in the Treaty of Tlatelolco.

— Not contributing "in any way to the performance of acts involving a violation of the obligations of Article 1 of the Treaty in the territories to which the Treaty applies".

— Not using or threatening to use "nuclear weapons against the contracting parties of the Treaty".

III. *Conclusions*

The importance of nuclear-weapon-free zones has been emphasised several times by the United Nations. The General Assembly in its Resolution 3472 B (XXX) of 11 December 1975 stated that "nuclear-weapon-free zones constitute one of the most effective means for preventing the proliferation, both horizontal and vertical, of nuclear weapons and for contributing to the elimination of the danger of a nuclear holocaust".

Subsequently, on 30 June 1978 the General Assembly, in the Programme of Action adopted by consensus as its first special session devoted to disarmament, stressed the significance of the establishment of nuclear-weapon-free zones as a disarmament measure.

The weight which the international community attaches to the Latin American nuclear-weapon-free zone was manifest from the very moment the Treaty of Tlatelolco was presented to the General Assembly. In its Resolution 2286 (XXII) of 5 December 1967, the General Assembly welcomed it "with particular satisfaction" and declared that it "constitutes an event of historic significance in the efforts to prevent the proliferation of nuclear weapons and to promote international peace and security". Such weight has been once again evidenced when, in the general debate of the first special disarmament Assembly, no less than forty-five States had supportive comments for the treaty.

The Treaty of Tlatelolco has shown the crucial importance of *ad hoc* preparatory efforts, such as those carried out for two years by COPREDAL, in attaining the desired goal. Furthermore, the Latin American nuclear-weapon-free zone which is now nearing completion has become in several respects an example which, notwithstanding the different characteristics of each region, is rich in inspiration. It provides profitable lessons for all states wishing to contribute to the broadening of the areas of the world from which those terrible instruments of mass destruction that are the nuclear weapons would be forever proscribed, process which, as unanimously declared by the General Assembly in 1978, "should be encouraged with the ultimate objective of achieving a world entirely free of nuclear weapons".

ENDNOTES

1. This paragraph is taken from Myrdal's *Game of Disarmament*, p. 224. General Maxwell Taylor became President John F. Kennedy's military adviser in 1961 and was appointed chairman of the joint chiefs of staff in 1962. McGeorge Bundy was special assistant for national security affairs to Presidents Kennedy and Lyndon B. Johnson. Herbert York was director of defense research and engineering in the Department of Defense under President Dwight Eisenhower and Kennedy.
2. In 1985 the Nobel Peace Prize was granted to the International Physicians for the Prevention of Nuclear War. See pages 123–154.
3. Lech Wałesa, the Polish leader of Solidarity, was granted the Nobel Peace Prize in 1983. See pages 71–95.
4. At the Dumbarton Oaks Conference, August–October 1944, the United States, Great Britain, China and the USSR drafted specific proposals for what was to be the Charter of the United Nations.

SELECTED BIBLIOGRAPHY

By Alva Myrdal:

Dynamics of European Nuclear Disarmament. Nottingham: Spokesman, 1981.

The Game of Disarmament: How the United States and Russia Run the Arms Race. 1976. Rev. ed. New York: Pantheon, 1982.

Nation and Family. 2nd ed. Cambridge: MIT Press, 1965.

War, Weapons and Everyday Violence. Manchester: University of New Hampshire Press, 1977.

Women's Two Roles. With V. Klein. Rev. ed. London: Routledge & Kegan Paul, 1968.

Other sources:

Bok, Sissela. *Alva Myrdal: A Daughter's Memoire.* Reading Massachusetts: Addison-Wesley, 1991. (Highly recommended.)

Herman, Sondra R. "From International Feminism to Feminist Internationalism. The Emergence of Alva Myrdal, 1936–1955" *Peace & Change* **18**, 4 (1993): 325–346. (An important interpretation, carefully researched.)

By Alfonso García Robles:

The Denuclearisation of Latin America. New York: Carnegie Endowment for International Peace, 1967.

"Mésures de Désarmament dans des Zones Particuliéres". In Academy of International Law, The Hague, *Recueil des Cours 1971.* Vol. 133. Leyden: Sijthoff, 1972, **2**: 43–134.

México en las Nacionas Unidas. 2 vols. Ciudad Universitaria: Universidad Nacional Autónoma de México, 1970. (Speeches at the United Nations, with introductions.)

El Tratado de Tlatelolco. Mexico City: El Colegio de México, 1967. (Speeches and documents.)

Peace 1983

LECH WAŁESA

INTRODUCTION

In its October announcement the Committee declared that the winner of the 1983 prize was Lech Wałesa, leader of the Solidarity labour movement in Poland and campaigner for the right of workers to organise, "a human right as defined by the United Nations". The Committee reaffirmed its position that "a campaign for human rights is a campaign for peace" and emphasised Wałesa's efforts to achieve this goal through negotiation "without resorting to violence".

The Solidarity movement had won this right from the Communist government in 1980, bringing elation in the West, but growing concern to Moscow. In December 1981, however, General Wojciech Jaruzelski, head of the government and of the Communist Party, set up a military dictatorship based on martial law, outlawed Solidarity and jailed most of its leaders. Wałesa, because of his international reputation, was not imprisoned, but he was detained in an isolated spot for almost a year. In July 1983 martial law was lifted and Wałesa was released, but strict controls remained in place.

When Wałesa learned about the prize in October, he decided to send his wife Danuta to represent him in Oslo, fearing that if he left Poland to receive the prize, he could be prevented from returning.

At the award ceremony Committee Chairman Egil Aarvik begins by quoting the UN Declaration of Human Rights, which declared these inalienable rights to be "the foundation of freedom, justice and peace in the world". In accordance with this principle, Aarvik explains, the Committee has granted earlier prizes to Lutuli (1960), King (1964), Sakharov (1975) and Pérez Esquivel (1980), and it now names Wałesa to "take his place among this gathering of campaigners for human rights".

Wałesa has chosen the path of peaceful negotiation, in itself an act of courage. His struggle draws strength from the support of the Catholic Church, and as the name of his movement, Solidarity, suggests, this struggle for workers' rights in Poland has universal implications. While at the moment he has the force of the Polish government against him, Aarvik is sure that Wałesa will be the ultimate victor, since he is a world spokesman "for the longing after freedom that can never be silenced... . The presentation of the Peace Prize to him today is a homage to the power of victory which abides in one person's belief, in his vision and in his courage to follow his call".

Representing her husband, Danuta Wałesa with clarity and emphasis reads his acceptance speech in his native language, in which he declares that he accepts the prize in the name of Solidarity, with the joy and hope of its millions of workers, but with sorrow for those who have died and suffered in its struggle. He notes that in 1905 when Henryk Sienkiewicz received the

Nobel prize for literature, Poland did not appear on the map of Europe, yet Sienkiewicz could insist that "here is proof that She lives on". Wałesa declares that today's prize has a similar meaning. Far away in Gdansk Lech listens to his wife's voice on the radio and is overcome by emotion.

The next day Wałesa's lecture in its original Polish is read by his Solidarity comrade Bogdan Cywinski. In it Wałesa speaks from his experience as a Polish worker, whose nation has fallen, but always to rise again, and whose life span has included "memorable and dramatic dates": 1944, when Warsaw rose against the German occupiers, but the uprising was suppressed and the city destroyed; 1956, when workers demonstrated in Poznan; 1970, when there were strikes on the Baltic coast; 1976, when the workers' movement in Ursus and Radom was suppressed; and 1980, when Solidarity won "irreversable" recognition of the rights of workers in the Gdansk Agreement.

"When I recall my own path of life", Wałesa says, "I cannot but speak of the violence, hatred and lies". But he has learned the lesson from such experiences "that we can effectively oppose violence, only if we ourselves do not resort to it". In the fifteen months of Solidarity's legal existence, it did not seek to overturn the government by force, and it still asks for peaceful negotiation today. In support of this request for dialogue, Wałesa cites the words of Pope John Paul II, who recently visited his Polish homeland.

Poland, like every nation, has the right to live in dignity, Wałesa maintains. Every nation has the inalienable right to peace and justice, "the two are like bread and salt for mankind". He concludes with the words of Psalm 29, which are inscribed on the monument at the entrance to the Gdansk shipyard in honour of the workers who died in the uprising there in December 1970, declaring: "Let these words be our message of brotherhood and hope".

ANNOUNCEMENT

The Norwegian Nobel Committee has awarded the Nobel Peace Prize for 1983 to Lech Wałesa.

In reaching this decision the Committee has taken into account Wałesa's contribution, made with considerable personal sacrifice, to ensure the workers' right to establish their own organisations.

This contribution is of vital importance in the wider campaign to secure the universal freedom to organise — a human right as defined by the United Nations.

Lech Wałesa's activities have been characterised by a determination to solve his country's problems through negotiation and cooperation without resorting to violence. He has attempted to establish a dialogue between the organisation he represents — Solidarity — and the authorities. The Committee regards Wałesa as an exponent of the active longing for peace and freedom which exists, in spite of unequal conditions, unconquered in all the peoples of the world.

The Committee has on several occasions when awarding the Peace Prize emphasised that a campaign for human rights is a campaign for peace. Furthermore the Committee believes that Wałesa's attempt to find a peaceful solution to his country's problems will contribute to a relaxation of international tension.

In an age when détente and the peaceful resolution of conflicts are more necessary than ever before, Lech Wałesa's contribution is both an inspiration and an example.

PRESENTATION

Speech by EGIL AARVIK, Chairman of the Norwegian Nobel Committee

Your Majesty, Your Royal Highnesses, Your Excellencies, Ladies and Gentlemen:

"Whereas recognition of the inherent dignity and of the equal and inalienable rights of all members of the human family is the foundation of freedom, justice and peace in the world".

Thus begins the text of the United Nations' Declaration of Human Rights, a declaration which, with its definition of the concept of peace, forms the basis of the Norwegian Nobel Committee's decision to award this year's Peace Prize to the Polish trade union leader, Lech Wałesa.

The campaign for human rights is, necessarily, an inseparable part of the struggle for peace. The selection of a Peace Prize winner on these grounds is not new: laureates such as the South African Albert Lutuli, Martin Luther King from the U.S.A., Andrei Sakharov from the U.S.S.R., and the Argentinian Adolfo Pérez Esquivel received their awards on just these grounds. The Committee believes that this year's prizewinner can justly take his place among this gathering of campaigners for human rights.

Consideration of the question of human rights raises the well-known problem: "Why does humanity advance so slowly?" It has, however, become more generally recognised that a peace which is won and defended through the violation of human rights, is a peace which neither can nor ought to be permanent.

The present generation has perhaps learned this in a way no previous generation experienced. Military occupation and foreign domination, together with the associated evils of physical and mental terror, have led more and more people to understand the great truth — that "freedom and life are one". Peace is created where people live and breathe in freedom, and where one does as one would be done by.

We can assume that such thoughts lie behind the United Nations' Declaration of Human Rights — which the world community has adopted as the basis for peaceful coexistence between peoples and nations. For the Norwegian Nobel Committee it was a natural development to consider the Peace Prize in the light of this declaration. Through the presentation of this year's award the Committee once again draws the attention of the world community to its own definition of the concept of peace.

It follows from this that the Committee's deliberations and decisions are necessarily independent of national and political boundaries. The guidelines given to the Committee in Alfred Nobel's will stipulate that the presentation of the Peace Prize is the responsibility of the Committee alone, and cannot be influenced by outside forces. Thus the Nobel Peace Prize can never be more — or less — than a hand stretched out to individuals or groups who give expression to the longing for peace and freedom felt by all the peoples of the world, wherever they live. We believe that it is in the spirit of Alfred Nobel's legacy that the Peace Prize should be a gesture of solidarity with those who, in the service of peace, campaign for humanity's highest ideals.

Human dignity is an important concept in this connection. The phrase has two central connotations: firstly, that the dignity of humanity is inviolable, and, secondly, that each and every human being has the same, everlasting value. A natural corollary of this is that we all have a common duty to defend human dignity. All thoughts of solidarity — even the command to love one another — have their foundation here. Human dignity is humanity's shared possession, a possession which we all have both a part in and a responsibility for. We are bound together in a common lot which makes it impossible for us to be unaffected by the fate of others.

Another Nobel Prize winner, Ernest Hemingway, opens one of his novels with a famous quotation from the English poet John Donne which illustrates this point with an almost shocking clarity:

> "No man is an island, intire of its selfe; every man is a piece of the Continent, a part of the maine; if a clod bee washed away by the sea, Europe is the lesse, as well as if a Promontorie were; as well as if a Mannor of thy friends or of thine owne were; any mans death diminishes me, because I am involved in Mankind: And therefore never send to know for whom the bell tolls; It tolls for thee".

This is the way in which we ought to experience humanity's oneness. "Any man's death diminishes me". Every brother being in chains is my shame. Every longing for freedom which is suppressed, every human right which is violated is a personal defeat for me — because we are united in humankind and share one another's fate.

Up from this ideal of human oneness this year's prizewinner has raised a burning torch, a shining name, the name of Solidarity. He has lifted the torch unarmed; the word, the spirit and the thought of freedom and human rights were his weapons. And, as is so often the case, the struggle involved great personal sacrifice, even though the object was something as simple as the workers' right to establish their own organisations. This is a right which, again, is confirmed in the world community's declaration of human rights.

The Norwegian Nobel Committee has evaluated Lech Wałesa's contribution in this field as being of essential importance in the campaign to establish the universal freedom of organisation in all countries. It is in just this context that the name "Solidarity" has its deepest and most wide-ranging meaning. Lech Wałesa's contribution is more than a domestic Polish concern; the solidarity for which he is spokesman is an expression of precisely the concept of being at one with humanity; therefore he belongs to us all. The world has heard his voice and understood his message; the Nobel Peace Prize is merely a confirmation of this.

Lech Wałesa has made the name "Solidarity" more than an expression of the unity of a group campaigning for special interests. Solidarity has come to represent the determination to resolve conflicts and obliterate disagreement through peaceful negotiation, where all involved meet with a mutual respect for one another's integrity.

Conflicts and disagreements can be various, and can lead to many different reactions. Those involved will inevitably be faced with complicated decisions. This was the situation on August day in 1980, when Lech Wałesa climbed over the steel fence of the Lenin yards in Gdansk, took the microphone and at a stroke became the leader of Polish solidarity. He was faced with overwhelming difficulties; the choice of strategy was not easy. The goal was clear enough: the workers' right to organise and the right to negotiate with the country's officials on the workers' social and economic situation. But which of the many available paths would lead him to this goal?

This is not the occasion to evaluate the political situation Lech Wałesa found himself in. Suffice it to say that it was difficult. More interesting to us now is the fact that Wałesa's chosen strategy was that of peace and negotiation. And, as always in such situations, the willingness to negotiate implied the willingness to compromise — here because it was obvious that the opponent was also fighting adverse conditions, both economic and political. Solidarity came to represent, as a result of a mobilisation of the national will — the so-called "Polish social opposition", the possibility of a solidarity of opinion in the whole nation. This was not an opposition which involved the use of physical power. Rather, it was a question of a spiritual or intellectual power which, because of its universal acceptance in the populace, would permeate the system and dissolve conflicts from within.

By following this peaceful course, without resorting to violence, Solidarity became a rapidly expanding movement. The courage which Lech Wałesa showed in stepping forward openly and unarmed was overwhelmingly rewarded by the millions of Polish workers and farmers who joined him in his struggle.

Thus, in awarding the Peace Prize to Lech Wałesa today, the Committee wishes it not only to be seen as a token of respect, but also as an expression of gratitude for the peaceful courage he showed when choosing his course.

That Wałesa and the movement he leads are in keeping with the highest of human ideals is confirmed not least by the close connections which have existed between Solidarity and the Polish church. This interdependence is based not on common political interests, but rather on an ideological unity in the perception of human value and human rights.

It has not escaped the Committee's notice that the Polish church, which is a popular church in a way that few European churches are, has been so consistent in its support of Lech Wałesa; this has given Solidarity an invaluable moral strength. One has great expectations of the role the church can come to play in Polish society given its standing among the people.

As outsiders we are particularly aware of the way in which Solidarity — also through its attachment to the church — has shown its willingness for peace and reconciliation. We have seen them gather in their tens of thousands in and around the churches in prayer for their land and cause. We have seen them water with their tears the wreaths of the victims of the fight for freedom. And we have understood that their unarmed battle is a battle they fight not only for their own sake, but also for all liberty-loving people the world over.

It is in this perspective that the Norwegian Nobel Committee has seen Lech Wałesa's contribution. The way he chose was the way of negotiation, peace and reconciliation.

In the world we live in it is shockingly clear that détente and the peaceful resolution of conflicts are more necessary than ever before. We have seen too much of what the brutal use of power can lead to. If history has taught us anything, it is that the use of violence and power can, in the long run, only mobilise the powers of death.

Unfortunately, we have also learned that the voice of history does not always tell of victory for humanity and peace. It is pertinent to ask whether idealistic and morally sound attitudes do, in fact, have any chance of success.

This question can, of course, also be raised in the case of Lech Wałesa. True enough, it would be strange if the causes he represents did not succeed, if only in the long run. He was not a political troublemaker: his concerns were rather the Polish workers' interests and current demands. But such demands are not always successful, even when they are as justified as they are in Lech Wałesa's case.

No, Lech Wałesa raised no revolutionary banner, and espoused no other weapon than the peaceful strike weapon which is recognised by the world community. Neither did he claim support from the declarations of human rights emanating from the United Nations and the Helsinki agreement. He wished only to negotiate. Two things alone were of pressing interest: the workers' social conditions and their right to negotiate.

The background to this singlemindedness was the simple fact that these rights were not recognised. This had led to outbreaks of universal bitterness on several occasions previously — in 1956, in 1970, and so again in 1980. All of these outbreaks were concerned with precisely these problems: social conditions, freedom of expression and the right to organise.

One can reasonably wonder why it should be so difficult to achieve recognition for such aims. Those who know but a little of the history of the international labour movement will be aware that such difficulties have always been present. It is still remarkable, however, that working people's elementary rights can be denied, irrespective of which ideology or economic system the respective countries belong to. One ought, perhaps, to be able to believe that there are boundaries behind which it is not necessary to campaign for workers' rights; such boundaries obviously don't exist.

It is clear that, although Lech Wałesa primarily campaigned for elementary social rights without challenging the established power structure, his campaign had inevitable political and ideological overtones. His campaign was also necessarily a campaign for human rights and, as such, inevitably interpreted as an obstruction against the system by the political authorities.

As the political opposition to Solidarity grew, its own consciousness of standing for humanity and human rights became clearer. It became increasingly obvious that Lech Wałesa's campaign for workers' rights was from the very beginning a contribution to the general campaign for human rights in the world. This connection was emphasised more and more — especially by intellectual groups within the movement, and also by the Polish church.

Campaigners for human rights, independent of where in the world they have lived and worked, have always had one common problem: How can the idealistic goal be realised when one is obliged, at the same time, to take into account the practical possibilities in the given situation. Is it wise to moderate demands and campaign for a step-by-step improvement?

This problem faced Lech Wałesa. Was a cautious course — with the possibility of gaining some ground — the right one? Or should one risk — and stand to loose — everything? It is impossible to understand the Polish Solidarity movement without being aware of this problem.

A realistic evaluation of the existing situation would suggest that the best course was to aim for a combination of the existing one-party government with a social pluralism which permitted the freedom to organise and negotiate — at any rate in the future. Such a solution was the first negotiating model.

We know now that even this moderate strategy failed. Solidarity is today a forbidden organisation. The negotiations and the strikes which were designed to emphasise the seriousness of the negotiations led to the state of emergency and the arrest and imprisonment of Lech Wałesa.

And, even though the state of emergency is rescinded and Wałesa is freed, his freedom is limited. His own evaluation of the situation has not permitted him to be present here today. The Peace Prize laureate's seat is empty; it won't be his voice we hear. Let us therefore try even harder to listen to the silent speech from his empty place.

At the present time, Lech Wałesa cannot be presented as a victor at the end of a struggle full of sacrifice. His chosen course was not as short and easy as that. And it could seem that the goals he set himself are just as distant still.

But is Lech Wałesa really silent today? Is he completely without victory? Has his cause suffered defeat? Many are of the opinion that his voice has never been stronger and reached further than it does now. The electrician from Gdansk, the carpenter's son from the Vistula valley, has managed to lift the banner of freedom and humanity so high that the whole world can once again see it. The power of his belief and vision is unweakened. His actions have become a chapter in the history of international labour, and the future will recognise his name among those who contributed to humanity's legacy of freedom. Once again the stone rejected by the builder has become a cornerstone; this time a cornerstone in the building of freedom and democracy which humanity, with varying degrees of success, is attempting to raise in our world.

It is in any case certain that Lech Wałesa's efforts have an important message for our times. It is the Committee's opinion that he stands as an inspiration and a shining example to all those who, under different conditions, fight for freedom and humanity.

If, in a future which we hope is not too distant, there should again be attempted a compromise between the Polish authorities and the country's workers and farmers, Lech Wałesa's participation will be both necessary and indispensable.

For he is a victor in the eyes of the ordinary worker or farm labourer; he is a victor in the eyes of the people and their church. And he is one of the great spokesman in the world today for the longing for freedom that can never be silenced.

Lech Wałesa has made humanity bigger and more inviolable. His ambivalent good fortune is that he has won a victory which is not of this, our political, world. The presentation of the Peace Prize to him today is a homage to the power of victory which abides in one person's belief, in his vision and in his courage to follow his call.

LECH WAŁESA

Lech Wałesa was born on September 29, 1943 in Popowo, Poland. After graduating from vocational school, he worked as a car mechanic at a machine center from 1961 to 1965. He served in the army for two years, rose to the rank of corporal, and in 1967 was employed in the Gdansk shipyards as an electrician. In 1969 he married Danuta Goloś and they have eight children.

During the clash in December 1970 between the workers and the government, he was one of the leaders of the shipyard workers and was briefly detained. In 1976, however, as a result of his activities as a shop steward, he was fired and had to earn his living by taking temporary jobs.

In 1978 with other activists he began to organise free non-communist trade unions and took part in many actions on the sea coast. He was kept under surveillance by the state security service and frequently detained.

In August 1980 he led the Gdansk shipyard strike which gave rise to a wave of strikes over much of the country with Wałesa seen as the leader. The primary demands were for workers' rights. The authorities were forced to capitulate and to negotiate with Wałesa the Gdansk Agreement of August 31, 1980, which gave the workers the right to strike and to organise their own independent union.

The Catholic Church supported the movement, and in January 1981 Wałesa was cordially received by Pope John Paul II in the Vatican. Wałesa himself has always regarded his Catholicism as a source of strength and inspiration. In the years 1980–81 Wałesa travelled to Italy, Japan, Sweden, France and Switzerland as guest of the International Labour Organisation. In September 1981 he was elected Solidarity Chairman at the First National Solidarity Congress in Gdansk.

The country's brief enjoyment of relative freedom ended in December 1981, when General Jaruzelski, fearing Soviet armed intervention among other considerations, imposed martial law, "suspended" Solidarity, arrested many of its leaders, and interned Wałesa in a country house in a remote spot.

In November 1982 Wałesa was released and reinstated at the Gdansk shipyards. Although kept under surveillance, he managed to maintain lively contact with Solidarity leaders in the underground. While martial law was lifted in July 1983, many of the restrictions were continued in the civil code. In October 1983 the announcement of Wałesa's Nobel prize raised the spirits of the underground movement, but the award was attacked by the government press.

The Jaruzelski regime became even more unpopular as economic conditions worsened, and it was finally forced to negotiate with Wałesa and his Solidarity colleagues. The result was the holding of parliamentary elections which, although limited, led to the establishment of a non-communist government.

Under Mikhail Gorbachev the Soviet Union was no longer prepared to use military force to keep communist parties in satellite states in power.

Wałesa, now head of the revived Solidarity labour union, began a series of meetings with world leaders. In November 1989 he became the third person in history, after the Marquis de Lafayette and Winston Churchill, to address a joint session of the United States Congress.

In April 1990 at Solidarity's second national congress, Wałesa was elected chairman with 77.5% of the votes. In December 1990 in a general ballot he was elected President of the Republic of Poland. He served until defeated in the election of November 1995.

Wałesa has been granted many honorary degrees from universities, including Harvard University and the University of Paris. Other honors include the Medal of Freedom (Philadelphia, U.S.A.); the Award of Free World (Norway); and the European Award of Human Rights.

ACCEPTANCE*

LECH WAŁESA
(Translation)

Your Majesty, Honourable Representatives of the Norwegian people,

You are aware of the reasons why I could not come to your Capital city and receive personally this distinguished prize. On that solemn day my place is among those with whom I have grown and to whom I belong — the workers of Gdansk.

Let my words convey to you the joy and the never extinguished hope of the millions of my brothers — the millions of working people in factories and offices, associated in the union whose very name expresses one of the noblest aspirations of humanity. Today all of them, like myself, feel greatly honoured by the prize.

With deep sorrow I think of those who paid with their lives for the loyalty to "Solidarity"; of those who are behind prison bars and who are victims of repressions. I think of all those with whom I have travelled the same road and with whom I shared the trials and tribulations of our time.

For the first time a Pole has been awarded a prize which Alfred Nobel founded for activities towards bringing the nations of the world closer together.

The most ardent hopes of my compatriots are linked with this idea — in spite of the violence, cruelty and brutality which characterise the conflicts splitting the present-day world.

We desire peace — and that is why we have never resorted to physical force. We crave for justice — and that is why we are so persistent in the struggle for our rights. We seek freedom of convictions — and that is why we have never attempted to enslave man's conscience nor shall we ever attempt to do so.

We are fighting for the right of the working people to association and for the dignity of human labour. We respect the dignity and the rights of every man and every nation. The path to a brighter future of the world leads through honest reconciliation of the conflicting interests and not through hatred and bloodshed. To follow that path means to enhance the moral power of the all-embracing idea of human solidarity.

I feel happy and proud that over the past few years this idea has been so closely connected with the name of my homeland.

In 1905, when Poland did not appear on the map of Europe, Henryk Sienkiewicz said when receiving the Nobel prize for literature: "She was

*Read by Mrs Danuta Wałesa

pronounced dead — yet here is a proof that She lives on; She was declared incapable to think and to work — and here is proof to the contrary; She was pronounced defeated — and here is proof that She is victorious".

Today nobody claims that Poland is dead. But the words have acquired a new meaning.

May I express to you — the illustrious representatives of the Norwegian people — my most profound gratitude for confirming the vitality and strength of our idea by awarding the Nobel Peace Prize to the chairman of "Solidarity".

NOBEL LECTURE*

11 December 1983
by
LECH WAŁESA
(Translation)

Ladies and Gentlemen,

Addressing you, as the winner of the 1983 Nobel Peace Prize, is a Polish worker from the Gdansk Shipyard, one of the founders of the independent trade union movement in Poland. It would be the simplest thing for me to say that I am not worthy of that great distinction. Yet, when I recall the hour when the news of the prize has spread throughout my country, the hour of rising emotions and universal joy of the people who felt that they have a moral and spiritual share in the award, I am obligated to say that I regard it as a sign of recognition that the movement to which I gave all my strength has served well the community of men.

I accept the award with my deepest respects for its meaning and significance, and, at the same time, I am conscious that the honour is bestowed not on me personally, but upon "Solidarity", upon the people and the ideas for which we have fought and shall continue to do so in the spirit of peace and justice. And there is nothing I desire more than that the granting of the award should help the cause of peace and justice in my country and the world over.

My first words which I address to you, and through you to all people, are those which I have known since my childhood days: *Peace to men of goodwill* — all and everywhere, in the North and South, East and West.

I belong to a nation which over the past centuries has experienced many hardships and reverses. The world reacted with silence or with mere sympathy when Polish frontiers were crossed by invading armies and the sovereign state had to succumb to brutal force. Our national history has so often filled us with bitterness and the feeling of helplessness. But this was, above all, a great lesson in hope. Thanking you for the award I would like, first of all, to express my gratitude and my belief that it serves to enhance the Polish hope. The hope of the nation which throughout the nineteenth century had not for a moment reconciled itself with the loss of independence, and fighting for its own freedom, fought at the same time for the freedom of other nations. The hope whose elations and downfalls during the past forty years — i.e. the span of my own life — have been marked by the memorable and dramatic dates: 1944, 1956, 1970, 1976, 1980.

*Read by Bogdan Cywinski.

And if I permit myself at this juncture and on this occasion to mention my own life, it is because I believe that the prize has been granted to me as to one of many.

My youth passed at the time of the country's reconstruction from the ruins and ashes of the war in which my nation never bowed to the enemy paying the highest price in the struggle. I belong to the generation of workers who, born in the villages and hamlets of rural Poland, had the opportunity to acquire education and find employment in industry, becoming in the course conscious of their rights and importance in society. Those were the years of awakening aspirations of workers and peasants, but also years of many wrongs, degradations and lost illusions. I was barely 13 years old when, in June 1956, the desperate struggle of the workers of Poznan for bread and freedom was suppressed in blood. Thirteen also was the boy — Romek Strzalkowski — who was killed in the struggle. It was the "Solidarity" union which 25 years later demanded that tribute be paid to his memory. In December 1970 when workers' protest demonstrations engulfed the towns of the Baltic coast, I was a worker in the Gdansk Shipyard and one of the organisers of the strikes. The memory of my fellow workers who then lost their lives, the bitter memory of violence and despair has become for me a lesson never to be forgotten.

Few years later, in June 1976, the strike of the workers at Ursus and Radom was a new experience which not only strengthened my belief in the justness of the working people's demands and aspirations, but has also indicated the urgent need for their solidarity. This conviction brought me, in the summer of 1978, to the Free Trade Unions — formed by a group of courageous and dedicated people who came out in the defense of the workers' rights and dignity. In July and August of 1980 a wave of strikes swept throughout Poland. The issue at stake was then something much bigger than only material conditions of existence. My road of life has, at the time of the struggle, brought me back to the shipyard in Gdansk. The whole country has joined forces with the workers of Gdansk and Szczecin. The agreements of Gdansk, Szczecin and Jastrzebie were eventually signed and the "Solidarity" union has thus come into being.

The great Polish strikes, of which I have just spoken, were events of a special nature. Their character was determined on the one hand by the menacing circumstances in which they were held and, on the other, by their objectives. The Polish workers who participated in the strike actions, in fact represented the nation.

When I recall my own path of life I cannot but speak of the violence, hatred and lies. A lesson drawn from such experiences, however, was that we can effectively oppose violence only if we ourselves do not resort to it.

In the brief history of those eventful years, the Gdansk Agreement stands out as a great charter of the rights of the working people which nothing can ever destroy. Lying at the root of the social agreements of 1980 are the courage, sense of responsibility, and the solidarity of the working people.

Both sides have then recognised that an accord must be reached if bloodshed is to be prevented. The agreement then signed has been and shall remain the model and the only method to follow, the only one that gives a chance of finding a middle course between the use of force and a hopeless struggle. Our firm conviction that ours is a just cause and that we must find a peaceful way to attain our goals gave us the strength and the awareness of the limits beyond which we must not go. What until then seemed impossible to achieve has become a fact of life. We have won the right to association in trade unions independent from the authorities, founded and shaped by the working people themselves.

Our union — the "Solidarity" — has grown into a powerful movement for social and moral liberation. The people freed from the bondage of fear and apathy, called for reforms and improvements. We fought a difficult struggle for our existence. That was and still is a great opportunity for the whole country. I think that it marked also the road to be taken by the authorities, if they thought of a state governed in cooperation and participation of all citizens. "Solidarity", as a trade union movement, did not reach for power, nor did it turn against the established constitutional order. During the 15 months of "Solidarity's" legal existence nobody was killed or wounded as a result of its activities. Our movement expanded by leaps and bounds. But we were compelled to conduct an uninterrupted struggle for our rights and freedom of activity while at the same time imposing upon ourselves the unavoidable self-limitations. The programme of our movement stems from the fundamental moral laws and order. The sole and basic source of our strength is the solidarity of workers, peasants and the intelligentsia, the solidarity of the nation, the solidarity of people who seek to live in dignity, truth, and in harmony with their conscience.

Let the veil of silence fall presently over what happened afterwards. Silence, too, can speak out.

One thing, however, must be said here and now on this solemn occasion: the Polish people have not been subjugated nor have they chosen the road of violence and fratricidal bloodshed.

We shall not yield to violence. We shall not be deprived of union freedoms. We shall never agree with sending people to prison for their convictions. The gates of prisons must be thrown open and persons sentenced for defending union and civic rights must be set free. The announced trials of eleven leading members of our movement must never be held. All those already sentenced or still awaiting trials for their union activities or their convictions — should return to their homes and be allowed to live and work in their country.

The defense of our rights and our dignity, as well as efforts never to let ourselves to be overcome by the feeling of hatred — this is the road we have chosen.

The Polish experience, which the Nobel Peace Prize has put into limelight, has been a difficult, a dramatic one. Yet, I believe that it looks to the future.

The things that have taken place in human conscience and re-shaped human attitudes cannot be obliterated or destroyed. They exist and will remain.

We are the heirs of those national aspirations thanks to which our people could never be made into an inert mass with no will of their own. We want to live with the belief that law means law and justice means justice, that our toil has a meaning and is not wasted, that our culture grows and develops in freedom.

As a nation we have the right to decide our own affairs, to mould our own future. This does not pose any danger to anybody. Our nation is fully aware of the responsibility for its own fate in the complicated situation of the contemporary world.

Despite everything that has been going on in my country during the past two years, I am still convinced that we have no alternative but to come to an agreement, and that the difficult problems which Poland is now facing can be resolved only through a real dialogue between state authorities and the people.

During his latest visit to the land of his fathers, Pope John Paul II had this to say on this point:

> "Why do the working people in Poland — and everywhere else for that matter — have the right to such a dialogue? It is because the working man is not a mere tool of production, but he is the subject which throughout the process of production takes precedence over the capital. By the fact of his labour, the man becomes the true master of his workshop, of the process of labour, of the fruits of his toil and of their distribution. He is also ready for sacrifices if he feels that he is a real partner and has a say in the just division of what has been produced by common effort".

It is, however, precisely this feeling that we lack. It is hardly possible to build anything if frustration, bitterness and a mood of helplessness prevail. He who once became aware of the power of solidarity and who breathed the air of freedom will not be crushed. The dialogue is possible and we have the right to it. The wall raised by the course of events must not become an insurmountable obstacle. My most ardent desire is that my country will recapture its historic opportunity for a peaceful evolution and that Poland will prove to the world that even the most complex situations can be solved by a dialogue and not by force.

We are ready for the dialogue. We are also prepared, at any time, to put our reasons and demands to the judgement of the people. We have no doubts as to what verdict would be returned.

I think that all nations of the world have the right to life in dignity. I believe that, sooner or later, the rights of individuals, of families, and of entire communities will be respected in every corner of the world. Respect for civic and human rights in Poland and for our national identity is in the best interest of all Europe. For, in the interest of Europe is a peaceful

Poland, and the Polish aspirations to freedom will never be stifled. The dialogue in Poland is the only way to achieving internal peace and that is why it is also an indispensable element of peace in Europe.

I realise that the strivings of the Polish people gave rise, and still do so, to the feelings of understanding and solidarity all over the world. Allow me from this place to express my most profound thanks to all those who help Poland and the Poles. May I also voice my desire that our wish for the dialogue and for respect of human rights in Poland should be strengthened by a positive thought. My country is in the grips of a major economic crisis. This is causing dramatic consequences for the very existence of Polish families. A permanent economic crisis in Poland may also have serious repercussions for Europe. Thus, Poland ought to be helped and deserves help.

I am looking at the present-day world with the eyes of a worker — a worker who belongs to a nation so tragically experienced by the war. I most sincerely wish that the world in which we live be free from the threat of a nuclear holocaust and from the ruinous arms race. It is my cherished desire that peace be not separated from freedom which is the right of every nation. This I desire and for this I pray.

May I repeat that the fundamental necessity in Poland is now understanding and dialogue. I think that the same applies to the whole world: we should go on talking, we must not close any doors or do anything that would block the road to an understanding. And we must remember that only peace built on the foundations of justice and moral order can be a lasting one.

In many parts of the world the people are searching for a solution which would link the two basic values: peace and justice. The two are like bread and salt for mankind. Every nation and every community have the inalienable right to these values. No conflicts can be resolved without doing everything possible to follow that road. Our times require that these aspirations which exist the world over must be recognised.

Our efforts and harsh experiences have revealed to the world the value of human solidarity. Accepting this honourable distinction I am thinking of those with whom I am linked by the spirit of solidarity:

— first of all, of those who in the struggle for the workers' and civic rights in my country paid the highest price — the price of life;
— of my friends who paid for the defense of "Solidarity" with the loss of freedom, who were sentenced to prison terms or are awaiting trial;
— of my countrymen who saw in the "Solidarity" movement the fulfillment of their aspirations as workers and citizens, who are subjected to humiliations and ready for sacrifices, who have learnt to link courage with wisdom and who persist in loyalty to the cause we have embarked upon;
— of all those who are struggling throughout the world for the workers' and union rights, for the dignity of a working man, for human rights.

Inscribed on the monument erected at the entrance to the Gdansk Shipyard in memory of those who died in December 1970 are the words of the Psalm:

"The Lord will give power to His people;
The Lord will give His people the blessing of peace".

Let these words be our message of brotherhood and hope.

SELECTED BIBLIOGRAPHY

By Wałesa:

The Struggle and the Triumph. New York: Arcade, 1992.

A Way of Hope. New York: Henry Holt, 1987.

Other Sources:

Craig, Mary. *Lech Wałesa and His Poland.* New York: Continuum, 1987. (By a popular writer who knows Poland well. Based on extensive research and interviews with Wałesa and others. Covers the period through 1986. Highly recommended.)

Goodwyn, Lawrence. *Breaking the Barrier: The Rise of Solidarity in Poland.* New York: Oxford University Press, 1991.

Kurski, Jaroslaw. *Lech Wałesa: Democrat or Dictator.* Boulder, Colorado: Westview Press, 1993. (Translated by Peter Obst. The period July 1989 to March 1992. By Wałesa's press spokesman, whose purpose is "to portray Lech in motion".)

Peace 1984

REVEREND DESMOND MPILO TUTU

INTRODUCTION

In its October announcement, the Committee declared that Bishop Desmond Tutu had been chosen as the 1984 prizewinner as "a unifying figure" in the nonviolent struggle against apartheid ("apartness" of the races) in his country. The Committee wished to recognise "the courage and heroism shown by black South Africans in their use of peaceful methods" in this "campaign for racial equality as a human right" and at the same time to recognise others throughout the world engaged in such a struggle and using similar methods.

In the presentation speech, Chairman Aarvik of the Committee emphasises the importance to Africa and the world that this campaign "is being fought with the weapons of the spirit and reason". He recalls the earlier prize given to the black South African leader Albert Lutuli in 1961 on similar grounds.

Aarvik refers to such baneful elements of the apartheid system as the removal of persons officially classified as black to special areas denoted as their "homelands", and the Pass Laws, which required blacks to carry a "passbook" to identify themselves whenever they went to a "white" area for work or another purpose. He tells how Tutu took up the struggle against apartheid, but he "never learned to hate", and he chose to work for racial justice by peaceful means.

To Aarvik, apartheid is "totally incompatible with human civilisation", and he declares that the prize for Tutu is "an attempt to awaken consciences". It also may be seen as an omen that although the way may be difficult, the campaign for freedom and peace will eventually win. Aarvik concludes with words of the song of the American civil rights movement, "We shall overcome".

Before Aarvik can present to Tutu the Nobel diploma and medal, there is a bomb scare, and the hall must be cleared. When the audience reassembles, Tutu has several of his friends sing Gospel songs before the ceremony continues.

The next day Tutu in his Nobel lecture vividly described many aspects of the oppression in "the land I love passionately", the beautiful richly endowed land, where there would be enough for everybody, were it not for the greed of the minority, who take a disproportionate share. He compares apartheid to Hitler's "final solution" for the Jews. There cannot be peace, Tutu maintains, without justice, and South Africa in this way is a microcosm of a world in which in many lands in different degrees, "when there is injustice, invariably peace becomes a casualty".

"When will we learn", Tutu asks, "that human beings are of infinite value because thety have been created in the image of God, and that it is a blasphemy to treat them as if they were less than this?" He concludes, his arms in the air, citing the passage he is so fond of quoting, the vision of world peace in the Revelation of St. John the Divine (Rev. 6: 9–12).

ANNOUNCEMENT

The Norwegian Nobel Committee has chosen to award the Nobel Peace Prize for 1984 to Bishop Desmond Tutu, General Secretary of the South African Council of Churches.

The Committee has attached importance to Desmond Tutu's role as a unifying leader in the campaign to resolve the problem of apartheid in South Africa. The means by which this campaign is conducted is of vital importance for the whole of the continent of Africa and for the cause of peace in the world. Through the award of this year's Peace Prize the Committee wishes to direct attention to the nonviolent struggle for liberation to which Desmond Tutu belongs, a struggle in which black and white South Africans unite to bring their country out of conflict and crisis.

The Nobel Peace Prize has been awarded to a South African once before, in 1960 when it was awarded to the former president of the African National Congress, Albert Lutuli. This year's award should be seen as a renewed recognition of the courage and heroism shown by black South Africans in their use of peaceful methods in the struggle against apartheid. This recognition is also directed to all who, throughout the world, use such methods to stand in the vanguard of the campaign for racial equality as a human right.

It is the committee's wish that the Peace Prize now awarded to Desmond Tutu should be regarded not only as a gesture of support to him and to the South African Council of Churches of which he is leader, but also to all individuals and groups in South Africa who, with their concern for human dignity, fraternity and democracy, incite the admiration of the world.

PRESENTATION

Speech by EGIL AARVIK, Chairman of the Norwegian Nobel Committee

Your Majesty, Your Royal Highnesses, Your Excellencies, Ladies and Gentlemen:

The Norwegian Nobel Committee wishes, through the presentation of this year's Nobel Peace Prize, to direct attention to a unifying leader figure in the campaign to solve South Africa's apartheid problem by peaceful means. The situation as it is today is such that a peaceful solution is by no means inevitable — the repression is so brutal that a violent rebellion would be an understandable reaction. The South African has more reason now than ever before to exclaim "Cry the beloved country".

Given this situation it is all the more remarkable that human beings are able to choose a peaceful way to freedom.

It is the Nobel Committee's opinion that the means by which the South African liberation process is conducted will have wide-ranging consequences for the whole of the African continent, and therefore also for the cause of peace in the world. This is an opinion which is also expressed in a number of United Nations resolutions — most recently that passed by the Security Council in October this year. Racial discrimination in South Africa is rightly regarded as a threat to peace and as an outrageous violation of basic human rights.

Fortunately, a peaceful alternative exists. On a broad front a campaign is being fought with the weapons of the spirit and reason — a campaign for truth, freedom and justice. In recognition of the fact that it is this alternative which must succeed, the South African bishop, Desmond Tutu, has been selected as this year's Peace Prize laureate.

The contribution he has made, and is still making, represents a hope for the future, for the country's white minority as well as the black majority. Desmond Tutu is an exponent of the only form for conflict solving which is worthy of civilised nations.

It is today 23 years since the Nobel Peace Prize was last awarded to a South African. On that occasion it was Albert Lutuli, then president of the African National Congress, who was presented with the prize. It is the Committee's wish that this year's award should be seen as a renewed recognition of the courage and heroic patience shown by black South Africans in their use of peaceful means to oppose the apartheid system. This recognition is also extended to all who, throughout the world, stand in the forefront of the campaign for racial equality as a human right.

It is unfortunately not only in South Africa that human rights are violated. Another former prizewinner, Amnesty International, informs us that it is known to occur in 117 countries, and that prisoners of conscience are tortured in 60 countries. Too frequently, the brutal features of power and violence mar the face of our times. But if we are willing to look for it, we can also see the face of peace — even if we have to peer through prison bars and barbed wire to find it. And, in spite of everything, new hope is raised, on each occasion we see how the spirit of man refuses to be conquered by the forces of hate.

Some time ago television enabled us to see this year's laureate in a suburb of Johannesburg. A massacre of the black population had just taken place — the camera showed ruined houses, mutilated human beings and crushed children's toys. Innocent people had been murdered. Women and children mortally wounded. But, after the police vehicles had driven away with their prisoners, Desmond Tutu stood and spoke to a frightened and bitter congregation: "Do not hate", he said, "let us choose the peaceful way to freedom".

It is with admiration and humility we today present the Nobel Peace Prize to this man.

Desmond Tutu's contribution to the liberation struggle was given a special significance in 1978 when he became the first black secretary of the South African Council of Churches. This Council of Churches is both a joint forum for the churches of South Africa and the national representative for the World Council of Churches. It includes all the major churches in the country — with the exception of the Boer Church which withdrew as a result of disagreement with the Council over the question of apartheid. The Catholic Church is a so-called associate member, but is also one of the Council's strongest supporters.

As around 75 percent of all citizens of South Africa are members of a church, the body is a very representative organisation. Few other organisations can make the same claim to speak for the black population.

As the dynamic leader of this Council, Desmond Tutu has formulated as his goal "a democratic and just society without racial segregation". His minimum demands are: equal civil rights for all, the abolition of the Pass Laws, a common system of education and the cessation of the forced deportation of blacks from South Africa to the so-called "homelands".

Both through these objectives and through its practical activities the South African Council of Churches has obviously exceeded the normal scope of such an organisation. The Council has become a trailblazer in the campaign for human rights, a central force in a liberation struggle and an increasingly wide-ranging support organisation for the many victims of the present system's racial discrimination. Consider what happens when millions of human beings are deported. Their homes are razed to the ground. Their personal possessions are taken from them. They lose their jobs, and are physically transported and deposited in the empty veld with just a tent and a sack of maize as their only hopes of survival.

3 millions have been deported in this way, while new millions await their turn.

If we ignore for a moment the personal humiliation, the question remains

— who is there to help these people to survive in their new existence? Who will help them house themselves, find water, tend to the sick or educate their children?

The system also has — obviously — its political prisoners. Their crime is the necessary one of wanting a society with freedom and respect for human rights! They are imprisoned — but who is there to help their families?

There is also the so-called "migration labour" system under which underpaid labourers are obliged to live away from their families. The Pass Laws are also notorious; they burden the black population with a collective captivity and make them foreigners in their own country. Anyone breaking these laws risks group arrest and indefinite imprisonment without legal help.

It is not difficult to imagine that, as a result of this system, there are considerable social, medical and legal problems which necessitate help from the South African Council of Churches. It is a pleasure to note that over 90 percent of the Council's budget is covered by contributions from churches in the Western world, while it is with anxiety we note that new laws are being prepared which will deprive the Council of the right to administer its own funds.

As already mentioned, racial discrimination is by no means limited to South Africa. Before the Second World War such discrimination was relatively common, and world opinion was not particularly concerned with it. The situation changed, however, after 1945: new ideas were expressed in the Atlantic Charter and the Declaration of Human Rights.[1]

During the war it was possible to see signs of a more liberal policy evolving in South Africa. The ideas from the Atlantic Charter, however, had little effect there, and when the Nationalist Party won the election of 1948 the situation worsened. It was in this period that the apartheid laws were formulated and ratified, a move which has correctly been described as a counter-revolution against pre-1948 tendencies.

History is never without a certain sense for the ironic — the man who more than anyone else was responsible for the implementation of the apartheid system, the Nationalist Party's first prime minister Dr. Daniel Malan, was a churchman, an ordained priest in the Dutch Reformed Church. And now we see that the most dynamic opponent of the apartheid system is also a churchman — in fact a bishop! In this way history corrects its own mistakes.

The irony of history is even more wide-ranging. The apartheid system is the indirect reason for the fact that Desmond Tutu became a churchman with the position he has today. His first wish was to become a doctor, but this was impossible with his parents' financial situation. He became, therefore, a teacher — as his father had been. In 1957 when the government introduced the state "Bantu education" — in many ways an abolition of education for the black population — Tutu felt himself driven from the teaching profession and began to study to be a priest. He has himself said that he did not feel himself called to take this step by high ideals, "it just occurred to me that, if the Church would have me, the profession of priest could be a good way of serving my people".

Yes — it seems that the Church was willing to take him!

Obviously, Desmond Tutu was not without high ideals. And, like so many others, he had these ideals from the family home. In his childhood in Klerksdorp in the West Rand district he was taught tolerance and sympathy. He has himself said that "I never learnt to hate". The idealism of his parents was thus reflected in Tutu's upbringing.

When Tutu was twelve years old his family moved to Johannesburg, where his father was a teacher and his mother a cleaner and cook at a school for the blind. Here he learned sympathy for the weakest and most underprivileged. It was also here that he met the man who probably exercised the strongest influence over his formative years, the white priest Trevor Huddleston, who was parish priest in the black slum of Sophiatown. "One day", says Tutu, "I was standing in the street with my mother when a white man in a priest's clothing walked past. As he passed us he took off his hat to my mother. I couldn't believe my eyes — a white man who greeted a black working class woman!" When Tutu has in later years been asked why he doesn't hate whites, he usually replies that it is because he was fortunate in the whites he met when young.

But, although he has never learnt to hate, none has opposed injustice with a more burning anger. Courageous and fearless he opposes his country's authorities. He is to be found at the front of the demonstration processions, regardless of the danger to his own life. His clear standpoints and his fearless attitude have made his name a unifying symbol for all groups of freedom campaigners in Africa.

Desmond Tutu has shown that to campaign for the cause of peace is not a question of silent acceptance, but rather of arousing consciences and a sense of indignation, strengthening the will and inspiring the human spirit so that it recognises both its own value and its power of victory. To this fight for peace we give our affirmative "yes" today.

The actress Liv Ullmann has told of a Lebanese boy who was asked if he believed in revenge. "Yes", replied the boy, he believed in revenge. "And to revenge", he was asked, "what is that?" "To revenge", replied the boy, "is to make a bad person a good person."

Thoughts of this nature are the human spirit's bulwark against barbarism. It is those who have such thoughts who are the real peacemakers and the meek, who are not only blessed, but who shall also inherit the earth — also the earth of South Africa. The 23 million coloured people shall at least have the same right of inheritance of this earth as the 4.5 million whites.

The question has been raised whether the award of the Peace Prize to Desmond Tutu is to be seen as a judgement on the South African apartheid system. The answer is that the system has judged itself. Racial discrimination can never be anything but an expression of shameful contempt for humankind. Racial discrimination used and defended as a political system is totally incompatible with human civilisation. This year's Peace Prize is therefore an attempt to awaken consciences. It is, and has to be, an illusion that privileged groups can maintain their position through repression. That such things can have a place in our future is a lie which nobody should allow themselves to believe.

In his famous book *Roots*, the black author Alex Hailey tells of his African ancestor, the negro slave Kunta Kinte, who attained the position of coachman with his white master. One of his duties was to drive his white masters to luxurious parties held at neighbouring farms. One evening, as he sat outside and waited, he began to philosophise over his experiences. According to the author, he couldn't understand that such an unbelievable luxury really existed and that the whites really lived the way they did. After a long time and many such parties, he began to realise that the whites' existence was, in a remarkable way, unreal — a sort of beautiful dream built on a lie which the whites told themselves: that good can come of evil, and that it is possible to lead a civilised existence while not acknowledging as human beings those whose sweat and blood made their privileges possible.

Kunta Kinte was right. Negro slavery was incompatible with American civilisation — in the same way as the apartheid system is in reality incompatible with South African.

There are few if any recorded examples in history of privileged groups who voluntarily relinquish privileges to the advantage of the repressed. In all probability it won't happen in South Africa either. The possibility of an unbloody resolution of the conflict is nevertheless still there. It is such a solution that Desmond Tutu fights for. The presentation of the Peace Prize to him is, therefore, not a judgement, rather it is a challenge, a hand stretched out — in the same way as Desmond Tutu's hand is stretched out to conciliation and atonement. If only the dominant minority would recognise this opportunity and take the chance before history's amnesty runs out.

It will be understood that to present Desmond Tutu's Nobel Peace Prize with a white man's hands is in some ways an oppressive experience. On such an occasion it is impossible not to allow one's thoughts to consider what the white man has prepetrated against his coloured cousins. It is depressing to think of the list of debts which is written with the African's suffering, tears and blood. Think of the humiliation and exploitation which human beings from this continent have had to endure — from the first slave traffic, through centuries of colonialism to today's discrimination. On a day like this our memories are indeed painful — not only on account of what the white man has done and still does, but also on account of what he, to this day, has neglected to do.

Thus, as we now present the Nobel Peace Prize to the African Desmond Tutu, our immediate feeling is that our first word to the Prize Laureate ought to be a word describing our sorrow over the wounds which injustice and racial hatred has inflicted on his people.

The dominating feeling is, however, one of thankfulness and respectful joy, and this is because we feel ourselves united with him in the belief in the creative power of love. With his warmhearted Christian faith he is a representative of the best in us all.

Additionally, there is a factor which the Nobel Committee has placed great emphasis on — that in the liberation process which Desmond Tutu leads black and white stand shoulder to shoulder in the common cause against injustice. In this we see a moving confirmation of the words in Alfred Nobel's testament on the brotherhood of mankind.

In the light of this we bring our homage to Desmond Tutu. Because his struggle is — and has to be — our struggle, we recognise him as a brother. He receives today the Peace Prize as a sign of the thankfulness of millions — perhaps also as an omen of black and white Africans' final victory over the last remnants of opposition in the campaign for freedom and peace. It is appropriate to remember the words of Martin Luther King just before his martyrdom: "I have seen the Promised Land!"

Even though the black South African's way forward to freedom's promised land can still be long and difficult, it is a way of humanity which we shall traverse together in the sound knowledge that "we shall overcome". Therefore our first word to the Peace Prize laureate will be a word of hope and victory: "oh yes, deep in my heart I do believe that we shall overcome — some day!"

REVEREND DESMOND MPILO TUTU

Born	:	7 October 1931, Klerksdorp, Transvaal
Parents	:	Father a school teacher. Mother relatively uneducated
Married	:	2 July 1955
Wife	:	Leah Nomalizo (né Shenxane)
Children	:	Trevor Thamsanqa, Theresa Thandeka, Naomi Nontombi, Mpho Andrea
1945–50	:	High school education — Johannesburg Bantu High School, Western Native Township up to Matric
1951–53	:	Teacher's Diploma at Pretoria Bantu Normal College
1954	:	BA (University of South Africa)
1954	:	Teacher at Johannesburg Bantu High School
1955–58	:	Teacher at Munsieville High School, Krugersdorp
1958–60	:	St Peter's Theological College, Rosettenville, Johannesburg Ordination Training — Licentiate in Theology
1960	:	Ordained Deacon — served title in Benoni Location
1961	:	Ordained Priest
1962–65	:	Part-time curate St Alban's — lived at Golders Green, London
1965	:	BD Hon (London)
1966	:	Part-time curate St Mary's, Blechingley, Surrey
1966	:	M. Th. (London)
1967–69	:	Federal Theological Seminary, Alice, Cape — member of staff Chaplain University of Fort Hare
1970–72	:	UBLS, Roma, Lesotho — Lecturer in Department of Theology
1972–75	:	Associate Director — Theological Education Fund of the World Council of Churches based in Bromley, Kent. Lived in Grove Park, London and was honorary curate of St Augustine's
1975–76	:	Dean of Johannesburg
1976–78	:	Bishop of Lesotho
1978–85	:	General Secretary, South African Council of Churches
1985–86	:	Bishop of Johannesburg
1986–	:	Archbishop of Cape Town

Other offices held:

1987	:	President — All Africa Conference of Churches
1988	:	Chancellor — University of the Western Cape

Honorary Degrees

1978	:	Elected Fellow of King's College, London, UK
		Honorary Doctor of Divinity, General Theological Seminary, USA
		Honorary DCL, Kent University, UK
1979	:	Honorary Doctor of Laws, Harvard University, USA

1981   :   Honorary Doctor of Theology, Ruhr University, Bochum, Germany
            Federal Republic
1982   :   Honorary Doctor of Sacred Theology, Columbia University, USA
1984   :   Honorary Doctor of Humane Letters, St Paul's College Lawrenceville,
            USA
            Honorary Doctor of Sacred Theology, Dickinson College, USA
            Honorary Doctor of Law, Claremont Graduate School, USA
            Honorary Doctor of Divinity, Aberdeen University, Scotland
            Honorary Doctor of Humane Letters, Howard University, USA
1985   :   Honorary LLD, Temple University, Philadelphia, USA
            Honorary Doctor of Humanities, Wilberforce University, Ohio, USA
            Honorary Doctor of Divinity, Trinity Lutheran Seminary, Columbus,
            Ohio, USA
1986   :   Honorary Doctor of Divinity, Trinity College, Hartford, USA
            Honorary Doctor of Divinity, Chicago Theological Seminary, USA
            Honorary Doctor of Humane Letters, More House College, Atlanta,
            USA
            Honorary Doctor of Humane Letters, Central University, Durham,
            North Carolina, USA
            Honorary Doctor of Laws, Temple University, Philadelphia, USA
            Honorary Doctor of Humane Letters, Hunter College, University
            of New York
            Honorary Doctorate, University of Rio, Rio de Janiero, Brazil
            Honorary Doctor of Divinity, University of the West Indies, Trinidad
            Honorary Doctor of Divinity, Oberlin College, Davenport Iowa, USA
1988   :   Honorary Doctor of Divinity, University of the South Sewanee, USA
            Honorary Doctor of Laws, Mount Allison University, Sackville,
            Canada
            Honorary Doctor of Laws, North Eastern University, Boston, USA
            Honorary Doctor of Divinity, Emory University, Atlanta, USA
            Honorary Doctorate, University of Strasbourg, France
1989   :   Honorary Fellowship of the Selly Oak Colleges, Birmingham, UK
1990   :   Honorary Doctor of Divinity, Wesleyan University, Connecticutt,
            USA
            Honorary Doctor of Divinity, Lincoln University, Pennsylvania, USA
            Honorary Doctor of Divinity, Oxford University, UK
            Honorary Doctorate, University of Missouri, Kansas City, USA
            Honorary Doctor of Humane Letters, University of New Rochelle,
            NY, USA
            Honorary Doctorate, Brown University, Rhode Island, USA
            Honorary Doctor of Laws, Seton Hall University, New Jersey, USA
            Honorary Doctorate, University of Puerto Rico, Rio Piedra
            Honorary Doctor of Laws, Stetson University, Florida, USA
            Docteur Honoris Causa de L'Universite Nationale du Benin

Awards

1980 : Prix d'Athene (Onassis Foundation)
1983 : The Family of Man Gold Medal Award
Designated Member of International Social Prospects Academy
1984 : Martin Luther King Jr. Humantarian Award, Annual Black American Hero and Heroines Day;
Nobel Peace Prize, Oslo, Norway
1985 : Life Member, National Association for Advancement of Coloured People
1986 : International Integrity Award from John-Roger Foundation, Los Angeles, USA;
USA President's Award, Glassboro State College, New Jersey, USA;
Martin Luther King Jr. Peace Award, Atlanta, USA;
World Public Forum Award from San Rafael, California, USA
1987 : Order of the Southern Cross, Brazil;
Order of Merit of Brasilia, Brazil;
"Pacem in Terris" Peace and Freedom Award from the Quad Cities;
"Pacem in Terris" Coalition, Cleveland, Ohio, USA
1988 : Albert Schweitzer Humanitarian Award, Emmanuel College, Boston, USA
1989 : Joint recipient of the Third World Prize awarded jointly to Rev. Tutu, Rev. Dr. F. Chikane, Rev. Dr. A. Boesak and Dr. B. Naudé
1990 : Distinguished Peace Leadership Award, Nuclear Age Peace Foundation; President's Medal, Claremont Graduate School, California, USA
1985 : Freedom of the City of Florence, Italy
1986 : Freedom of the City of Methyr Tydfil, UK
1987 : Freedom of the City of Durham, UK
1989 : Freedom of the City of Hull, UK
1990 : Freedom of the Borough of Lewisham, UK
1990 : Freedom of the City of Kinshasa, Zaire

Organisations and Committees

1986 : Vice Chairman, International Alert
1987 : Patron, World Council of Global Cooperation, Canada
1988 : Member of the Committee of Honour for the Memorial to Imre Nagy and his companions, Hungarian Human Rights League, International Patron, Global Cooperation for a Better World, UK Patron, Orchestra of the World;
Member of the Disbursements Advisory Committee, Fund for Education in South Africa, New York;
Member of the International Advisory Committee of the Robert F. Kennedy Memorial Human Rights Award

1990   : Member of the Honorary Committee of the Special Fund for
               Health in Africa;
               Advisor to the Editorial Board of "On the Cutting Edge" — a
               publication dedicated to redefining rights, obligations and dignity
               in the post-nuclear age;
               Patron, District Six Museum Foundation
1991   : Patron, Pan-African Book Foundation;
               Honorary Chairman of Advisory Board of Children of War

The Nobel Prize gave Tutu a greater international stature and made more
effective his appeal for maintaining economic sanctions against South Africa
until apartheid was liquidated. As a churchman, Archbishop of Capetown
since 1986, his courageous and unceasing call for freedom, justice and reconciliation
within South Africa gave emphasis to the moral character of the opposition
to that system.

When Nelson Mandela was freed from prison in 1990 and assumed leadership
of the movement, Tutu gave strong moral support to his efforts but did not
take a major political role. He was master of ceremonies at the celebration
following Mandela's election as President of South Africa by the new democratic
legislature in May 1994, and at the inauguration ceremony the next day he
gave the closing prayer of thankfulness.

In 1993 Tutu took part in the unsuccessful mission of Nobel peace
laureates attempting to secure the freedom from detention in Burma (Myanmar)
of fellow laureate Aung San Suu Kyi.

NOBEL LECTURE[2]

December 11, 1984
by
DESMOND TUTU

Ladies and Gentlemen,

Before I left South Africa, a land I love passionately, we had an emergency meeting of the Executive Committee of the South African Council of Churches with the leaders of our member churches. We called the meeting because of the deepening crisis in our land, which has claimed nearly 200 lives this year alone. We visited some of the troublespots on the Witwatersrand. I went with others to the East Rand. We visited the home of an old lady. She told us that she looked after her grandson and the children of neighbors while their parents were at work. One day the police chased some pupils who had been boycotting classes, but they disappeared between the township houses. The police drove down the old lady's street. She was sitting at the back of the house in her kitchen, whilst her charges were playing in the front of the house in the yard. Her daughter rushed into the house, calling out to her to come quickly. The old lady dashed out of the kitchen into the living room. Her grandson had fallen just inside the door, dead. He had been shot in the back by the police. He was 6 years old. A few weeks later, a white mother, trying to register her black servant for work, drove through a black township. Black rioters stoned her car and killed her baby of a few months old, the first white casualty of the current unrest in South Africa. Such deaths are two too many. These are part of the high cost of apartheid.

Everyday in a squatter camp near Cape Town, called K.T.C., the authorities have been demolishing flimsy plastic shelters which black mothers have erected because they were taking their marriage vows seriously. They have been reduced to sitting on soaking mattresses, with their household effects strewn round their feet, and whimpering babies on their laps, in the cold Cape winter rain. Everyday the authorities have carried out these callous demolitions. What heinous crime have these women committed, to be hounded like criminals in this manner? All they have wanted is to be with their husbands, the fathers of their children. Everywhere else in the world they would be highly commended, but in South Africa, a land which claims to be Christian, and which boasts a public holiday called Family Day, these gallant women are treated so inhumanely, and yet all they want is to have a decent and stable family life. Unfortunately, in the land of their birth, it is a criminal offence for them to live happily with their husbands and the fathers of their children. Black family life is thus being undermined, not accidentally, but by deliberate Government policy. It is part of the price human beings, God's children, are called to pay for apartheid. An unacceptable price.

I come from a beautiful land, richly endowed by God with wonderful natural resources, wide expanses, rolling mountains, singing birds, bright shining stars out of blue skies, with radiant sunshine, golden sunshine. There is enough of the good things that come from God's bounty, there is enough for everyone, but apartheid has confirmed some in their selfishness, causing them to grasp greedily a disproportionate share, the lion's share, because of their power. They have taken 87% of the land, though being only about 20% of our population. The rest have had to make do with the remaining 13%. Apartheid has decreed the politics of exclusion. 73% of the population is excluded from any meaningful participation in the political decision-making processes of the land of their birth. The new constitution, making provision of three chambers, for whites, coloureds, and Indians, mentions blacks only once, and thereafter ignores them completely. Thus this new constitution, lauded in parts of the West as a step in the right direction, entrenches racism and ethnicity. The constitutional committees are composed in the ratio of 4 whites to 2 coloureds and 1 Indian. 0 black. 2 + 1 can never equal, let alone be more than, 4. Hence this constitution perpetuates by law and entrenches white minority rule. Blacks are expected to exercise their political ambitions in unviable, poverty-stricken, arid, bantustan homelands, ghettoes of misery, inexhaustible reservoirs of cheap black labour, bantustans into which South Africa is being balkanised. Blacks are systematically being stripped of their South African citizenship and being turned into aliens in the land of their birth. This is apartheid's final solution, just as Nazism had its final solution for the Jews in Hitler's Aryan madness. The South African Government is smart. Aliens can claim but very few rights, least of all political rights.

In pursuance of apartheid's ideological racist dream, over 3,000,000 of God's children have been uprooted from their homes, which have been demolished, whilst they have then been dumped in the bantustan homeland resettlement camps. I say dumped advisedly: only things or rubbish is dumped, not human beings. Apartheid has, however, ensured that God's children, just because they are black, should be treated as if they were things, and not as of infinite value as being created in the image of God. These dumping grounds are far from where work and food can be procured easily. Children starve, suffer from the often irreversible consequences of malnutrition — this happens to them not accidentally, but by deliberate Government policy. They starve in a land that could be the bread basket of Africa, a land that normally is a net exporter of food.

The father leaves his family in the bantustan homeland, there eking out a miserable existence, whilst he, if he is lucky, goes to the so-called white man's town as a migrant, to live an unnatural life in a single sex hostel for 11 months of the year, being prey there to prostitution, drunkenness, and worse. This migratory labour policy is declared Government policy, and has been condemned, even by the white Dutch Reformed Church,[3] not noted for being quick to criticise the Government, as a cancer in our society. This cancer, eating away at the vitals of black family life, is deliberate Government policy. It is part of the cost of apartheid, exorbitant in terms of human suffering.

Apartheid has spawned discriminatory education, such as Bantu Education, education for serfdom, ensuring that the Government spends only about one tenth on one black child per annum for education what it spends on a white child. It is education that is decidedly separate and unequal. It is to be wantonly wasteful of human resources, because so many of God's children are prevented, by deliberate Government policy, from attaining to their fullest potential. South Africa is paying a heavy price already for this iniquitous policy because there is a desperate shortage of skilled manpower, a direct result of the short-sighted schemes of the racist regime. It is a moral universe that we inhabit, and good and right equity matter in the universe of the God we worship. And so, in this matter, the South African Government and its supporters are being properly hoisted with their own petard.

Apartheid is upheld by a phalanx of iniquitous laws, such as the Population Registration Act, which decrees that all South Africans must be classified ethnically, and duly registered according to these race categories. Many times, in the same family one child has been classified white whilst another, with a slightly darker hue, has been classified coloured, with all the horrible consequences for the latter of being shut out from membership of a greatly privileged caste. There have, as a result, been several child suicides. This is too high a price to pay for racial purity, for it is doubtful whether any end, however desirable, can justify such a means. There are laws, such as the Prohibition of Mixed Marriages Act, which regard marriages between a white and a person of another race as illegal. Race becomes an impediment to a valid marriage. Two persons who have fallen in love are prevented by race from consummating their love in the marriage bond. Something beautiful is made to be sordid and ugly. The Immorality Act decrees that fornication and adultery are illegal if they happen between a white and one of another race. The police are reduced to the level of peeping Toms to catch couples red-handed. Many whites have committed suicide rather than face the disastrous consequences that follow in the train of even just being charged under this law. The cost is too great and intolerable.

Such an evil system, totally indefensible by normally acceptable methods, relies on a whole phalanx of draconian laws such as the security legislation which is almost peculiar to South Africa. There are the laws which permit the indefinite detention of persons whom the Minister of Law and Order has decided are a threat to the security of the State. They are detained at his pleasure, in solitary confinement, without access to their family, their own doctor, or a lawyer. That is severe punishment when the evidence apparently available to the Minister has not been tested in an open court — perhaps it could stand up to such rigorous scrutiny, perhaps not; we are never to know. It is a far too convenient device for a repressive regime, and the minister would have to be extra special not to succumb to the temptation to circumvent the awkward process of testing his evidence in an open court, and thus he lets his power under the law to be open to the abuse where he is both judge and prosecutor. Many, too many, have died mysteriously in detention. All this is too costly in terms of human lives. The minister is able, too, to place people under banning orders without being subjected to the annoyance of the checks and balances of due process. A banned person for 3 or 5 years becomes a non-person, who cannot be quoted during the period of her banning order. She cannot attend a gathering, which means more than one other person. Two persons together talking to a banned person are a gathering! She cannot attend the wedding or funeral of even her own child without special permission. She must be at home from 6:00 PM of one day to 6:00 AM of the next and on all public holidays, and from 6:00 PM on Fridays until 6:00 AM on Mondays for 3 years. She cannot go on holiday outside the magisterial area to which she has been confined. She cannot go to the cinema, nor to a picnic. That is severe punishment, inflicted without the evidence allegedly justifying it being made available to the banned person, nor having it scrutinised in a court of law. It is a serious erosion and violation of basic human rights, of which blacks have precious few in the land of their birth. They do not enjoy the rights of freedom of movement and association. They do not enjoy freedom of security of tenure, the right to participate in the making of decisions that affect their lives. In short, this land, richly endowed in so many ways, is sadly lacking in justice.

Once a Zambian and a South African, it is said, were talking. The Zambian then boasted about their Minister of Naval Affairs. The South African asked, "But you have no navy, no access to the sea. How then can you have a Minister of Naval Affairs?" The Zambian retorted, "Well, in South Africa you have a Minister of Justice, don't you?"

It is against this system that our people have sought to protest peacefully since 1912 at least, with the founding of the African National Congress. They have used the conventional methods of peaceful protest — petitions, demonstrations, deputations, and even a passive resistance campaign. A tribute to our people's commitment to peaceful change is the fact that the only South Africans to win the Nobel Peace Prize are both black. Our people are peace-loving to a fault. The response of the authorities has been an escalating intransigence and violence, the violence of police dogs, tear gas, detention without trial, exile, and even death. Our people protested peacefully against the Pass Laws in 1960, and 69 of them were killed on March 21, 1960, at Sharpeville, many shot in the back running away. Our children protested against inferior education, singing songs and displaying placards and marching peacefully. Many in 1976, on June 16th and subsequent times, were killed or imprisoned. Over 500 people died in that uprising. Many children went into exile. The whereabouts of many are unknown to their parents. At present, to protest that self-same discriminatory education, and the exclusion of blacks from the new constitutional dispensation, the sham local black government, rising unemployment, increased rents and General Sales Tax, our people have boycotted and demonstrated. They have staged a successful two-day stay away. Over 150 people have been killed. It is far too high a price to pay. There has been little revulsion or outrage at this wanton destruction of human life in the West. In parenthesis, can somebody please explain to me something that has puzzled me. When a priest goes missing and is subsequently found dead, the media in the West carry his story in very extensive coverage.[4] I am glad that the death of one person can cause so much concern. But in the self-same week when this priest is found dead, the South African Police kill 24 blacks who had been participating in the protest, and 6,000 blacks are sacked for being similarly involved, and you are lucky to get that much coverage. Are we being told something I do not want to believe, that we blacks are expendable and that blood is thicker than water, that when it comes to the crunch, you cannot trust whites, that they will club together against us? I don't want to believe that is the message being conveyed to us.

Be that as it may, we see before us a land bereft of much justice, and therefore without peace and security. Unrest is endemic, and will remain an unchanging feature of the South African scene until apartheid, the root cause of it all, is finally dismantled. At this time, the Army is being quartered on the civilian population. There is a civil war being waged. South Africans are on either side. When the African National Congress and the Pan-Africanist Congress[5] were banned in 1960, they declared that they had no option but to carry out the armed struggle. We in the South African Council of Church have said we are opposed to all forms of violence — that of a repressive and unjust system, and that of those who seek to overthrow that system. However, we have added that we understand those who say they have had to adopt what is a last resort for them. Violence is not being introduced into the South African situation *de novo* from outside by those who are called terrorists or freedom fighters, depending on whether you are oppressed or an oppressor. The South African situation is violent already, and the primary violence is that of apartheid, the violence of forced population removals, of inferior education, of detention without trial, of the migratory labour system, etc.

There is war on the border of our country. South African faces fellow South African. South African soldiers are fighting against Namibians who oppose the illegal occupation of their country by South Africa, which has sought to extend its repressive system of apartheid, unjust and exploitative.

There is no peace in Southern Africa. There is no peace because there is no justice. There can be no real peace and security until there be first justice enjoyed by all the inhabitants of that beautiful land. The Bible knows nothing about peace without justice, for that would be crying "peace, peace, where there is no peace". God's Shalom, peace, involves inevitably righteousness, justice, wholeness, fullness of life, participation in decision-making, goodness, laughter, joy, compassion, sharing and reconciliation.

I have spoken extensively about South Africa, first because it is the land I know best, but because it is also a microcosm of the world and an example of what is to be found in other lands in differing degree — when there is injustice, invariably peace becomes a casualty. In El Salvador, in Nicaragua, and elsewhere in Latin America, there have been repressive regimes which have aroused opposition in those countries. Fellow citizens are pitted against one another, sometimes attracting the unhelpful attention and interest of outside powers, who want to extend their spheres of influence. We see this in the Middle East, in Korea, in the Philippines, in Kampuchea, in Vietnam, in Ulster, in Afghanistan, in Mozambique, in Angola, in Zimbabwe, behind the Iron Curtain.

Because there is global insecurity, nations are engaged in a mad arms race, spending billions of dollars wastefully on instruments of destruction, when millions are starving. And yet, just a fraction of what is expended so obscenely on defence budgets would make the difference in enabling God's children to fill their stomachs, be educated, and given the chance to lead fulfilled and happy lives. We have the capacity to feed ourselves several times over, but we are daily haunted by the spectacle of the gaunt dregs of humanity shuffling along in endless queues, with bowls to collect what the charity of the world has provided, too little too late. When will we learn, when will the people of the world get up and say, Enough is enough. God created us for fellowship. God created us so that we should form the human family, existing together because we were made for one another. We are not made for an exclusive self-sufficiency but for interdependence, and we break the law of our being at our peril. When will we learn that an escalated arms race merely escalates global insecurity? We are now much closer to a nuclear holocaust than when our technology and our spending were less.

Unless we work assiduously so that all of God's children, our brothers and sisters, members of our one human family, all will enjoy basic human rights, the right to a fulfilled life, the right of movement, of work, the freedom to be fully human, with a humanity measured by nothing less than the humanity of Jesus Christ Himself, then we are on the road inexorably to self-destruction, we are not far from global suicide; and yet it could be so different.

When will we learn that human beings are of infinite value because they have been created in the image of God, and that it is a blasphemy to treat them as if they were less than this and to do so ultimately recoils on those who do this? In dehumanising others, they are themselves dehumanised. Perhaps oppression dehumanises the oppressor as much as, if not more than, the oppressed. They need each other to become truly free, to become human. We can be human only in fellowship, in community, in koinonia, in peace.

Let us work to be peacemakers, those given a wonderful share in Our Lord's ministry of reconciliation. It we want peace, so we have been told, let us work for justice. Let us beat our swords into ploughshares.

God calls us to be fellow workers with Him, so that we can extend His Kingdom of Shalom, of justice, of goodness, of compassion, of caring, of sharing, of laughter, joy and reconciliation, so that the kingdoms of this world will become the Kingdom of our God and of His Christ, and He shall reign forever and ever. Amen. Then there will be a fulfullment of the wonderful vision in the Revelation of St. John the Divine (Rev. 6:9ff):

9. After this I beheld, and lo, a great multitude, which no man could number, of all nations and kindreds and people and tongues, stood before the throne and before the Lamb, clothed with white robes, and palms in their hands,

10. And cried with a loud voice saying, "Salvation to our God, who sitteth upon the throne, and unto the Lamb".

11. And all the angels stood round about the throne, and about the elders and the four beasts, and fell before the throne on their faces, and worshipped God

12. saying, "Amen; Blessing and glory and wisdom and thanksgiving and honour and power and might, be unto our God forever and ever. Amen".

ENDNOTES

1. The Atlantic Charter was a program of peace aims jointly signed by Prime Minister Winston Churchill of Great Britain and President Franklin Roosevelt of the United States on August 14, 1941. It was drawn up at sea, off the coast of Newfoundland, and included principles of economic and social betterment and individual freedom. The Universal Declaration of Human Rights was adopted by the General Assembly of the United Nations on December 10, 1948.
2. The lecture is reprinted in Tutu's *Rainbow People of God* as "Apartheid's 'Final Solution'", using a phrase from the address.
3. The white Dutch Reformed Church was the principal church of the Afrikaner ruling minority.
4. Tutu refers to a recent event in Poland, when Father Jerzy Popieluszko was murdered by the Secret Police in October 1984.
5. The African National Congress (ANC), established in 1912, of which the Nobel laureate Albert Lutuli had been President-General, wanted a racially just South Africa of blacks and whites. The "Africanists" split off to establish the Pan-Africanist Congress (PAC), which wanted government "of the African, by the African, for the African".

SELECTED BIBLIOGRAPHY

By Tutu:

Crying in the Wilderness. The Struggle for Justice in South Africa. Edited by John Webster. Grand Rapids, Michigan: Eerdmans, 1982. (Sermons, speeches, articles, press statements, 1978–1980.)

Hope and Suffering: Sermons and Speeches. Edited by John Webster. Grand Rapids, Michigan: Eerdmans, 1984. (From the period 1976–1982.)

The Rainbow People of God: The Making of a Peaceful Revolution. Edited by John Allen. New York: Doubleday, 1994. (Speeches, letters and sermons from 1976 to 1994, woven together in narrative by his media secretary.)

Other Sources:

du Boulay, Shirley. *Tutu, Voice of the Voiceless.* London: Penguin Books, 1989.

Sparks, Allister. *The Mind of South Africa.* New York: Knopf, 1990. (Historical interpretation by a distinguished South African journalist.)

Peace 1985

INTERNATIONAL PHYSICIANS FOR THE PREVENTION OF NUCLEAR WAR (IPPNW)

INTRODUCTION

In its October statement, the Norwegian Nobel Committee announced that the 1985 prize was to be awarded to the organisation International Physicians for the Prevention of Nuclear War (IPPNW), which "has performed a considerable service to mankind by spreading authoritative information and by creating an awareness of the catastrophic consequences of atomic warfare". IPPNW, the Committee declared, has contributed to arousing public opinion to oppose the proliferation of atomic weapons and given support to the current arms limitation negotiation between the USSR and the USA.

The Committee stated that it attached special importance to the fact that IPPNW was formed as a joint initiative by Soviet and American physicians and in an unprecedented move invited the two founding co-presidents, Dr. Yevgeny Chazov, Director-General of the National Cardiological Research Centre in Moscow, and Dr. Bernard Lown, Professor of Cardiology, Harvard University School of Public Health, to be the organisation's representatives to receive the tokens of the award at the December ceremony.

On this occasion Committee Chairman Egil Aarvik explains that this award is especially consistent with those provisions of Nobel's will which refer to work for human brotherhood and for disarmament. Brotherhood is the key to disarmament, he says, and IPPNW disregards ideological divisions and national borders and strives for a cause common to all humanity, the prevention of a nuclear war which could mean extinction of the human race. The very structure of IPPNW bears witness to this universality, initiated by the cooperation of American and Soviet physicians and now including doctors from forty countries.

Following the Oath of Hippocrates, the Greek father of medicine, which is often recited at medical school graduation ceremonies, these physicians, "dedicated without compromise to the protection of life and health", have warned what the consequences of a nuclear war would be, basing their statements on the irrefutable evidence of medical science.

The great physicist Albert Einstein has urged that to survive the atomic age, "a new manner of thinking" is required of mankind. By showing that an atomic war cannot be won, IPPNW attempts to dissuade governments from seeking security by adding to their nuclear armaments.

In conclusion Aarvik refers to the conservatives who have criticised the award by claiming that IPPNW is disregarding the Soviet Union's abuse of human rights. Aarvik declares that the Committee's concern for human rights is attested by many of its awards, and the most fundamental human right is the right to live. It is in concern for this right first of all that IPPNW has chosen its course.

Both Lown and Chazov give brief speeches of acceptance. Lown refers hopefully to the recent summit meeting of President Ronald Reagan and General Secretary Mikhail Gorbachev in Geneva on November 19–21, where they declared their determination to prevent nuclear war and decided to expand Soviet-American exchanges. No progress, however, was made on disarmament, even though at the same time a majority of United Nations member states called for amending the Limited Test Ban Treaty of 1963 to make it comprehensive. Lown now calls for the two superpowers to agree to an immediate moratorium on all nuclear explosions, to remain in effect until a comprehensive test ban treaty is concluded. It is curious that neither Aarvik nor either laureate mentions Linus Pauling, who was granted the postponed 1962 Nobel Peace Prize in 1963 for mobilising the world scientists against atom bomb tests and helping achieve the Limited Test Ban Treaty of that year.

Chazov, reading his Oslo speeches in English, says, "True to the Hippocratic Oath, we cannot keep silent knowing what the final epidemic — nuclear war — can bring to humankind". He emphasises the importance of cooperation, although he admits that it is not always easy, that the five years of IPPNW "were not all roses". The way of confrontation is the road to the end of civilisation. Even today it deprives the world of untold riches which could solve social problems and combat hunger and disease.

On the next day the co-presidents give their Nobel lectures, reiterating familiar IPPNW themes. Chazov's lecture is entitled, "Tragedy and Triumph of Reason". What is tragic is the widely held theory of preserving peace through "deterrence" and the belief in the defensive significance of a "space shield", which would not only provide the temptation for a first strike with impunity, but would produce an incentive to overcome it and keep the arms race on its upward spiral. Yet Chazov has himself experienced the triumph of reason in the peaceful cooperation of Soviet and American medical scientists, which has led to significant achievements, and he is confident that the world will eventually heed the message of IPPNW, based on solid scientific fact, to listen to reason and abandon the "nuclear illusion". In accordance with their duty "to protect life on Earth", the doctors must continue to present the grim picture of their total inadequacy to cope with the medical consequences of nuclear warfare, which Chazov does so effectively in his lecture.

Lown is also optimistic, entitling his lecture, "A Prescription for Hope", and declaring: "For the physician, whose role is to affirm life, optimism is a medical imperative". There was optimism as the twentieth century dawned, but hope was shattered in World War I, and the brutalities of total war in World War II culminating in the atomic incineration of Hiroshima brought prophecies of the doom of civilisation, based this time on objective scientific analyses by the very physicists who created the bomb.

The medical profession, committed by the Hippocratic Oath to assuage human misery and preserve life, could not remain silent. Lown pictures graphically the consequences of diverting resources to the military instead of using them to combat global poverty, malnutrition and disease: "We are already living in the rubble of World War III".

Yet the science and technology which have brought us to the brink of extinction have also "brought humankind to the boundary of an age of abundance". Never before was it possible to feed all the hungry, shelter all the homeless, diminish drudgery and pain. The physicians' movement, Lown declares, will not be discouraged. The imminence of danger will itself bring the human family together in a common pursuit of peace. "The reason, the creativeness and the courage that human beings possess foster an abiding faith that what humanity creates, humanity can and will control".

ANNOUNCEMENT

The Norwegian Nobel Committee has decided to award the Nobel Peace Prize for 1985 to the organisation International Physicians for the Prevention of Nuclear War.

It is the committee's opinion that this organisation has performed a considerable service to mankind by spreading authoritative information and by creating an awareness of the catastrophic consequences of atomic warfare. The committee believes that this in turn contributes to an increase in the pressure of public opposition to the proliferation of atomic weapons and to a redefining of priorities, with greater attention being paid to health and other humanitarian issues. Such an awakening of public opinion, as is now apparent both in the East and in the West, in the North and in the South, can give the present arms limitation negotiations new perspectives and a new seriousness.

In this connection the committee attaches particular importance to the fact that the organisation was formed as a result of a joint initiative by Soviet and American physicians and that it now draws support from physicians in over forty countries all over the world.

It is the committee's intention to invite the organisation's two founders, who now share the title of president — Professor Bernard Lown from the USA and Professor Yevgeny Chazov from the Soviet Union — to receive the Peace Prize on behalf of their organisation.

PRESENTATION

Speech by EGIL AARVIK, Chairman of the Norwegian Nobel Committee

Your Majesty, Your Royal Highnesses, Your Excellencies, Ladies and Gentlemen:

This year's award of the Nobel Peace Prize gives us once again an opportunity to reconsider a well known detail in the wording of Alfred Nobel's will. The prize, it is stated, is to be awarded to the individual or group who has "done the most or the best work for fraternity between nations, for the abolition or reduction of standing armies, and for the holding and promotion of peace congresses".

What is especially important here is the way in which the question of disarmament is given a direct relationship to the attitudes of peoples and nations to one another. Brotherhood and disarmament are two aspects of the same issue. Work aimed at giving international relationships a quality of unity rather than conflict can therefore be seen as a step on the way to a bilateral and controlled disarmament.

Through this year's award of the Peace Prize, the Norwegian Nobel Committee wishes to emphasise this aspect of the struggle for peace — to direct attention to the way in which the problem of disarmament is a concern, not only of politicians, but also of the general public in all countries.

No one can avoid being aware of the anxious interest shown in this problem today — not least among children and young people. The reason for this is obvious: with the development of atomic weapons the question of disarmament has been given a new dimension, we could almost say an eternal dimension. The prevention of an outbreak of war is increasingly regarded as a question of life or death for the human race.

It is in this connection that this year's Peace Prize laureate, International Physicians for the Prevention of Nuclear War, has, in the opinion of the Nobel Committee, made a commendable contribution. In accordance with the ancient Hippocratic Oath, which demands a dedication without compromise to the protection of life and health, this organisation has indicated, using the evidence of medical science, the dangers to life and health which atomic weapons represent. These physicians have told us what will happen if these weapons were to be used. We know now about the "atomic winter" with its destruction of the biosphere and of all conditions necessary for life. The physicians have also shown the absence of any escape route, and that there is no feasible protection available against such an atomic catastrophe. Home defence and medical services would inevitably collapse: it would be impossible to help the injured and the dying, and survivors would be subjected to the murderous long-term consequences.

Another aspect of this matter is that the resources which are today used in the development of new weapons, could have been used to help the millions of people who die of hunger and lack of adequate health care. What can be more true to the spirit of the Hippocratic Oath than this campaign for new priorities in the use of the available resources — from military ends to health and other development causes?

Also in this area International Physicians for the Prevention of Nuclear War has presented an informative and convincing documentation.

The Norwegian Nobel Committee believes that the organisation in this way has made an important contribution to activating the general opposition to nuclear armaments and contributes therefore to a mobilisation of opinion which is now taking place all over the world.

It is also true that the question of bilateral and controlled reduction of nuclear arsenal has been offered a considerable amount of attention at innumerable disarmament conferences. The results have not been particularly encouraging. Possibly the former laureate Alva Myrdal (1982) was correct in believing that all we can hope for now is a stronger mobilisation of public opposition and a corresponding strengthening of pressure on the political authorities. However that may be, a contribution to an increased public opposition to the continued atomic arms race can only be seen as a contribution to the cause of peace. International Physicians for the Prevention of Nuclear War has, in the opinion of the Nobel Committee, made such a contribution.

It is obvious that, if such a public opposition is to have real value as a peace inducing force, it has to be built up independently of ideological systems, political viewpoints or geographical divisions. It has to be universal. One has to begin with the simple fact that, faced with the threat of a nuclear war, the whole of the world's population is in the same boat. Or, as Nikita Krushchev once expressed it: "After the first exchange of atomic bombs, no one will be able to see the difference between capitalist and communist ashes".

Face to face with the threat of nuclear war there is one common interest which will assert itself over all others: the will to survive. In other words, there is a common human interest in preventing nuclear war. The feeling for this common interest is now beginning to be so strong that a watchword seems to be evolving: People of all lands who wish to survive — unite!

It is precisely in the light of the fact that this public opinion has to be universal that the Norwegian Nobel Committee regards as particularly important the fact that International Physicians for the Prevention of Nuclear War is the result of a common initiative from American and Soviet doctors. Together, they have created a forum for cooperation which transcends borders which are otherwise all too often sealed. Building on their realistic evaluation of the situation, these physicians have chosen to stand shoulder to shoulder and to work together in a cooperation founded on trust and confidence. The Nobel Committee believes this was a good decision.

This opinion is obviously shared by many. Although the organisation has only existed for five years, it now has active support from physicians in more than forty countries all over the world. And this support is growing. One thousand delegates from fifty countries are expected to take part in next year's annual congress, which is to be held in Cologne, West Germany. The organisation has achieved widespread recognition for its work. At the third annual congress in Amsterdam, declarations of support were received from, among others, the Secretary-General of the United Nations and from Pope John Paul II, as well as from a number of heads of government in both East and West. In 1984 International Physicians for the Prevention of Nuclear War was awarded UNESCO's Peace Education Prize "for its remarkable contribution to informing public opinion and mobilising the conscience of the human race in the cause of peace", as the citation stated.

International Physicians for the Prevention of Nuclear War receives active support from the World Health Organisation, which acts as distributor for the organisation's reports on the medical consequences of nuclear explosions. From March of this year the organisation has been recognised as a so-called "non-governmental organisation" officially connected to the World Health Organisation. In a statement from the WHO the point is made that the prevention of an atomic war is the most important task in the field of health politics, a task which all physicians should have a duty to contribute to.

The award of the Nobel Peace Prize to International Physicians for the Prevention of Nuclear War should be seen as yet another recognition of a trans-national contribution to the cause of peace, coming from physicians who see it as their duty to mobilise the strongest possible public opposition to atomic annihilation.

It is permissible to wonder whether we don't already know enough about the terrible consequences of a nuclear war. The answer is, of course, that we know more than enough. While visiting the Peace Museum which the Japanese have erected on the spot where the first atomic bomb fell forty years ago, however, I came across the following epitaph: "We know 100 times more than we need to know. What we lack is the ability to experience and to be moved by what we know, what we understand and what we see and believe".

One can see that this epitaph touches the heart of the matter. A theoretic knowledge of the megaton-bomb's explosive power is not enough. It isn't enough to be frightened to sleeplessness by fiction films on the atomic Ragnarok.[2] The question is: "What shall we do about it? Do we have the ability to begin to act? Is it possible to force a change of direction?" This is the question which has become our time's "to be or not to be".

Albert Einstein wrote in connection with the development of atomic weapons: "We shall require a substantially new manner of thinking if mankind is to survive".

International Physicians for the Prevention of Nuclear War has, in addition to its information work, attempted to create such a new way of thinking. Here again it is apposite to recall the way in which Nobel's will emphasises the connection between the problem of disarmament and the people's attitude to one another.

All the many bloody chapters in the history of mankind tell us of this connection. It starts when groups of peoples and nations begin to regard each other as enemies. In time, each side considers the oppositions to be evil incarnate. The enemy has become a monster capable of unscrupulously attacking and destroying. History — especially European history — has, unfortunately, far too many examples of this "philosophy's" self-fertilising effect.

What sort of results would this philosophy have today? With the murderous potential the various groups now have control over, we have to conclude that the need for a new direction is now categorical — or, as Einstein said, it is now a question of life or death for mankind.

Alongside the atomic weapons a new reality has been created, based on the fact that an atomic war cannot be won. It is no longer possible to solve problems through a power-political confrontation. And, if a war were to be begun, the question of who was to blame would be totally uninteresting afterwards. The world's conflicts would have found what Hitler called "the final solution".

Is it possible to find a responsible politician who desires such a solution? Obviously not. We have to believe all politicians who declare that this is precisely what we must avoid. Because it is the truth.

The riddle is, of course, to explain why the arms race continues. How is it possible, in a world ravaged by famine, poverty and sickness, that anyone has the conscience to use more than 800 million dollars a year on armaments?

The explanation is simple. The reason is fear, a fear created and kept alive by the well-known "enemy philosophy" which, more or less consciously, sets its mark on both ideas and attitudes. Nobody dares to take the risk of relying on the other side. Without this bilateral fear, it would be difficult to find any rational argument for the buildup of armaments. Nobody with any knowledge of the information and propaganda which support our age's balance of terror can be in doubt: the driving force behind the arms race is the two sides' fear and lack of confidence in one another. The extent to which this lack of confidence is promoted as a political doctrine is an indicator of the dangerous nature of today's world as a place in which to live one's life.

Another aspect of the same picture is the fact that, from time to time, things are both said and done which can easily be interpreted as confirmation of the doubts the various parties have of one another. As a general rule, we have a tendency to believe the enemy when he says something which confirms our suspicions. If he, on the other hand, says something which indicates that he is interested in peace and friendship, it is argued that we would be stupid to believe him, as his intention is to give us a false sense of security in order to be able to destroy us all the more easily.

It is easy to see how such a mode of thinking creates problems for arms reduction negotiations. The result is all too well known: For our own security's sake we have to have more weapons because we cannot trust the opposition, and they have to have at least as many weapons because they cannot trust us. And thereby the evil circle is made whole.

Meanwhile, fear and insecurity grow in all countries, and resources which could have been used in the fight against famine and sickness are used to further increase an arsenal which was more than big enough before.

It was once fashionable to talk about "the inevitable conflict". It is universally accepted today that such an argument cannot be maintained. The unavoidable truth is that our little planet could not survive an atomic war. Nobody today dares to think of an atomic confrontation as unavoidable.

This makes the question which is being raised in more and more countries even more urgent: Why do we develop more and more sophisticated atomic weapons when we know that each new development makes their use seem even more absurd? There is, of course, no political or ideological objective which can justify the use of such weapons, for who would be able to enjoy the fruits of our wonderful political or ideological systems if the price of their introduction is a common annihilation?

Among all the complications which abound in our world, there remains one simple fact: we have the choice between living together or ceasing to live at all. Irrespective of what we call ourselves or to which political philosophy we subscribe, it is this reality which has to be the starting point for our thoughts and actions — that is, if we want to survive. This is becoming increasingly more recognised. We have to assume that the fear of atomic war and the will to prevent it is just as strong in all human beings, wherever in the world they live. The absurdity of the atomic arms race is ever more apparent and its necessity ever more doubtful. It ought to be simple to argue that resource ought to be diverted to causes like health care or used for the benefit of those in need.

The creation of a new way of thinking and acting based on this common opinion ought not to be too difficult.

It is regrettable that the world is divided in the way we know it is. It is just as regrettable that atomic weapons were ever invented. This is, however, the unfortunate reality with which we have to live. The technological development of weapons cannot be reversed, and it is even questionable that our divided world can be united through a power-political confrontation. It is in the light of this reality that we have to define our own involvement, and it is this reality which now presents humankind with a decisive test. Nobody can opt out by resorting to the easy excuse that it is the other side which is responsible, and that it is their philosophy and actions which make ours an unfortunate necessity. The problem is that those on the other side reason in precisely the same way. The fear which oppresses mankind today is the possibility that both sides are right, and that we can begin to build the future on the basis of a strategy which would be disastrous precisely at the moment it showed itself to be correct.

It is in the light of this reality that we have to regard the engagement in the cause of peace which has been shown by International Physicians for the Prevention of Nuclear War.

The Norwegian Nobel Committee does not regard the evaluation of this organisation's — or any other's — concrete proposals for disarmament to be part of its duties. The committee is primarily interested in the way in which International Physicians for the Prevention of Nuclear War has directed its efforts towards the brotherhood which is the key to the problem of disarmament. A forum has been created where discussions and actions can be raised out of ideological blind alleys. The organisation has recognised the consequences of the fact that only by uniting in a common cause today is it possible to make even things that are impossible today, possible tomorrow.

In the opinion of the Nobel Committee, International Physicians for the Prevention of Nuclear War has shown that this is a feasible course. And it is our duty to believe that the cause of peace can only be promoted through common interests and brotherhood.

The Nobel Peace Prize has, especially in latter years, often been awarded to campaigners for human rights. The Committee has followed — and follows — the fate of these prizewinners with interest, but also in the hope that the concept of human value they represent will be successful and will be consummated in the universal recognition of the freedom which is every human being's birthright.

This year's prize is more concerned with the problem of disarmament, but is also at a deeper level concerned with human rights — perhaps even the most fundamental human right of them all — the right to live. The right to a life and a future for us all, for our children and for our grandchildren. Yes, it is concerned with the unborn generations' right to inherit that earth which we today tend on their behalf.

It is in the light of this fundamental right of man that the organisation International Physicians for the Prevention of Nuclear War has chosen its course. And, as it now receives the Peace Prize, it is in recognition of a constructive work in the cause of peace. But the prize also expresses a hope — a hope for the steady advance of a new way of thinking, so that bridges can be built over the chasms that represent our fear of the future.

Mankind in all countries is united in that hope.

INTERNATIONAL PHYSICIANS FOR THE PREVENTION OF NUCLEAR WAR (IPPNW)

IPPNW is a non-partisan international federation of physicians' organisations dedicated to research, education and advocacy relevant to the prevention of nuclear war. To this end IPPNW seeks to prevent all wars, to promote nonviolent conflict resolution, and to minimise the effects of war on health, development and the environment. (Mission Statement adopted by IPPNW's International Council, October 1993.)

Currently, there are over 80 IPPNW-affiliated national groups. The total number of physicians and health professionals worldwide who are members or supporters is over 200,000.

The impetus for the formation of IPPNW was a long-standing professional association between two leading cardiologists, Dr. Bernard Lown of the Harvard School of Public Health and Dr. Yevgeny Chazov of the USSR Cardiological Institute. They arranged for a meeting, extraordinary during the Cold War, of six Soviet and American physicians in December 1980 in Geneva, which laid the foundation for the organisation.

While this unusual Soviet-American cooperation remained a central factor in the early years, from the beginning physicians from all over the world were invited "to work to prevent nuclear war as a consequence of their professional commitments to protect life and preserve health". The organisers were careful to declare "that IPPNW would restrict its focus to nuclear war", thus avoiding political issues on which there were important differences between the two superpowers, such as human rights. After the end of the Cold War, this focus was considerably broadened, as is evident from the 1993 Mission Statement.

IPPNW's Central Office is in Cambridge, Massachusetts, USA. Since 1981 it has organised a number of World Congresses, the eleventh having been held in Mexico City in 1993. In 1995 IPPNW initiated the Abolition 2000 Campaign, building worldwide support for abolition of nuclear weapons, culminating in a signed global agreement by the year 2000. Meanwhile, the World Court Project, which IPPNW co-founded with the International Association of Lawyers Against Nuclear Arms and the International Peace Bureau, has led to a resolution of the United National General Assembly, asking the International Court of Justice to render an advisory opinion on whether the threat or use of nuclear weapons is permitted under international law. Similar efforts brought a resolution of the World Health Organisation requesting an advisory opinion of the Court on the legality of the use of nuclear weapons.

ACCEPTANCE

YEVGENY CHAZOV

Ladies and Gentlemen, dear Colleagues,

I am convinced that today is a great and exciting day not only for the members of our international movement but also for all physicians on our planet, irrespective of their political and religious beliefs. For the first time in history, their selfless service for the cause of maintaining life on Earth is marked by the high Nobel Prize. True to the Hippocratic Oath, we cannot keep silent knowing what the final epidemic — nuclear war — can bring to humankind. The bell of Hiroshima rings in our hearts not as funeral knell but as an alarm bell calling out to actions to protect life on our planet.

We were among the first to demolish the nuclear illusions that existed and to unveil the true face of nuclear weapons — the weapons of genocide. We warned the peoples and governments that medicine would be helpless to offer even minimal relief to the hundreds of millions of victims in nuclear war.

However, our contacts with patients inspire our faith in the human reason. Peoples are heedful of the voice of physicians who warn them of the danger and recommend the means of prevention. From the first days of our movement we suggested our prescription for survival which envisaged a ban on tests of nuclear weapons, a freeze, reduction and eventual elimination of nuclear weapons, non-first-use of nuclear weapons, ending the arms race on Earth and preventing it from spreading to outer space, creation of the atmosphere of trust between peoples and countries, promotion of close international cooperation.

Let us recall the words of the remarkable French author A. de Saint-Exupéry who said: "Why should we hate each other? We are all in one, sharing the same planet, a crew of the same ship. It is good when dispute between different civilisations gives birth to something new and mature, but it is outrageous when they devour each other".

Confrontation is the road to war, destruction and end of civilisation. Even today it deprives the world's peoples of hundreds of millions of dollars which are so badly needed for solving social problems, combating hunger and diseases.

Cooperation is the road to increased well-being of peoples, and flourishing of life. Medicine knows many examples when joint efforts of nations and scientists contributed to successful combat against diseases such as, for instance, as smallpox.

The five years of International Physicians for the Prevention of Nuclear War were not all roses. We had to cope with mistrust, scepticism, indifference and sometimes animosity. Our aspirations are pure: from time immemorial the physician was and remains the one who dedicates his life to the happiness of fellow men. And we are happy that today broad public and, what is especially important for the cause of peace, the Nobel Committee show high appreciation of the noble and humane endeavours of each of the 145,000 physicians persistent in their work to prevent nuclear war. For this we are grateful to the Committee.

The award of the Nobel Prize to our movement invigorates all the forces calling for the eradication of nuclear weapons from Earth. We are thankful to numerous public, political, state and religious figures all over the world for their support of our movement and our ideas. It was physically impossible to reply in writing to everyone; therefore I use this opportunity to express my sincere gratitude to all who sent their warm congratulations.

At this moment I recall the telegram I received at the time of our first congress from an ordinary woman in Brooklyn. It was short: "Thank you on behalf of children".

As adults we are obliged to avert transformation of the Earth from a flourishing planet into a heap of smoking ruins. Our duty is to hand it over to our successors in a better state than it was inherited by us. Therefore, it is not for fame, but for the happiness and for the future of all mothers and children, that we — International Physicians for the Prevention of Nuclear War — have worked, are working and will work.

TRAGEDY AND TRIUMPH OF REASON

Nobel Lecture, December 11, 1985
by
YEVGENY CHAZOV

Ladies and Gentlemen, Dear Colleagues,

Physicist Leo Szilard, one of those who persuaded Albert Einstein to appeal to President Franklin D. Roosevelt to go on with the development of A-bomb, in his last years wrote science fiction stories. In one of them he describes newcomers from a distant star who arrived to find the cities and towns of Earth destroyed and devastated. One of the visitors recalled he had observed a series of enigmatic explosions on the planet Earth; these must have been uranium explosions, he suggested, which annihilated every living thing. Another member of the crew objected it could not be possible. Uranium by itself is not an explosive; a very sophisticated technology is required to make it explode. Only highly intelligent beings, however, could have known this technology and built beautiful cities. It is hard to believe they made all these efforts and processed uranium for self-destruction.

That was written by one of those who was instrumental in the creation of the two-faced Janus of the chain reaction capable of solving mankind's energy problem and at the same time being the basis of the weapon of genocide — the atom bomb.

Did you ever ponder upon the fact that the first active opponents of nuclear weapons were those who created or helped to develop it — Einstein, Szilard, Bohr, Jolio-Curie, Kurchatov and others?[3] The atom bomb was created by the reason of these men, but that same reason rebelled against it.

In medical science arguments are going on between behaviourists who perceive the function of brain as a multitude of simple and unconscious conditioned reflexes, and cognitivists who insist that humans sensing the surrounding world create its mental image which can be considered as memory of facts.

I do not intend to argue the essence of these processes, all the more so because it has been proved that both types of memory function in the brain. However, I am convinced that those who once saw a nuclear explosion or imagined the victims of Hiroshima and Nagasaki will forever maintain the mental picture of horror-stricken and dust-covered Earth, burned bodies of the dead and wounded and people slowly dying of radiation disease. Prompted by the sense of responsibility for the fortunes of the human race, Einstein addressed the following warning to his colleagues: "Since we, scientists, face the tragic lot of further increasing the murderous effectiveness of the means of destruction, it is our most solemn and noble duty to prevent the use of these weapons for the cruel ends they were designed to achieve".

Unfortunately, this appeal, like the warnings voiced by many leading scientists, has not reached the public conscience or the conscience of political and state figures. Nuclear arsenals on our planet have been increasing with every year, with every day. Ten new nuclear warheads appear daily on Earth now.

Put forward by some state and military figures, the theory of preserving peace through "deterrence" led to the situation where nuclear might transcended the limits of human perception. Indeed, no one in this audience can really imagine one million Hiroshimas — a statistic designed to depict figuratively the destructive power of nuclear weapons stockpiled today.

Keep in mind that when the first A-bomb was developed as a defence against Nazism, moral objections and conscience of scientists and many others involved were lulled by assurances that everything would be over after production of a few bombs.

Is not the same rationale applied today when they speak about the research objectives of the space militarisation programme, about its defensive significance? Can we not discern that it is an attempt to gradually make us accept the idea of weapons over our heads, in outer space? The minds of honest scientists, of all men, cannot be reconciled with turning the vicinity of our planet, so far weapons-free, into an arena of military competition. The "space shield" will mean one more step toward nuclear catastrophe, not only because it would create the temptation to effect a first strike with impunity, but because any defence will inevitably lead to the creation of the means to overcome it. Thus the spiral of the arms race — nuclear, conventional, laser and other — will again soar steeply undermining strategic stability.

The peril from space should not be underestimated. In the late 1940s humanity entered the military-nuclear era, which for the first time in history confronted the human civilisation with the threat of total annihilation. Can we allow the 1980s to become the starting point of the military-nuclear-space era which would lead the present-day brinkmanship to utmost unsteadiness? It is time we say a decisive "NO" to the arms race in space and stop it on Earth.

We do not fully know the material basis of the brain function, we do not know whether adrenalin, acetylcholine or opioid peptides determine human senses and behavioural reactions. However, we do know (such is, unfortunately, the nature of human consciousness) that most people, absorbed by anxieties of everyday life and with solving their daily problems tend to forget the global problems of life on Earth which concern all of us, all inhabitants of our beautiful Planet — first of all the problem of the nuclear arms race and the threat of nuclear war. Many people, even if they think about it, regard it as some kind of a fairy tale.

Let us recall the situation as it was five years ago when three American and three Soviet physicians met in Geneva to decide jointly what physicians should do to prevent the "final epidemic" — nuclear war. Like the songs of sirens who lured Odysseys, soothing voices of state figures and military leaders, commentators and even some scientists were heard from parliaments and congresses, from TV screens and periodicals. They created and disseminated nuclear illusions to the effect that nuclear war is just another war (they added diffidently that it might involve a larger scale of destruction); that a limited nuclear war is possible; that nuclear ware is not only survivable but also winnable. One could even hear assertions that there are things more important than peace.

It is difficult for me to speak about the feelings of our American colleagues and friends, but we, Soviet physicians, who know what a devastating war is like, not from history textbooks but from our own experience, who together with all our people imbibed hatred to war — we were troubled by the indifference demonstrated by many people towards these irresponsible statements justifying the nuclear arms race. It was necessary to arouse the indifferent and turn them into active opponents of nuclear weapons. It was not simply our obligation as honest men, it was our professional duty. As Hippocrates said: the physician must inform the patient about every thing that threatens his life.

In our medical practice we not infrequently come across patients who are careless about their own health. In such cases we appeal to their reason. If I receive a patient who is a smoker suffering from endoarthritis, I will tell him that if he does not give up smoking the outcome might be lethal. Likewise, we, participants in our movement of International Physicians for the Prevention of Nuclear War, appealed to the reason of humankind by drawing the real picture, without colouring the truth, of what would happen to our Earth if nuclear war is unleashed. In a way, it was a heroic deed on the part of tens of thousands of physicians from many countries of the world, adhering to different political and religious views and belonging to various nationalities, to raise their voice to defend life on Earth. We could not have acted otherwise. As Anton Chekhov,[4] a remarkable author and physician, wrote about our profession: "The profession of physicians is an exploit, it requires self-confirmation and purity of soul and thought. One should be mentally lucid and morally pure".

At the end of 1980 a meeting was held in Geneva, mentioned above, of Soviet and American physicians — Ilyin, Kuzin and myself, Lown, Muller and Chivian.[5] In the course of a two-day discussion the representatives of the two countries that so often confront each other, were unanimous in supporting the creation of a broad-based international movement of physicians for the prevention of nuclear war. Despite their differences they came to the conclusion that physicians cannot and indeed have no right to stay silent and remain at the sidelines when the preservation of life and health of hundreds of millions is at stake.

Our movement, which has come to be called "International Physicians for the Prevention of Nuclear War" has grown rapidly: physicians from 11 countries participated in its first international congress in the USA in 1981; the fifth congress in Budapest in 1985 attracted delegates from over 50 countries. The small group of Soviet and American physicians grew to become a multinational army of 145,000 activists, who devote their free time to research on the possible consequences of nuclear war and to explain the data obtained to governments, politicians, scientists, the public and international organisations.

Our annual congress and regional seminars constitute important milestones of this research and information activities, which mobilise world public opinion to act against the unprecedented threat in our civilisation's history.

Over a million and a quarter physicians have signed the Amsterdam congress appeal against the nuclear arms race. We suggested the inclusion in the Hippocratic Oath a commitment to fight against the danger of a nuclear war (such an amendment has already been officially made to the Soviet physicians' oath).[6] A "Message to My Patients" is distributed in hospitals, clinics and physicians' offices to help prevent nuclear war.

IPPNW is aware of the fact that wars start not from bombs dropped or shots fired — they start in the minds of people and are the result of political decisions. That is why our congresses regularly address world leaders, particularly of the USSR and the USA, calling upon them to do the utmost to exclude the very possibility of a nuclear war and to reverse the nuclear arms race. The messages received by us from these and other leaders show that the voice of physicians is being heeded.

We are aware that in order to eradicate nuclear illusions and impart hatred of war to the peoples, one should be based, like in our medical practice, on solid scientific data. I do not wish to dwell on the results of our studies confirmed by the authoritative expert group of the World Health Organisation. Physicians have demonstrated to the whole world that not only would nuclear war spell the end of civilisation, it would also prejudice the existence of life on Earth. My conscience, and I am sure the same applies to many of my colleagues in IPPNW, was staggered primarily by the total number of victims in nuclear war. The human mind finds it difficult to comprehend the figure of 2,000 million victims. As they say, one death is death, but a million deaths are statistics. For us, physicians, life is the aim of our work and each death is a tragedy. As people constantly involved in the care of patients, we felt the urge to warn governments and peoples that the critical point has been passed: medicine will be unable to render even minimal assistance to the victims of a nuclear conflict — the wounded, the burned, the sick — including the population of the country which unleashes nuclear war. Even rough estimates show it would require efforts of at least 30 million physicians, 100 million nurses and technical personnel. These, of course, are absolutely unrealistic figures. In the world today there are around 3.5 million physicians and about 7.5 million nurses. Treatment of a few hundred patients suffering from burns as a result of a major fire can rapidly exhaust the burn cure resources of a large city. Where, then, can the resources be found to treat thousands and millions of casualties? Physicians and hospitals will face an insoluble problem, even if we discount the appalling conditions of "nuclear winter" which is bound to cap the catastrophe. Besides, in a nuclear war many physicians and nurses will be killed and many hospitals destroyed.

Our data were widely circulated and produced a sobering effect the world over on a broad range of public, political and religious figures and common men who had underestimated the scale of a nuclear catastrophe. The threat to humanity posed by nuclear weapons is being perceived by hundreds of millions on our planet. Of course a lot of people are still under a delusion, consciously or involuntarily, as regards the significance of the arms race and its proliferation to outer space. However, as Cicero put it, "Each man can err, but only fools persist in their errors".

Every morning tens of thousands of newly-born babies in Europe and America, in Asia and Africa for the first time see the sky and the sun, enjoy their mothers' loving care. We, physicians, are to protect their health and life. But what is there ahead for them? What will their life be like? Will they live to see the twenty-first century? There is a nuclear bomb in stock for each of them. Back in 1951 French author André Maurois aptly expressed the aspirations of all honest men on Earth. He wrote: "Are we really deprived of all hope? Will the wretched human race destroy itself together with the planet that harboured it? I believe the catastrophe can be avoided... Salvation of the humankind is in its own hands ... The strength of our convictious, the promptness of our decisions will disarm those who threaten the future of humanity ... Will the globe live or die — that is the choice we face. Either we join hands, or we exterminate each other in an atomic war".

These ideas are consonant with our views. Our intellect cannot be reconciled with the situation when the world is heading toward nuclear death. We physicians are neither politicians, nor military experts. However, we have analysed the present uneasy situation thoroughly enough to suggest to governments our medical prescription for the survival of humankind. Our programme has been elaborated, discussed and approved by IPPNW Congresses. It envisages a ban on tests of nuclear weapons and, as the inital step, a moratorium on nuclear explosions; a nuclear weapons freeze and the subsequent reduction and eventual liquidation of nuclear weapons; the non-proliferation of the arms race to outer space, no first use of nuclear weapons and the creation of an atmosphere of trust and cooperation.

It is not a political declaration of either communists or capitalists — it is what is demanded by reason, by people the world over who want to live. More than 400 years ago the Dutch thinker Erasmus of Rotterdam wrote about war: "By the way, what can be sillier than to join a competition for whatever reason, when each side would inevitably experience more awkwardness than it would receive benefits".[7] Today we are talking not just about warring sides but about humanity at large. Any reasonable man finds it hard to believe that while hunger, diseases, social inequality, economic underdevelopment and illiteracy are in existence, hundreds of billions of dollars are wasted to feed the insatiable monster — the arms race.

On the other hand, I recall the days when the triumph of reason and political atmosphere of trust provided for close peaceful cooperation and joint studies by Soviet and American scientists. I cannot say about other spheres, but in cardiology, which is my province, this atmosphere contributed to accelerated study of such acute problems as atherosclerosis, myocardial infarction, sudden death and arrhythmia and facilitated introduction of new methods of diagnosis and therapy. A space bridge discussion of Soviet and American scientists on the problem of prevention and treatment of atherosclerosis will take place in the near future. This discussion will acquaint scientists the world over with achievements in this field. These achievements make it possible to assert that the problem of atherosclerosis will be largely solved within the next ten years. It will be a commendable example of cooperation between the USSR and the USA for the benefit of the peoples of the world. It is a vital necessity to continue and extend this cooperation. What we need is cooperation, not confrontation. Therefore, I was deeply satisfied with the Soviet-American arrangement arrived at during the recent meeting in Geneva between General Secretary Gorbachev and President Reagan, to extend exchanges and contact in the field of medicine and, in particular, to resume cooperation in combating cancer diseases. We are ready for such cooperation.

Today is a meaningful and festive day for over 140,000 physicians from 41 nations, those who united in the movement of International Physicians for the Prevention of Nuclear War. And not only for them but for all honest men and women dedicated to maintaining life on Earth as members of the most humane profession — medicine. The Nobel Prize awarded to our movement is not only a recognition of physicians' services in denouncing the nuclear illusions and promoting a true perception of nuclear weapons and effects of their use, but also a symbol of international trust and belief in the infinite value and uniqueness of the human mind. As Ibsen[8] wrote in Peer Gynt "Only he who has nothing to lose in life can risk it". Nuclear war, unless it is prevented, would lead to the extinction of life on Earth and possibly in the Universe. Can we take such a risk?

In our medical practice when we deal with a critical patient in order to save him, we mobilise all our energies and knowledge, sacrifice part of our hearts and enlist the cooperation of our most experienced colleagues. Today we face a seriously ill humanity, torn apart by distrust and fear of nuclear war. To save it we must arouse the conscience of the world's peoples, cultivate hatred for nuclear weapons, repudiate egoism and chauvinism, and create favourable atmosphere of trust. In the nuclear age we are all interdependent. The Earth is our only common home which we cannot abandon. The new suicidal situation calls for the new thinking. We must convince those who take political decisions.

Our professional duty is to protect life on Earth. True to the Hippocratic Oath, physicians will dedicate their knowledge, their hearts and their lives to the happiness of their patients and the well-being of the peoples of the world.

ACCEPTANCE

BERNARD LOWN

Your Majesty, Your Royal Highnesses, Mr. Chairman, Colleagues in the International Physicians for the Prevention of Nuclear War, Friends, Distinguished Ladies and Gentlemen,

Dr. Chazov and I are filled with deep emotions of gratitude, of humility, and of pride as we accept this most prestigious prize on behalf of our movement. We are both cardiologists and usually speak about the heart. If we are to succeed in our goal of ridding military arsenals of instruments of genocide, we need the extraordinary energising strength that comes when mind and heart are joined to serve humankind.

We physicians who shepherd human life from birth to death have a moral imperative to resist with all our being the drift toward the brink. The threatened inhabitants on this fragile planet must speak out for those yet unborn, for posterity has no lobby with politicians.

The official announcement of the Nobel Committee on October 11th commended IPPNW for performing "a considerable service to mankind by spreading authoritative information and by creating an awareness of the catastrophic consequences of atomic warfare". The statement continued: "... this, in turn, contributes to an increase in the pressure of public opposition". The distinguished award honours physicians of our movement, who are responsible for such noteworthy accomplishments. It empowers the 135,000 members worldwide with a new *elan* and determination to prevent what cannot be cured. This new-found inspiration is demonstrated by the presence here in Oslo of 300 members, many of whom have travelled from halfway around the world, from faraway Australia, Latin America, Bangladesh, India, and Japan, representing 38 of our 41 national affiliates! The enormous prestige of the Nobel Prize provides a unique opportunity for further mobilising and educating a still larger public. Thus the reason for awarding the prize will be enhanced by receiving the prize.

The committee's citation took note of the "awakening of public opinion", and the thought was expressed that this new force can "give the present arms limitation negotiations new perspectives and new seriousness". Much has transpired since to provide reason for guarded optimism. At the meeting in Geneva three weeks ago, the leaders of the two great powers affirmed their determination to prevent nuclear war. They have expanded Soviet-American exchanges to promote a wide-ranging dialogue essential to foster understanding and to build trust. Cooperation on any scale is far preferable to relentless confrontation.

Summits like those in Geneva promote hope. But hope without action is hopeless. Our enthusiasm for the positive spirit in these deliberations must not blind us to the absence of genuine progress toward disarmament. Twenty-four nuclear bombs are being added weekly to world arsenals.

We physicians protest the outrage of holding the entire world hostage. We protest the moral obscenity that each of us is being continuously targeted for extinction. We protest the ongoing increase in overkill. We protest the expansion of the arms race to space. We protest the diversion of scarce resources from aching human needs. Dialogue without deeds brings the calamity ever closer, as snail-paced diplomacy is outdistanced by missile-propelled technology. We physicians demand deeds to implement further deeds which will lead to the abolition of all nuclear weaponry.

We recognise that before abolition can become a reality, the nuclear arms race must be halted. At our Fourth Congress in Helsinki 18 months ago, I urged a policy of reciprocating initiatives, the process compelled by popular understanding and public pressure. As its first medical prescription IPPNW endorsed the cessation of all nuclear testing. Our analysis leads to the inescapable conclusion that nuclear testing has a central role in the development of new, more sophisticated and more destabilising weapons.

From this world podium we call upon the governments of the United States and the Soviet Union to agree to an immediate mutual moratorium on all nuclear explosions to remain in effect until a comprehensive test ban treaty is concluded. A moratorium is verifiable, free of risk to either party, simple in concept yet substantive, has wide public support, and is conducive to even more dramatic breakthroughs. On November 21st an overwhelming majority of members of the United Nations favored amending the Limited Test Ban Treaty to make it more comprehensive. If enacted, a moratorium will begin unwinding the potential doomsday process.

We physicians have focused on the nuclear threat as the singular issue of our era. We are not indifferent to other human rights and hard-won civil liberties. But first we must be able to bequeath to our children the most fundamental of all rights, which preconditions all others; the right to survival.

Alfred Nobel believed that the destructiveness of dynamite would put an end to war. He deeply believed that the tragic reality of mass carnage would achieve results which all the preaching of peace and goodwill had so far failed to achieve. His prophecy now must gain fulfillment. Recoiling from the abyss of nuclear extermination, the human family will finally abandon war. May we learn from barbaric and bloody deeds of the twentieth century and bestow the gift of peace to the next millenium. Perhaps in that way we shall redeem some measure of respect from generations yet to come. Having achieved peace, in the sonorous phrase of Martin Luther King spoken here twenty-one years ago, human beings will then "rise to the majestic heights of moral maturity".

A PRESCRIPTION FOR HOPE

Nobel Lecture, December 11, 1985
by
BERNARD LOWN

When Alfred Nobel drafted his final will in late 1895, providing this enduring and monumental legacy, the world was charged with anticipation and optimism for the twentieth century. Mind and hand, the distinctive attributes of our species, were at last finding their intertwined fulfillment in science and technology. Science, at the "fin de siècle", promised mastery of a hostile environment and an end to chaotic societal relations punctuated by war and brutality. Advancing technology augured unlimited potential for human power, inspiring a dream for an end to drudgery and an age of abundance.

The hope of a benevolent civilisation was shattered in the blood-soaked trenches of the First World War. The "war to end all wars" claimed sixteen million lives, and left embers which kindled an even more catastrophic conflagration.

Over the sorry course of 5,000 years of endless conflicts, some limits had been set on human savagery. Moral safeguards proscribed killing unarmed civilians and health workers, poisoning drinking waters, spreading infection among children and the disabled, and burning defenseless cities. But the Second World War introduced total war, unprincipled in method, unlimited in violence, and indiscriminate in victims. The ovens of Auschwitz and the atomic incineration of Hiroshima and Nagasaki inscribed a still darker chapter in the chronicle of human brutality. The prolonged agony which left 50 million dead did not provide an enduring basis for an armistice to barbarism. On the contrary, arsenals soon burgeoned with genocidal weapons equivalent to many thousands of World War II's.

The advent of the nuclear age posed an unprecedented question: not whether war would exact yet more lives but whether war would preclude human existence altogether.

Every historic period has had its Cassandras. Our era is the first in which prophecies of doom stem from objective scientific analyses. Nearly a quarter of a century ago, a study by American physicians concluded that medicine, which in past wars mitigated misery and saved lives, had nothing to offer following nuclear war. This conclusion was extrapolated from the destruction wrought by blast, fire and radiation on Hiroshima and Nagasaki. Astonishingly, nearly 40 years elapsed before scientists first discovered additional ecologic consequences. Nuclear war, they found, could blanket the sky with smoke, dust, and soot, creating a pall of all-pervasive darkness and frigid cold. The impact on climate could last for several years, not sparing the Southern Hemisphere.

But there is more. Since cities are enormous storehouses of combustible synthetics, raging fire storms would release into the air a Pandora's box of deadly toxins. When dust, poisons, and soot finally cleared, another plague would be visited on the unfortunate survivors; high levels of ultraviolet light caused by depletion of atmospheric ozone would take an additional toll.

Martin Buber[9] suggested that evil prevailed because of the inability of man to imagine the real. Yet human beings do have that capacity. Lord Byron, a poet favored by Alfred Nobel, captured the stark essence of a post-nuclear world in his poem "Darkness":

"I had a dream, which was not all a dream.
The bright sun was extinguished, and the stars
Did wander darkling in the eternal space,
Rayless, and pathless; and the icy Earth
Swung blind and blackening in the moonless air;
Morn came and went — and came, and brought no day,...

All earth was but one thought — and that was Death
Immediate and inglorious; and the pang
Of famine fed upon all entrails — men
Died, and their bones were tombless as their flesh.

The world was void,
The populous, and the powerful was a lump,
Seasonless, herbless, treeless, manless, lifeless —
A lump of death — a chaos of hard clay...

And the clouds perished; Darkness had no need
Of aid from them — She was the Universe!"

Byron composed this poem in 1816, known as the "year without a summer". Mt Tambora in the East Indies had erupted the year before, spewing 100 cubic kilometers of earth and rock into the atmosphere. The United States witnessed snow and ice in August. Worldwide crop failures induced mass starvation. A typhus epidemic in England, ascribed to cold and hunger, resulted in 65,000 deaths. The volcanic eruption lowered the earth's surface temperature by a mere 0.6 of a degree centigrade. A twenty-fold greater cooling of the Northern Hemisphere has been predicted for a nuclear winter.

This scenario may not constitute a complete appraisal of the dire biologic and ecologic aftermath. We know little or nothing of the synergistic effects on our fragile ecosystem of subfreezing temperatures, darkness, high levels of radiation, massive release of toxins, excessive ultraviolet emissions, and other events still unforeseen. It is sheer hybris to pretend that there would be human survival after such a man-made catastrophe.

We know, therefore, that a nuclear war must never occur. Is this merely a hope or a certainty?

As no national interest would justify inflicting genocide on the victim and suicide on the aggressor, a prevalent misconception is that nuclear war will never be fought. But the realities of our age compel an opposite assessment. In no previous epoch were adversaries so continuously and totally mobilised for instant war. It is a statistical certainly that hair-trigger readiness cannot endure as a permanent condition. Furthermore, the unrelenting growth in nuclear arsenals, the increasing accuracy of missiles, and the continuing computerisation of response systems all promote instabilities which court nuclear war by technical malfunction; by miscalculation, human aberration or criminal act. The ever decreasing time between missile launch and nuclear detonation relegates critical decision-making to computers programmed by fallible human beings.

The possession of these weapons has been justified by the theory of deterrence. Such a view of human affairs has held sway throughout the ages. But the Roman adage *si vis pacem, para bellum* has been consistently a prelude to war, not a guarantor of peace. No more untenable view of human affairs has ever gained such widespread public acceptance. In order to be effective, nuclear deterrence must operate perfectly and forever. No such expectations are permissible for any human activities. The pretension to inhibit aggression by threatening to inflict unacceptable damage is jarred with contradictions. How is one to account for an overkill capacity equivalent to more than one million Hiroshimas? Would annihilation of only a few major cities not inflict unacceptable damage? A single modern submarine has approximately 8 times the total firepower of World War II, sufficient to destroy every major city in the Northern Hemisphere. Why then the stockpiling of 18,000 strategic weapons? In this race the runners are no longer in control of their limbs.

This buildup is like a cancer, the cells of which multiply because they have been genetically programmed to do no other. Pointing nuclear-tipped missiles at entire nations is an unprecedented act of moral depravity. The horror is obscured by its magnitude, by the sophistication of the means of slaughter, and by the aseptic Orwellian language crafted to describe the attack — "delivery vehicles" promote an "exchange" in which the death of untold millions is called "collateral damage". Bertrand Russell[10] called attention to the ethical bankruptcy that afflicts this era: "Our world has sprouted a weird concept of security and a warped sense of morality. Weapons are sheltered like treasures while children are exposed to incineration".

How did we reach such a dangerous and tragic impasse? From the dawn of history the tools humans forged have imposed their laws on behavior. As tools were transformed into ever more complex machines, technology shaped our consciousness while providing mastery over our environment. This was not to be some Faustian bargain. Technology was intended to serve human interests, to enlarge the domain of freedom against life's compelling necessities. Increasingly, though, as Thoreau[11] observed, "We are becoming the tools of our tools". Worse still, our tools are beginning to operate against our will and threaten our existence.

An additional misperception propels the arms race. Throughout human history, when confronted with what was deemed a deadly enemy, the fixed human response has been to gather more rocks, muskets, cannons, and now nuclear bombs. While nuclear weapons have no military utility — indeed they are not weapons but instruments of genocide — this essential truth is obscured by the notion of an "evil enemy". The "myth of the other", the stereotyping and demonising of human beings beyond recognition, is still pervasive and now exacts inordinate economic, psychologic, and moral costs. The British physicist P.M.S. Blackett[12] anticipated this state of paranoia: "Once a nation bases its security on an absolute weapon, such as the atom bomb, it becomes psychologically necessary to believe in an absolute enemy". The imagined enemy is eventually banished from the human family and reduced to an inanimate object whose annihilation loses all moral dimension.

The nuclear threat haunts our age. Among the first to alert humanity to the peril were the physicists who let the atomic genie out of the bottle. Interestingly, though, the public is beginning to listen not to the military experts but to the physicians who are the custodians of public health. Now it may be argued that nuclear war is a social and political issue and we may address it only as concerned citizens. But we physicians have taken a sacred and ancient oath to assuage human misery and preserve life. This commitment imposes social and moral obligations for us to band together, to make our collective voices heard.

Furthermore, the medical profession cannot remain quiet in the face of the increasing diversion of scarce resources to the military compared to the meager efforts devoted to combatting global poverty, malnutrition and disease. In 1984 world military spending exceeded 800,000 million dollars, or 100 million dollars every hour. This occurred at a time when life expectancy at birth in Africa is 30 years less than in Europe, when more than 40,000 children die daily from malnutrition and infection, when annually more than 3.5 million children die and an equal number are permanently crippled because they are denied inexpensive immunisation. Two billion people have no access to a dependable and sanitary water supply. The litany of grief is long and painful to recite. Yet a single day's diversion of profligate military spending would diminish and even resolve many of these miseries. We are already living in the rubble of World War III.

How has International Physicians for the Prevention of Nuclear War (IPPNW) addressed the grim realities of the nuclear age? Remarkable is the youth of our endeavor. This week we celebrate only the fifth anniversary of our founding. In this brief time we have helped penetrate the fog of denial. We have persuaded millions of people, for the first time, to confront the unthinkable. We have exposed to public view the long list of horrors. We have convinced a large public that there can be no useful medical response. We have demonstrated the deception implicit in nuclear war civil defense preparations. We have provided persuasive data that nuclear war would constitute the ultimate human and ecologic disaster.

Perhaps the signal accomplishment of the IPPNW has been the broad-based, free-flowing dialogue between physicians of the two contending power blocs. We heed Einstein's words, "Peace cannot be kept by force. It can only be achieved by understanding". In a world riven with confrontation and strife, IPPNW has become a model for cooperation among physicians from East and West, from North and South. Paranoid fantasies of a dehumanised adversary cannot withstand the common pursuit of healing and preventing illness. Our success in forging such cooperation derives largely from an insistent avoidance of linkage with problems that have embittered relations between the great powers. We have resisted being sidetracked to other issues, no matter how morally lofty. Combatting the nuclear threat has been our exclusive preoccupation, since we are dedicated to the proposition that to insure the conditions of life, we must prevent the conditions of death. Ultimately, we believe people must come to terms with the fact that the struggle is not between different national destinies, between opposing ideologies, but rather between catastrophe and survival. All nations share a linked destiny; nuclear weapons are their shared enemy.

The physicians' movement is contributing to a positive world outlook, rejecting the view that human life is merely the molecular unwinding of a dismal biologic clock. For the physician, whose role is to affirm life, optimism is a medical imperative. Even when the outcome is doubtful, a patient's hopeful attitude promotes well-being and frequently leads to recovery. Pessimism degrades the quality of life and jeopardises the tomorrows yet to come. An affirmative world view is essential if we are to shape a more promising future.

The American poet Langston Hughes[13] urged:

"Hold on to dreams
For if dreams die,
Life is a broken winged bird
And cannot fly."

We must hold fast to the dream that reason will prevail. The world today is full of anguish and dread. As great as is the danger, still greater is the opportunity. If science and technology have catapulted us to the brink of extinction, the same ingenuity has brought humankind to the boundary of an age of abundance.

Never before was it possible to feed all the hungry. Never before was it possible to shelter all the homeless. Never before was it possible to teach all the illiterates. Never before were we able to heal so many afflictions. For the first time science and medicine can diminish drudgery and pain.

Only those who see the invisible can do the impossible. But in order to do the impossible, in the words of Jonathan Schell,[14] we ask "not for our personal survival: we ask only that we be survived. We ask for assurance that when we die as individuals, as we know we must, mankind will live on".

When questioned on his approach to sculpture, Michelangelo replied that he simply cut away the stone surrounding his vision. We in the physicians' movement will not grow discouraged as we chip away at the granite mass if that obstructs our vision of a world freed from the specter of nuclear war.

If we are to succeed, this vision must possess millions of people. We must convince each generation that they are but transient passengers on this planet earth. It does not belong to them. They are not free to doom generations yet unborn. They are not at liberty to erase humanity's past nor dim its future. Only life itself can lay claim to sacred continuity. The magnitude of the danger and its imminence must bring the human family together in common pursuit of peace denied throughout the century. On the threshold of a new millennium the achievement of world peace is no longer remote, for it is beckoned by the unleashing of the deepest spiritual forces embedded in humankind when threatened with extinction. The reason, the creativeness, and the courage that human beings possess foster an abiding faith that what humanity creates, humanity can and will control.

ENDNOTES

1. Nikita Krushchev (1894–1971), Soviet Communist leader 1953–64.
2. Ragnarok refers in Norse mythology to the doom of the gods.
3. Albert Einstein (1879–1955), American, born in Germany; Leo Szilard (1898–1964), American, born in Hungary; Niels Bohr (1885–1962) of Denmark; Frédéric Joliot-Curie (1900–1958) of France; Igor Kurchatov (1903–1960) of the Soviet Union.
4. Anton Pavlovich Chekhov (1860–1904), Russian short story writer, dramatist and physician.
5. Dr. Leonid Ilyin, Director of the Institute of Biophysics of the Soviet Union; Dr. Mikhail Kuzin, Director of the Vishnevsky Institute of Surgery; Dr. James Muller of the Harvard Medical School, who had studied and done research in Moscow; and Dr. Eric Chivian, staff psychiatrist at the Massachusetts Institute of Technology.
6. Following the Nobel lectures, Dr. Dagmar Sørbøe of Norway led the assembled physicians in reciting the amended oath of Hippocrates:

Oath of Hippocrates
The regimen I adopt shall be for the benefit of my patients according to my ability and judgment, and not for their hurt or for any wrong. I will give no deadly drug to any, though it be asked me, nor will I counsel such.

Whatsoever house I enter, there will I go for the benefit of the sick, refraining from all wrongdoing or corruption, and especially from any act of seduction, of male or female, of bond or free. Whatsoever things I see or hear concerning the life of men, in my attendance on the sick or even apart therefrom, which ought not to be noised abroad, I will keep silence thereon, counting such things to be as sacred secrets.

As a physician, I recognise that the only effective medical response to nuclear war is prevention. I believe that medical preparations for nuclear war increase its likelihood by strengthening the illusions of protection, survival, and recovery. Such measures promote the acceptability of a catastrophe which I will not accept. As a matter of individual conscience, I will refuse to participate in any medical preparations for nuclear war. I affirm my duty and willingness to provide care in all medical emergencies to the best of my ability. I commit myself to applying my medical knowledge and skills for the preservation of human life.

As a physician of the twentieth century, I recognise that nuclear weapons have presented my profession with a challenge of unprecedented proportions, and that a nuclear war would be the final epidemic for humankind. I will do all in my power to work for the prevention of nuclear war.

7. Desiderius Erasmus (1466?–1536), a Dutch humanist who wrote often on the folly and iniquity of war.
8. Henrik Ibsen (1828–1906), the Norwegian dramatist and poet.
9. Martin Buber (1878–1965), a Jewish philosopher born in Vienna, who taught in universities in Germany and Israel.
10. Bertrand Russell (1872–1970), the British philosopher and mathematician who won the Nobel Prize for Literature in 1950.
11. Henry David Thoreau (1817–1862), the American author and naturalist.
12. Patrick Maynard Stuart Blackett (1897–1974) of Great Britain won the Nobel Prize for Physics in 1948.
13. Langston Hughes (1902–1967) was a central figure of the Harlem Renaissance.
14. Jonathan Schell (1943–) wrote about the world's "nuclear predicament" in *The Fate of the Earth* (New York: Knopf, 1982).

SELECTED BIBLIOGRAPHY

By IPPNW:

A Global Guidebook for Nuclear Abolition. Cambridge, MA: IPPNW, 1995.

Other Sources:

Caldicott, Helen. *A Desperate Passion: An Autobiography*, New York: Norton, 1996.

Kleidman, Robert. *Organizing for Peace. Neutrality, the Test Ban and the Freeze.* Syracuse, New York: Syracuse University Press, 1993.

Nusbaumer, Michael R. and Judith A. Dilorio, "The Medicalization of Nuclear Disarmament Claims". in *Peace & Change* 11, 1 (1985): 63–73.

Warner, Gale and Michael Shulman. *Citizen Diplomats: From Main Street to Red Square and Back.* New York: Continuum, 1987. Chapter 1: "Physician to the World: Bernard Lown". (An excellent portrait.)

Peace 1986

ELIE WIESEL

INTRODUCTION

The October announcement declared that the 1986 prize would be awarded to Elie Wiesel, the author who had survived the Holocaust and now was a personal witness both to the potential of human evil and the promise of the human spirit.

In presenting the prize to Wiesel, Chairman Aarvik speaks of the award to the antimilitarist Carl von Ossietzky just fifty years before, whose advocacy of truth and justice brought him to a Nazi concentration camp. Wiesel has survived that experience to become a "powerful spokesman for the view of mankind and the unlimited humanitarianism which are, at all times, the basis of a lasting peace".

Aarvik tells of Wiesel's shattering experiences in the concentration camps, where his parents and younger sister died, and how in his literary works, "prisoner number A 7713 has become a human being once again — a human being dedicated to humanity". The Committee grants the prize to Wiesel, Aarvik declares, "in recognition of this particular human spirit's victory over the powers of death and degradation and as a support to the rebellion of good against the evil in the world".

The speech, as is customary, is in Norwegian. Then, speaking in English, Aarvik reminds Wiesel how he had once questioned bringing a child into this evil world, but had finally decided that he had no right to break the chain of generations which had lasted three thousand years, and so he had put them on the shoulders of a little child.

"Now", Aarvik declares, "your son, with such a precious burden on his shoulders, should follow you to the podium. As you stood with your father in the darkness, your son, Shlomo Elisha, with his grandfather's name, should be at your side in this moment of joy and brightness, as you receive the Peace Prize for 1986". So father and son stand together as Aarvik hands Wiesel the medal and the diploma, an unprecedented occurrence in the history of the Peace Prize.

Wiesel begins his acceptance speech by first asking King Olav's permission, then putting on his prayer cap and saying a Hebrew blessing. In accepting the award, Wiesel identifies himself with the victims, the survivors and the Jewish people. He still wonders at how the world could know of the death camps and yet be silent — "and that is why I swore never to be silent whenever and wherever human beings endure suffering and humiliation". Jews are naturally his priority, but there are others. Apartheid is an abhorrence to him, and he refers to the imprisonment of Nelson Mandela (who is to be given the Prize in 1993) and also to the mistreatment of laureates Andrei Sakharov (1975) and Lech Wałesa (1983), and to the suffering of the Palestinians. But one person can make a difference, an Albert Schweitzer (Prize winner 1952), a Raoul Wallenberg (the Swedish diplomat who saved thousands of Jews in Hungary from the Nazis and died in a Soviet prison).

"No one is capable of gratitude as one who has emerged from the kingdom of night", Wiesel says. He thanks the Nobel Committee and the people of Norway "for declaring on this singular occasion that our survival has meaning for mankind".

Other survivors have come to be with Wiesel, and when he introduces his lecture the next day with a Jewish song, they sing with him. The topic is "Hope, Despair and Memory". He illustrates the power of memory with a legend about Rabbi Baal-Shem-Tov (c.1698–1760), the founder of the Jewish religious movement of Hasidism. He speaks of his own despair during and after Auschwitz, which its survivors never have had the option to forget, or to let humanity forget. It is their duty to bear witness, to testify to the atrocities, so that humanity would never let such atrocities be committed again.

Yet Wiesel sees religious wars, racism and fanaticism, incidents of terrorism, Soviet Jews like Josef Biegun and other dissidents forbidden to leave their country. "We must remember the suffering of my people", he declares, "as we must remember that of the Ethiopians, the Cambodians, the boat people, Palestinians, the Mesquite Indians, the Argentinean 'disappeared ones'..."

Wiesel does not abandon hope: "Because I remember, I despair. Because I remember, I have the duty to reject despair". He concludes, "Mankind must remember that peace is not God's gift to his creatures, it is our gift to each other".

ANNOUNCEMENT

The Norwegian Nobel Committee has resolved that the Nobel Peace Prize for 1986 should be awarded to the author, Elie Wiesel. It is the Committee's opinion that Elie Wiesel has emerged as one of the most important spirtual leaders and guides in an age when violence, repression and racism continue to characterise the world.

Wiesel is a messenger to mankind; his message is one of peace, atonement and human dignity. His belief that the forces fighting evil in the world can be victorious is a hard-won belief. His message is based on his own personal experience of total humiliation and of the utter contempt for humanity shown in Hitler's death camps. The message is in the form of a testimony, repeated and deepened through the works of a great author.

Wiesel's commitment, which originated in the sufferings of the Jewish people, has been widened to embrace all repressed peoples and races.

The Norwegian Nobel Committee believes that Elie Wiesel, with his message and through his practical work in the case of peace, is a convincing spokesman for the view of mankind and for the unlimited humanitarianism which are at all times necessary for a lasting and just peace.

PRESENTATION

Speech by EGIL AARVIK, Chairman of the Norwegian Nobel Committee.

Your Majesty, Your Royal Highnesses, Your Excellencies, Ladies and Gentlemen,

It is today exactly 50 years since the Nobel Peace Prize was awarded to the German public figure and pacifist, Carl von Ossietzky.[1] That particular award was one of the most controversial ever made. The newly established Nazi regime in Germany was violently critical of the Norwegian Nobel Committee, and German citizens were forbidden to accept Nobel prizes in the future.

This type of reaction was in a way so predictable that it can be ignored. What we ought to be more interested in, on the other hand, is the type of reaction which came from countries other than Germany. Many were of course delighted, but there were also many commentators who were sceptical. Leading figures in politics and the press expressed the opinion that Ossietzky was too extreme in his warnings and revelations. Some believed him to be a communist. In any case, it was argued, the cause of peace was poorly served by a Peace Prize which seemed to be a direct provocation of the German government.

The existence of such reactions was obviously partly a result of judging the Hitler regime by current political and moral criteria. Most people were, in contrast to Ossietzky, unable to recognise the deadly threat to democracy which was developing. When the threat was at last recognised people were more or less paralysed by the "Hilter-roar", and had few resources to fight it with, other than the almost desperate appeasement politics represented by Chamberlain. During Nazism's formative years the general attitude was one of unsuspicious ambivalence. Of course one disagreed with Hitler, but when is one not in disagreement with politicians? And of course one was aware of the terrible rumours about the brownshirts' atrocities, but wasn't it necessary to evaluate this against the background of the extraordinary situation in the country? At least there was now a strong and active government, and Hilter was of course a democratically elected leader ... Most people feared some sort of unavoidable catastrophe. But only a few suspected the extent of what was happening — and it is precisely because of this blindness that the catastrophe was allowed to happen. Ibsen's buttonmaker was proved right once again: "... it's when insight is lacking that the fellow with the hoof takes his best prey".

Carl von Ossietzky had insight. He has the courage and ability to tell of what he saw, and therefore acted as an unafraid witness for truth and justice. All honour to the then Nobel Committee for awarding him the Nobel Peace Prize. His testimony was, however, also his doom — Ossietzky did not survive his meeting with the terrible regime which had established itself in the heart of Europe.

Today, fifty years later, the Peace Prize is to be presented to one who survived. In 1945, on the ashes left behind after the sacrificial flames which annihilated six million Jews, sat the seventeen-year-old Elie Wiesel, an only son of Abraham, an Isaac who once again had escaped a sacrificial death on Mount Moriah at the last moment. He will receive the Nobel Peace Prize today because he, too, has become a witness for truth and justice. From the abyss of the death camps he has come as a messenger to mankind — not with a message of hate and revenge, but with one of brotherhood and atonement. He has become a powerful spokesman for the view of mankind and the unlimited humanity which is, at all times, the basis of a lasting peace. Elie Wiesel is not only the man who survived — he is also the spirit which has conquered. In him we see a man who has climbed from utter humiliation to become one of our most important spiritual leaders and guides.

The Nobel Committee believes it is vital that we have such guides in an age when terror, repression, and racial discrimination still exist in the world.

With today's presentation of the Peace Prize, a bridge is built between the German who gave his life in the fight against what he saw was going to happen and the Jew who has dedicated his life to fighting anything that could lead to a recurrence of that same tragedy. It is appropriate that there is a Nobel Peace Prize at both ends of that bridge.

Elie Wiesel was born on the 30th of September 1928 in the Romanian town of Sighet in the Carpathians. He and his three sisters grew up in a peaceful family which was strongly bound by Jewish traditions and the Jewish religion. Elie was fourteen years old when the deportation of Hungarian Jews began. Sighet was now occupied by Hungary, and the town's Jewish population was packed, in the usual humiliating way, into goods wagons and transported to Auschwitz. There he saw his mother and youngest sister sent to the gas chambers. Later, his father died while being transported to Buchenwald.

Through his books Elie Wiesel has given us not only an eyewitness account of what happened, but also an analysis of the evil powers which lay behind the events. His main concern is the question of what measures we can take to prevent a recurrence of these events.

The terrors he encountered in the death camps, which were slowly revealed to the rest of the world, were something which was qualitatively new in the history of mankind. The Holocaust was a war within a war, a world in itself, a kingdom of darkness where there existed an evil so monstrous that it shattered all political and moral codes. It represented a new dimension. According to its theoretical basis, which could only have been the product of sick minds, it was a captial offence to belong to a certain race! This was previously unimaginable, but now the unimaginable was happening.

It is true that previous regimes had used brutal punishment against real or imagined opponents, but behind such measures there was always an element of logical — though perverted — reasoning. The punishment was the result of some injury or offence, either actual or potential.

But for the Jews — and, to a certain extent, the Romanies — the situation was different. Among the relics of the Nazi regime have been found registration forms used when arresting Jews. The usual details were noted down: name, age, sex, religion, address, and, of course, reason for arrest. In the last case only one word was entered, the word *JEW*.

The enormity of what happened is thus not only the sheer number of the victims; it is not only the existence of factory-like slaughter houses. No, the enormity lies in the philosophy which made this "industry" possible! It is this that Elie Wiesel wants us to understand. His mission is not to gain the world's sympathy for the victims or the survivors. His aim is to awaken our conscience. Our indifference to evil makes us partners in the crime. That is the reason for his attack on indifference and his insistence on measures aimed at preventing a new holocaust. We know that the unimaginable has happened. What are we doing now to prevent it happening again? Do not forget, do not sink into a new blind indifference, but involve yourselves in truth and justice, in human dignity, freedom, and atonement. That is this Peace Prize laureate's message to us.

Elie Wiesel's sojourn in the death camps ended in Buchenwald in the spring of 1945, when the prisoners were liberated by American troops. Together with a group of other Jewish children he was sent to France. His stay in France was part convalescence, part study: he learnt French and studied at the Sorbonne before becoming a correspondent with a Tel Aviv newspaper. He travelled to the USA as a journalist, became a correspondent with a New York Jewish paper, and took American citizenship in 1963. In the meantime he had published a number of books, of which *Night* (1956) was the first. His writings, which have been translated into many languages, now include twenty-six full-length books, together with a large number of articles, essays, and lectures. He has been awarded a number of honours and prizes.

Elie Wiesel is an honorary professor at City College in New York and has, in addition, a professorship in humanities at Boston University. He is the leader of the American Holocaust Commission instigated by the President of the USA. Biographical details are perhaps unnecessary in Elie Wiesel's case — he is best presented through his own writings and through his actions in pursuit of his call.

Naturally enough, it was his own people's fate which formed the starting point for his involvement. During the years, however, his message has attained a universal character. Presented as it is in different variations and in different contexts, it stands now as communication from one human being to humankind. Its involvement is limitless, and encompasses all who suffer, wherever they might be. The fight for freedom and human dignity — whether in Latin America, Asia, Europe or South Africa — has become his life's purpose.

This involvement is based on a strong feeling of duty to the lessons which history teaches us. It has been said that peoples or cultures who forget their history are doomed to repeat it, and it is against the background of his own experiences that Elie Wiesel now warns us of this. We cannot allow ourselves to forget the fate of those who died. If we do forget, we commit them to death once again, and become responsible ourselves for making their lives — and their deaths — meaningless. This warning has also a future perspective: we must not allow the unsuspicious ambivalence to return and open the way for an atomic holocaust. We cannot allow ourselves to be deluded into believing that the unthinkable will not happen. For it has happened once before. History has warned us.

The duty and responsibility which Elie Wiesel preaches are not primarily concerned with the fear of the terrors of the past repeating themselves. It is much more an engagement directed at preventing the possible victory of evil forces in the future. The creative force in this process is not hate and revenge, but rather a longing for freedom, a love of life and a respect for human dignity. Or as Elie Wiesel has said himself: "I will conquer our murderers by attempting to reconstruct what they destroyed".

No, Elie Wiesel's standpoint is not characterised by a passive obsession with a tragic history; rather it is a reconstructed belief in God, humanity, and the future. And it is truly a belief which is both hard-won and tested.

Elie Wiesel sat thus in the ashes after Auschwitz. The storm and fire had terrorised his life. Everything was in ruins. His family was annihilated. Two of his sisters were alive, though he was not aware of this at the time. He was homeless and without a fatherland. Even his identity as a human being was undermined — he was now prisoner number A 7713, a sort of shipwrecked sailor on a burnt coast, without hope, without a future. Only the naked memories remained. And, like Job in the ashes, he sat there and questioned his God — cast his agonised "WHY?" towards heaven: Why did this have to happen? And why should I have survived? Dear God, why were six million of your own chosen people sent to their deaths? Where were you when they hanged twelve-year-olds in Auschwitz, or burned small children alive in Birkenau?

He was seventeen years old, and how could a life be lived after what had happened? The sorrow was so great, and the experience of life so bitter. Indeed, he was only seventeen, but was already the lonely prophet of the *Lamentations*: "Is it nothing to you, all ye that pass by? Behold, and see if there be any sorrow like unto my sorrow".

But he was alive. And in time it occurred to him that there could be a purpose behind it — that he was to be a witness, the one who would pass on the account of what had happened so that the dead would not have died in vain and so that the living could learn.

The problem was that the story was impossible to tell. No human being could accurately describe the terror which existed in the death camps. To tell could thus easily become a betrayal of the dead. But to remain silent would be an even greater betrayal.

He remained silent for ten years. Then his profession as a journalist brought him into contact with the French poet and Nobel prizewinner, François Mauriac. This meeting led him to break his silence — at first with *Night* and then in the course of very short time with *Dawn, The Accident, The Town Beyond the Wall, The Gates of the Forest*, the play *Zalmen, A Beggar in Jerusalem*, and his credo *Ani Maamin* — "I believe".

All Elie Wiesel's books and publications are concerned with the same theme — the Holocaust is present in them all. As he himself says: "You can get out of Auschwitz, but Auschwitz can never get out of you". But, even though the theme is always the same, and even though the same story is repeated time after time, there is always a new approach which opens up new perspectives. There is a remarkable development in Wiesel's authorship. We see a forward looking development in a human being who regains his upright position and his individual identity.

In the beginning everything is night and dark. On the last page of *Night* he stands in front of the mirror and sees a face which is like a bleached skull. Even in *Dawn* the day doesn't dawn — the whole book is a fight with the darkness of night. The problem is constantly the same painful question: "How can one live a meaningful life under the weight of such agonising memories?" Is the German philosopher correct in stating that memory is in the service of everlasting agony? Was there no way forward to day and to light?

The answer comes slowly. We meet the first intimation of dawn in *The Town Beyond the Wall* where two prisoners, one of whom is mad and the other dumb, manage to find a means by which they can communicate with one another. The dumb prisoner breaks his silence and the lunatic shows that he perhaps isn't so insane after all. They build a relationship which is a salvation for both of them. The same thought is developed in *The Gate of the Forest* and *A Beggar in Jerusalem*, and, as the books progress, the light becomes brighter. The man raises himself up. The spirit conquers. The answer to the riddle of the night is not hate based on what has happened, but a believing and hopeful rebirth into future events. This is what he calls *The Refound Song* which appears in his credo, his *Ani Maamin: I believe in God — in spite of God! I believe in Mankind — in spite of Mankind! I believe in the Future — in spite of the Past!*

And with this hard-won belief he stands forward today with his message to all people on this earth. This is a message which not only awakens our conscience, but also inspires a limitless solidarity where individuals find one another in the labor of building a "Town Beyond the Wall" for the future — beyond the wall of evil and dark memories.

It is on account of this inspiration that Elie Wiesel has so successfully reached out with his message. I doubt whether any other individual, through the use of such quiet speech, has achieved more or been more widely heard. The words are not big, and the voice which speaks them is low. It is a voice of peace we hear. But the power is intense. Truly, the little spark will not be put out, but will become a burning torch for our common belief in the future. Truly, prisoner number A 7713 has become a human being once again — a human being dedicated to humanity.

And, once again, we have met the young Jew at the ford Jabbok in the book of *Genesis* — he who in the darkness of night wrestled with God, he who refused to release his opponent before his opponent blessed him and who left that place at dawn marked for life on his hip. It was to this man that the promise of the future was made from on high: "Thy name shall be called... Israel: for as a prince hast thou power with God and with men, and hast prevailed".

It is in recognition of this particular human spirit's victory over the powers of death and degradation, and as a support to the rebellion of good against the evil in the world, that the Norwegian Nobel Committee today presents the Nobel Peace Prize to Elie Wiesel. We do this on behalf of millions — from all peoples and races. We do it in deep reverence for the memory of the dead, but also with the deep felt hope that the prize will be a small contribution which will forward the cause which is the greatest of all humanity's concerns — the cause of peace.

ELIE WIESEL

Elie (Eliezer) Wiesel was born on September 30, 1928, in the town of Sighet, Romania. During World World II, he with his family and other Jews from the area were deported to the German concentration and extermination camps, where his parents and little sister perished. Wiesel and his two older sisters survived. Liberated from Buchenwald in 1945 by advancing Allied troops, he was taken to Paris where he studied at the Sorbonne and worked as a journalist.

In 1958, he published his first book, *La Nuit*, a memoir of his experiences in the concentration camps. He has since authored more than thirty books, some of which use these events as their basic material. In his many lectures Wiesel has concerned himself with the situation of the Jews and other groups who have suffered persecution and death because of their religion, race or national origin. He has been outspoken on the plight of Soviet Jewry, on Ethiopian Jewry and on behalf of the State of Israel today.

Now a United States citizen, Wiesel lives in New York City with his wife, Marion, who has translated most of his books into English, and their son, Shlomo Elisha. He has been a visiting scholar at Yale University, a Distinguished Professor of Judaic Studies at the City College of New York, and since 1976 the Andrew W. Mellon Professor in the Humanities and University Professor at Boston University.

Chairman of the United States Holocaust Memorial Council from 1980–86, Wiesel serves on numerous boards of trustees and advisors. He has received a great number of honorary degrees and many awards, including the Presidential Medal of Freedom, the United States Congressional Gold Medal, the French Legion of Honour, the Prix Médicis and the Grand Prize of Literature of the City of Paris.

Shortly after receiving the Nobel Peace Prize, he and Marion Wiesel established the Elie Wiesel Foundation for Humanity. Its mission is to promote human rights and peace through international conferences, such as the Oslo conference on "The Anatomy of Hate" and the Venice conference of young people on international understanding.

ACCEPTANCE

ELIE WIESEL

It is with a profound sense of humility that I accept the honour you have chosen to bestow upon me. I know: your choice transcends me. This both frightens and pleases me.

It frightens me because I wonder: do I have the right to represent the multitudes who have perished? Do I have the right to accept this great honour on their behalf?... I do not. That would be presumptuous. No one may speak for the dead, no one may interpret their mutilated dreams and visions.

It pleases me because I may say that this honour belongs to all the survivors and their children, and through us, to the Jewish people with whose destiny I have always identified.

I remember: it happened yesterday or eternities ago. A young Jewish boy discovered the kingdom of night. I remember his bewilderment, I remember his anguish. It all happened so fast. The ghetto. The deportation. The sealed cattled car. The fiery altar upon which the history of our people and the future of mankind were meant to be sacrificed.

I remember: he asked his father: "Can this be true?" This is the twentieth century, not the Middle Ages. Who would allow such crimes to be committed? How could the world remain silent?

And now the boy is turning to me: "Tell me", he asks, "What have you done with my future? What have you done with your life?"

And I tell him that I have tried. That I have tried to keep memory alive, that I have tried to fight those who would forget. Because if we forget, we are guilty, we are accomplices.

And then I explained to him how naive we were, that the world did know and remain silent. And that is why I swore never to be silent whenever and wherever human beings endure suffering and humiliation. We must always take sides. Neutrality helps the oppressor, never the victim. Silence encourages the tormentor, never the tormented. Sometimes we must interfere. When human lives are endangered, when human dignity is in jeopardy, national borders and sensitivities become irrelevant. Wherever men or women are persecuted because of their race, religion, or political views, that place must — at that moment — become the centre of the universe.

Of course, since I am a Jew profoundly rooted in my peoples' memory and tradition, my first response is to Jewish fears, Jewish needs, Jewish crises. For I belong to a traumatised generation, one that experienced the abandonment and solitude of our people. It would be unnatural for me not to make Jewish priorities my own: Israel, Soviet Jewry, Jews in Arab lands.... But there are others as important to me. Apartheid is, in my view, as abhorrent as anti-Semitism. To me, Andrei Sakharov's isolation is as much of a disgrace as Josef Biegun's imprisonment. As is the denial of Solidarity and its leader Lech Wałesa's right to dissent. And Nelson Mandela's interminable imprisonment.

There is so much injustice and suffering crying out for our attention: victims of hunger, of racism, and political persecution, writers and poets, prisoners in so many lands governed by the Left and by the Right. Human rights are being violated on every continent. More people are oppressed than free. And then, too, there are the Palestinians to whose plight I am sensitive but whose methods I deplore. Violence and terrorism are not the answer. Something must be done about their suffering, and soon. I trust Israel, for I have faith in the Jewish people. Let Israel be given a chance, let hatred and danger be removed from her horizons, and there will be peace in and around the Holy Land.

Yes, I have faith. Faith in God and even in His creation. Without it no action would be possible. And action is the only remedy to indifference: the most insidious danger of all. Isn't this the meaning of Alfred Nobel's legacy? Wasn't his fear of war a shield against war?

There is much to be done, there is much that can be done. One person — a Raoul Wallenberg, an Albert Schweitzer, one person of integrity — can make a difference, a difference between life and death. As long as one dissident is in prison, our freedom will not be true. As long as one child is hungry, our lives will be filled with anguish and shame. What all these victims need above all is to know that they are not alone; that we are not forgetting them, that when their voices are stifled we shall lend them ours, that while their freedom depends on ours, the quality of our freedom depends on theirs.

This is what I say to the young Jewish boy wondering what I have done with his years. It is in his name that I speak to you and that I express to you my deepest gratitude. No one is as capable of gratitude as one who has emerged from the kingdom of night. We know that every moment is a moment of grace, every hour an offering; not to share them would mean to betray them. Our lives no longer belong to us alone; they belong to all those who need us desperately.

Thank you, Chairman Aarvik. Thank you, members of the Nobel Committee. Thank you, people of Norway, for declaring on this singular occasion that our survival has meaning for mankind.

HOPE, DESPAIR AND MEMORY

Nobel Lecture, December 11, 1986
by
ELIE WIESEL

A Hasidic legend tells us that the great Rabbi Baal-Shem-Tov, Master of the Good Name, also known as the Besht, undertook an urgent and perilous mission: to hasten the coming of the Messiah. The Jewish people, all humanity were suffering too much, beset by too many evils. They had to be saved, and swiftly. For having tried to meddle with history, the Besht was punished; banished along with his faithful servant to a distant island. In despair, the servant implored his master to exercise his mysterious powers in order to bring them both home. "Impossible", the Besht replied. "My powers have been taken from me". "Then, please, say a prayer, recite a litany, work a miracle". "Impossible", the Master replied, "I have forgotten everything". They both fell to weeping.

Suddenly the Master turned to his servant and asked: "Remind me of a prayer — any prayer". "If only I could", said the servant. "I too have forgotten everything". "Everything — absolutely everything?" "Yes, except —" "Except what?" "Except the alphabet". At that the Besht cried out joyfully: "Then what are you waiting for? Begin reciting the alphabet and I shall repeat after you ...". And together the two exiled men began to recite, at first in whispers, then more loudly: "*Aleph, beth, gimel, daleth...*". And over again, each time more vigorously, more fervently; until, ultimately, the Besht regained his powers, having regained his memory.

I love this story, for it illustrates the messianic expectation — which remains my own. And the importance of friendship to man's ability to transcend his condition. I love it most of all because it emphasises the mystical power of memory. Without memory, our existence would be barren and opaque, like a prison cell into which no light penetrates; like a tomb which rejects the living. Memory saved the Besht, and if anything can, it is memory that will save humanity. For me, hope without memory is like memory without hope.

Just as man cannot live without dreams, he cannot live without hope. If dreams reflect the past, hope summons the future. Does this mean that our future can be built on a rejection of the past? Surely such a choice is not necessary. The two are not incompatible. The opposite of the past is not the future but the absence of future; the opposite of the future is not the past but the absence of past. The loss of one is equivalent to the sacrifice of the other.

A recollection. The time: After the war. The place: Paris. A young man struggles to readjust to life. His mother, his father, his small sister are gone. He is alone. On the verge of despair. And yet he does not give up. On the contrary, he strives to find a place among the living. He acquires a new language. He makes a few friends who, like himself, believe that the memory of evil will serve as a shield against evil; that the memory of death will serve as a shield against death.

This he must believe in order to go on. For he has just returned from a universe where God, betrayed by His creatures, covered His face in order not to see. Mankind, jewel of his creation, had succeeded in building an inverted Tower of Babel, reaching not toward heaven but toward an anti-heaven, there to create a parallel society, a new "creation" with its own princes and gods, laws and principles, jailers and prisoners. A world where the past no longer counted — no longer meant anything.

Stripped of possessions, all human ties severed, the prisoners found themselves in a social and cultural void. "Forget", they were told, "Forget where you came from; forget who you were. Only the present matters". But the present was only a blink of the Lord's eye. The Almighty himself was a slaughterer: it was He who decided who would live and who would die; who would be tortured, and who would be rewarded. Night after night, seemingly endless processions vanished into the flames, lighting up the sky. Fear dominated the universe. Indeed this was another universe; the very laws of nature had been transformed. Children looked like old men, old men whimpered like children. Men and women from every corner of Europe were suddenly reduced to nameless and faceless creatures desperate for the same ration of bread or soup, dreading the same end. Even their silence was the same for it resounded with the memory of those who were gone. Life in this accursed universe was so distorted, so unnatural that a new species had evolved. Waking among the dead, one wondered if one was still alive.

And yet real despair only seized us later. Afterwards. As we emerged from the nightmare and began to search for meaning. All those doctors of law or medicine or theology, all those lovers of art and poetry, of Bach and Goethe, who coldly, deliberately ordered the massacres and participated in them. What did their metamorphosis signify? Could anything explain their loss of ethical, cultural and religious memory? How could we ever understand the passivity of the onlookers and — yes — the silence of the Allies? And question of questions: Where was God in all this? It seemed as impossible to conceive of Auschwitz with God as to conceive of Auschwitz without God. Therefore, everything had to be reassessed because everything had changed. With one stroke, mankind's achievements seemed to have been erased. Was Auschwitz a consequence or an aberration of "civilisation"? All we know is that Auschwitz called that civilisation into question as it called into question everything that had preceded Auschwitz. Scientific abstraction, social and economic contention, nationalism, xenophobia, religious fanaticism, racism, mass hysteria. All found their ultimate expression in Auschwitz.

The next question had to be, why go on? If memory continually brought us back to this, why build a home? Why bring children into a world in which God and man betrayed their trust in one another?

Of course we could try to forget the past. Why not? Is it not natural for a human being to repress what causes him pain, what causes him shame? Like the body, memory protects its wounds. When day breaks after a sleepless night, one's ghosts must withdraw; the dead are ordered back to their graves. But for the first time in history, we could not bury our dead. We bear their graves within ourselves.

For us, forgetting was never an option.

Remembering is a noble and necessary act. The call of memory, the call *to* memory, reaches us from the very dawn of history. No commandment figures so frequently, so insistently, in the Bible. It is incumbent upon us to remember the good we have received, and the evil we have suffered. New Year's Day, *Rosh Hashana*, is also called *Yom Hazikaron*, the day of memory. On that day, the day of universal judgment, man appeals to God to remember: our salvation depends on it. If God wishes to remember our suffering, all will be well; if He refuses, all will be lost. Thus, the rejection of memory becomes a divine curse, one that would doom us to repeat past disasters, past wars.

Nothing provokes so much horror and opposition within the Jewish tradition as war. Our abhorrence of war is reflected in the paucity of our literature of warfare. After all, God created the Torah to do away with iniquity, to do away with war.[2] Warriors fare poorly in the Talmud: Judas Maccabeus is not even mentioned; Bar-Kochba is cited, but negatively.[3] David, a great warrior and conqueror, is not permitted to build the Temple; it is his son Solomon, a man of peace, who constructs God's dwelling place. Of course some wars may have been necessary or inevitable, but none was ever regarded as holy. For us, a holy war is a contradiction in terms. War dehumanises, war diminishes, war debases all those who wage it. The Talmud says, "*Talmidei hakhamim shemarbin shalom baolam*" (It is the wise men who will bring about peace). Perhaps, because wise men remember best.

And yet it is surely human to forget, even to want to forget. The Ancients saw it as a divine gift. Indeed if memory helps us to survive, forgetting allows us to go on living. How could we go on with our daily lives, if we remained constantly aware of the dangers and ghosts surrounding us? The Talmud tells us that without the ability to forget, man would soon cease to learn. Without the ability to forget, man would live in a permanent, paralysing fear of death. Only God and God alone can and must remember everything.

How are we to reconcile our supreme duty towards memory with the need to forget that is essential to life? No generation has had to confront this paradox with such urgency. The survivors wanted to communicate everything to the living: the victim's solitude and sorrow, the tears of mothers driven to madness, the prayers of the doomed beneath a fiery sky.

They needed to tell the child who, in hiding with his mother, asked softly, very softly: "Can I cry now?" They needed to tell of the sick beggar who, in a sealed cattle-car, began to sing as an offering to his companions. And of the little girl who, hugging her grandmother, whispered: "Don't be afraid, don't be sorry to die... I'm not". She was seven, that little girl who went to her death without fear, without regret.

Each one of us felt compelled to record every story, every encounter. Each one of us felt compelled to bear witness. Such were the wishes of the dying, the testament of the dead. Since the so-called civilised world had no use for their lives, then let it be inhabited by their deaths.

The great historian Shimon Dubnov served as our guide and inspiration. Until the moment of his death he said over and over again to his companions in the Riga ghetto: "*Yidden, shreibt un fershreibt*" (Jews, write it all down). His words were heeded. Overnight, countless victims become chroniclers and historians in the ghettos, even in the death camps. Even members of the *Sonderkommandos*, those inmates forced to burn their fellow inmates' corpses before being burned in turn, left behind extraordinary documents. To testify became an obsession. They left us poems and letters, diaries and fragments of novels, some known throughout the world, others still unpublished.

After the war we reassured ourselves that it would be enough to relate a single night in Treblinka, to tell of the cruelty, the senselessness of murder, and the outrage born of indifference: it would be enough to find the right word and the propitious moment to say it, to shake humanity out of its indifference and keep the torturer from torturing ever again. We thought it would be enough to read the world a poem written by a child in the Theresienstadt ghetto to ensure that no child anywhere would ever again have to endure hunger or fear. It would be enough to describe a death-camp "Selection", to prevent the human right to dignity from ever being violated again.

We thought it would be enough to tell of the tidal wave of hatred which broke over the Jewish people for men everywhere to decide once and for all to put an end to hatred of anyone who is "different" — whether black or white, Jew or Arab, Christian or Moslem — anyone whose orientation differs politically, philosophically, sexually. A naive undertaking? Of course. But not without a certain logic.

We tried. It was not easy. At first, because of the language; language failed us. We would have to invent a new vocabulary, for our own words were inadequate, anemic.

And then too, the people around us refused to listen; and even those who listened refused to believe; and even those who believed could not comprehend. Of course they could not. Nobody could. The experience of the camps defies comprehension.

Have we failed? I often think we have.

If someone had told us in 1945 that in our lifetime religious wars would rage on virtually every continent, that thousands of children would once again be dying of starvation, we would not have believed it. Or that racism and fanaticism would flourish once again, we would not have believed it. Nor would we have believed that there would be governments that would deprive a man like Lech Wałesa of his freedom to travel merely because he dares to dissent. And he is not alone. Governments of the Right and of the Left go much further, subjecting those who dissent, writers, scientists, intellectuals, to torture and persecution. How to explain this defeat of memory?

How to explain any of it: the outrage of Apartheid which continues unabated. Racism itself is dreadful, but when it pretends to be legal, and therefore just, when a man like Nelson Mandela is imprisoned, it becomes even more repugnant. Without comparing Apartheid to Nazism and to its "final solution" — for that defies all comparison — one cannot help but assign the two systems, in their supposed legality, to the same camp. And the outrage of terrorism: of the hostages in Iran, the coldblooded massacre in the synagogue in Istanbul, the senseless deaths in the streets of Paris. Terrorism must be outlawed by all civilised nations — not explained or rationalised, but fought and eradicated. Nothing can, nothing will justify the murder of innocent people and helpless children. And the outrage of preventing men and women like Andrei Sakharov, Vladimir and Masha Slepak, Ida Nudel, Josef Biegun, Victor Brailowski, Zakhar Zonshein, and all the others known and unknown from leaving their country. And then there is Israel, which after two thousand years of exile and thirty-eight years of sovereignty still does not have peace. I would like to see this people, which is my own, able to establish the foundation for a constructive relationship with all its Arab neighbors, as it has done with Egypt. We must exert pressure on all those in power to come to terms.

And here we come back to memory. We must remember the suffering of my people, as we must remember that of the Ethiopians, the Cambodians, the boat people, Palestinians, the Mesquite Indians, the Argentinian "*desaparecidos*" — the list seems endless.

Let us remember Job who, having lost everything — his children, his friends, his possessions, and even his argument with God — still found the strength to begin again, to rebuild his life. Job was determined not to repudiate the creation, however imperfect, that God had entrusted to him.

Job, our ancestor. Job, our contemporary. His ordeal concerns all humanity. Did he ever lose his faith? If so, he rediscovered it within his rebellion. He demonstrated that faith is essential to rebellion, and that hope is possible beyond despair. The source of his hope was memory, as it must be ours. Because I remember, I despair. Because I remember, I have the duty to reject despair.

I remember the killers, I remember the victims, even as I struggle to invent a thousand and one reasons to hope.

There may be times when we are powerless to prevent injustice, but there must never be a time when we fail to protest. The Talmud tells us that by saving a single human being, man can save the world. We may be powerless to open all the jails and free all the prisoners, but by declaring our solidarity with one prisoner, we indict all jailers. None of us is in a position to eliminate war, but it is our obligation to denounce it and expose it in all its hideousness. War leaves no victors, only victims. I began with the story of the Besht. And, like the Besht, mankind needs to remember more than ever. Mankind needs peace more than ever, for our entire planet, threatened by nuclear war, is in danger of total destruction. A destruction only man can provoke, only man can prevent.

Mankind must remember that peace is not God's gift to his creatures, it is our gift to each other.

ENDNOTES

1. Carl von Ossietzky (1889–1938) was a pacifist journalist, who opposed the secret rearming of Germany during the Weimar Republic. When Adolf Hitler came to power in 1933, he was thrown into a concentration camp. In 1936 he was awarded the postponed Nobel Peace Prize of 1935. See Irwin Abrams, *The Nobel Peace Prize and the Laureates,* pp. 125–129.

2. The Torah is the Hebrew name for the first five books of the Scriptures, in which God hands down the tablets of the Law to Moses on Mt. Sinai. In contradistinction to the Law of Moses, the Written Law, the Talmud is the vast compilation of the Oral Law, including rabbinical commentaries and elaborations.

3. Judas Maccabeus led the struggle against Antiochus IV of Syria. He defeated a Syrian expedition and reconsecrated the Temple in Jerusalem (c. 165 B.C.). Simon Bar-Kochba (or Kokba) was the leader of the Hebrew revolt against the Romans, 132–135 A.D.

SELECTED BIBLIOGRAPHY

By Elie Wiesel:

Against Silence: The Voice and Vision of Elie Wiesel. Ed., Irving Abrahamson. 3 vols. New York: Schocken, 1984.

All Rivers Run to the Sea: Memoirs. New York: Knopf, 1995.

From the Kingdom of Silence. New York: Summit, 1984. (Reminiscences, including text of Nobel speeches.)

The Night Trilogy: Night, Dawn, The Accident. New York: Hill & Wang, 1987. (Autobiographical novels.)

Other Sources:

Brown, Robert McAfee, *Elie Wiesel: Messenger to all Humanity.* South Bend, Ind.: University of Notre Dame Press, 1984.

Fine, Ellen S., *Legacy of Night: The Literary University of Elie Wiesel.* Albany, NY: State University of New York Press, 1982.

Peace 1987

OSCAR ARIAS SÁNCHEZ

INTRODUCTION

In its October announcement, the Committee declared that it had decided to award the 1987 prize to President Oscar Arias Sánchez of Costa Rica for his role in bringing about the peace accord signed by the five Central American presidents in the previous August. The agreement called for a cessation of hostilities, the granting of amnesty to political prisoners, and the holding of free democratic elections in each of the five countries.

As Chairman Egil Aarvik declares in his presentation address, the Committee regarded Arias as the most influential proponent for peace in that area of conflict, and his recognition that lasting peace must be based on democracy sends a message to the world.

Aarvik speaks of the new laureate's life and of Costa Rica and then discusses the Central American peace plan. The Committee's intention, he says, is not only to recognise Oscar Arias for this achievement, but also to use the prestige of the Noble Peace Prize to strengthen the efforts of all those "who struggle for democracy, for justice, for development and for the natural rights of the peoples in their countries".

In accepting the prize, Oscar Arias Sánchez, speaking in English, expresses his gratitude that the Committee through this prize is enhancing the chances for success of the peace plan. He has some very thoughtful and significant words to say about what peace means to him. He wants to say to his son, Oscar Felipe, whose eighth birthday is this very day of 10th December, and to all the children of Costa Rica, "We shall never resort to violence, we shall never support military solutions to the problems of Central America". Finally, he declares to the international community, especially to the superpowers, that Central America should be left alone to decide its own future: "Leave us in peace". Those familiar with his record know how he has opposed efforts of Nicaraguan anti-government forces, backed by a conservative United States administration, to use bases in Costa Rican territory.

The next day Oscar Arias Sánchez begins his Nobel lecture, "Only Peace Can Write the New History", with the words of the Dutch humanist, Erasmus of Rotterdam, "Peace consists, very largely, in the fact of desiring it with all one's soul".

Arias speaks as a Latin American, as a Central American, as a Costa Rican and as one of the five presidents who signed the accord. As a Latin American, sometimes referring to this area south of the United States as "America", he speaks of "a world in a hurry, because hunger cannot wait". There are many evils and problems, but freedom will come, freedom from dictators, freedom from misery.

As a Central American, he says that we have the choice "whether to suffer another century of violence, or to achieve peace by overcoming the fear of liberty. Only peace can write the new history". He has faith that "History can only move towards liberty" for "all oppression runs counter to man's spirit".

As a Costa Rican, he says with pride, "Mine is an unarmed country", which abolished its armed forces in 1948. "My country is a country of teachers" and "we believe in convincing our opponents, not defeating them". "Costa Rica's fortress... which makes it stronger than a thousand armies, is the power of liberty, of its principles, of the great ideals of our civilisation".

As one of the five presidents who signed the peace accord, Arias says that the peace plan will meet the challenges both from those without hope and from those fanatics controlled by dogmas. It is easier to predict the defeat of peace in Central America than victory, but "History was not written by men who predicted failure". "I am one of those five men", he concludes, "who signed an accord, a commitment which consists, very largely, in the fact of desiring peace with all one's soul".

ANNOUNCEMENT

The Norwegian Nobel Committee has decided to award the 1987 Nobel Peace Prize to President Oscar Arias Sánchez of Costa Rica, for his work for peace in Central America, efforts which led to the accord signed in Guatemala on 7 August this year.

As the main architect of the peace plan, President Arias made an outstanding contribution to the possible return of stability and peace to a region long torn by strife and civil war. He thereby carried on the constructive work begun by the Contadora group.

The Committee attaches importance to the fact that the accord is the result of responsible cooperation between the five signatory states. As such, it lays solid foundations for the further development of democracy and for open cooperation between peoples and states.

A prerequisite for lasting peace is the realisation of democratic ideals, with freedom and equality for all. In the opinion of the Committee, Oscar Arias is a strong spokesman for those ideals. The importance of his work for peace will extend beyond Central America.

PRESENTATION

Speech by EGIL AARVIK, Chairman of the Norwegian Nobel Committee

Your Majesty, Your Royal Highnesses, Your Excellencies, Ladies and Gentlemen,

This year's Peace Prize, one of the six Nobel Prizes which are to be presented today, is primarily a homage and an expression of thanks to Oscar Arias Sánchez for the praiseworthy work he has done in the cause of attaining a lasting peace in Central America.

Few regions of the world have had worse experiences of civil war and conflict during recent years. Insecurity, repression, lack of freedom and poverty have long been a part of everyday life for the majority of the 25 million people who live in the area.

For these people there is now a hope. On the 7th of August this year the presidents of Nicaragua, El Salvador, Guatemala, Honduras and Costa Rica signed a peace plan for Central America. The Norwegian Nobel Committee believes that this plan opens the way for a development which can replace bloody conflict with an open, trusting society.

The main architect behind this plan is this year's prizewinner, the President of Costa Rica, Oscar Arias. He stands today as the strongest exponent of the longing for peace among the peoples of Central America. He is also an exponent of the democratic ideals which, if they can be realised, are a decisive precondition for a long-lasting peace. This is the reason that the plan is a signpost in the work for peace the whole world over.

Victor Hugo said that "nothing is stronger than an idea when the time is ripe". We must believe that the time is now ripe for precisely the idea which has manifested itself in the Central American peace plan. Oscar Arias is one of those who had the vision to recognise this. The fact that the plan is the result of a cooperation between the five signatory states indicates that there is in fact a general recognition that the time is ripe. The Peace Prize to Oscar Arias is therefore to be interpreted as a recognition also of the work of the other heads of state and their work with the plan.

Oscar Arias is, at the age of 46, a relatively young Peace Prize laureate. It is probable that the bulk of his life's work is still to be done. But what he has already achieved indicates that he is one of the most important leaders in Latin America. He has the personal and theoretical background as well as the necessary experience to continue the work for peace which has been started in the area.

He began his political career seriously in 1970 at the age of 29, when he became an assistant to former President José Figueres, who was seeking re-election. The election campaign was successful. Figueres won the election in 1970, and Oscar Arias became a member of the government — as minister for national planning and political economy. In 1978 Arias was elected to the national assembly as a representative for the National Liberty party. At that time he was the party's international secretary, and from 1979 he was also its general secretary.

In 1985 he was nominated as his party's candidate for the presidency, and at the election the year after he became president.

It is probably not a coincidence that it is the president of Costa Rica who has become the principal force behind the work for peace in Central America. The country is in many ways a haven of peace in an area which unfortunately has been anything but peaceful. Even during the period of Spanish colonialism there was something special about Costa Rica. The country was not, as the name would suggest, a rich country. There was nothing there which could make the place interesting for gold prospectors or other fortune seekers. The country was too small for the establishment of large, profitable land holdings — the settlers in the first colony took enough land to secure their daily bread, and they worked themselves on the land. Slavery was neither necessary nor affordable. Even the founder of the colony was an ordinary, hardworking farmer.

In this way Costa Rica avoided the formation of a rich upper class of landowners with power over a landless and poverty-stricken majority — a pattern which is often found in the Third World. The small population — in 1821 there were only 65,000 — was thus mainly composed of land-owning small farmers.

The population was also homogeneous — both culturally and economically — and since the country was also relatively isolated from the bureaucratic, centralized Spanish administration, it developed a strong and resilient attitude towards freedom and independence. In other words, the country was an ideal centre for democratic traditions.

When Costa Rica became an independent republic at the beginning of the 1830s, the transition was made without the use of weapons or the shedding of blood. Throughout its whole history the use of military power has been unnecessary, and the country can be proud of having had a stable democratic system which has lasted since the 1890s.

This has set its mark on the country until the present time. After a short armed uprising in 1948 a new constitution was decreed. It declared that Costa Rica would be a country without a military force. Whatever one might think of such a body, one has to accept that the willingness to abolish it shows an interest in peace which is relatively unusual in this world.

Even though the country has armed guards at its borders, it is still without military forces in the usual sense of the word. It has been said that Costa Rica has more school teachers than soldiers. Some have even claimed that the country's artillery wouldn't even be able to fire a twenty-one gun salute in the event of a state visit, though this particular detail might now have been corrected. It has also been said that the country's two main products are good coffee and good and upright people. In truth a praiseworthy form of production.

The civil authorities in Costa Rica have traditionally given priority to investment in the education system, health and economic development. The result is that Costa Rica is exceptional in the area also with regard to economic growth and social equality. This is true even though Costa Rica has considerable economic problems as a result of the lower price of coffee and the rising price of oil in the decade from the mid-1970s.

Costa Rica's central role in the peace process in Central America has its background in the country's democratic traditions.

A positive turn in this work occurred in 1983 when the so-called Contadora group presented its 21-point preliminary agenda for a peace plan. The group was composed of Mexico, Venezuela, Colombia and Panama, and the plan included Nicaragua, El Salvador, Guatemala, Honduras and Costa Rica. It had also been approved by the leaders of these five countries before it was made public. For reasons too complicated to present here, the Contadora plan did not result in the planned peace treaty. But it did awaken interest and did receive support — especially from Western Europe and Canada. The Reagan administration announced that the plan was "the best foundation for a lasting solution of the problems in the area".

But the Contadora plan became a political backwater, while the military activity in the area grew.

When Oscar Arias became President of Costa Rica, he immediately began working on the completion of the Contadora group's intentions. Together with the presidents of Nicaragua, Guatemala, El Salvador and Honduras he worked on a new peace plan which was finally signed in August this year.

In principle, this plan is based on the same ideas as the Contadora plan, but the proposals are more definite. They are based on, among other things, a concurrent ceasefire in the civil wars of Nicaragua, El Salvador and Guatemala, an amnesty for all guerilla soldiers, the abolition of the state of emergency, the release of political prisoners and the establishment of freedom of the press and a democratic form of government.

There are two things about this plan which are particularly worth commenting on. The first is that the plan is the five signatory states' own plan — conceived and signed without involvement or pressure from outside. This is important, not least because it expresses a particular view of the situation in Central America — the view that the conflicts are an internal problem for the region, and that they are a result of the existing social and economic injustices.

As so often in the Third World, it is a question of injustice in the relationship between the big landowners and the poor landless. In addition it is a question of a brutal use of power against any form of opposition, and of a minority government which discriminates without mercy. This is once again the sad story of the privileged minorities who resist the demands of the poor for justice with armed resistance. And as always, this results in the release of revolutionary forces. When the authorities then react with repeated repression instead of political and social reforms, the result can never be anything other than conflict — perhaps it ought never to be anything else.

The Central American Peace Plan addresses itself to a different sort of problem. The intention is clear: since the conflict is the result of problems within the five states, it is the five states themselves who have to solve the problems. It is in accordance with this principle that the plan suggests that all outside help to the opposition forces has to cease. The peace plan's message in this connection can only be interpreted in one way: outside powers must — if they will serve the cause of peace in the area, stop any actions which can contribute to keeping the never-ending civil war alive. The combatting groups need help — help to change the underlying circumstances which are the root cause of the conflict.

It has been suggested that peace and stability have to be established before any reforms can be made. The weakness of this argument, even if it can be regarded as correct, is that efforts to create stability can be a support for the power groups who oppose reform; the process would therefore strengthen the revolutionary situation.

The solution is obviously to be found in the doctrine that the imbalances which are at the root of the conflict have to be changed. If that is successful, it will be possible to establish peace and stability based on a foundation acceptable to the people themselves. This is the reality all outside parties have to accept.

This leads us to the other remarkable aspect of the peace plan: the principle of the intimate relationship between peace and democracy.

Already in the speech he held at his inauguration as Costa Rica's president Oscar Arias made this principle a major point. Our experience, he said, has taught us that democracy is the form of government which gives the greatest possibilities for a future anchored on justice. Government through the decisions of correctly elected organs is the only way to a liberation from poverty and dependence.

What Oscar Arias is saying is that democracy is something more than a form of government. It is in reality an important tool in the work for peace.

We have to accept, however unwillingly — and independently of how old our own democratic traditions are — that the principle of majority rule is not perfect. In a number of areas we are only on the way towards the goals we have set ourselves. But democracy has the obvious advantage that it makes possible the further development of democracy. And because this is the case, we have also achieved goals which newly established democracies around the world can only dream of. It is important to have this historical perspective before us when we evaluate the quality of the young democracies. They have their difficult path to tread, just as we had.

The present situation in Central America gives us hope because democracy has been given a chance.

Democracy is, in contrast to totalitarian regimes, dependent on support from the people. This support is in its turn dependent on the experiences of the people. As long as democracy can be identified with free elections, freedom of expression, with honest measures for social justice and with a moderate improvement in economic status, the positive development can continue with the people's support.

The future of democracy will be dependent on the realisation of a minimum of the people's expectations. It can be difficult to accept the overturning of a dictatorship if the system which replaces it brings with it lack of freedom, corruption and injustice.

Government by the people makes demands — both on the individuals who govern and on the people who elect their leaders. There are demands for moral qualities, and there have to be ideals which nobody can reasonably deny.

With this as a background it is easy to see why the Central American peace plan is so strongly rooted in the connection between peace and democracy. Peace will be realised if democracy is realised. In this way the peace plan is something more than a dream and a hope. It is a powerful challenge — not only to the leaders of the five countries, but also to all of us. If we have anything to contribute which can affect the development of this area let it be a contribution to social and economic liberation and to the growth of a government by the people which is, in Central America as elsewhere, one of the keys to peace.

The award of the Peace Prize usually has two goals. This is particularly true this year. The prize to Oscar Arias is a recognition of an achieved result — the peace plan. It sets its sights also on the future and is a moral support in the work for peace which is based on that plan. The Norwegian Nobel Committee wishes, after much thought, to place the prestige of the Nobel Peace Prize in the scale to the advantage of those who struggle for democracy, for justice, for development and for the natural rights of the peoples in their countries.

Oscar Arias is one of the foremost of those who strive to achieve those goals. His name is today a focal point in the work for peace which is anchored in the will of the people and in respect for human rights. It is the Nobel Committee's hope that the Peace Prize will contribute to his success in the symbolic building dedicated to peace which is now being raised for the war-weary people of Central America.

Oscar Luis S.

OSCAR ARIAS SÁNCHEZ

Oscar Arias Sánchez was born in 1941. After studying in the United States, he read law and economics at the University of Costa Rica in the capital San José. As a student he engaged actively in the work of the National Liberation Party. Having completed his degree, he went on to take a doctorate in England, with a thesis on the subject of "Who rules Costa Rica?". He is the author of a number of books and articles on political and historical subjects.

Arias embarked on his political career in earnest in 1970, as an assistant to José Figueres, a former president who was again seeking election. When Figueres was elected in 1972, Arias was given a seat in the government as Minister of National Planning and Political Economy. In 1975 his party elected him International Secretary and in 1979 General Secretary. He represented the party at several Socialist International congresses.

In the 1978 elections, when the Christian Social Unity Party won the presidency, Arias was elected to the Legislative Assembly, but withdrew in 1981 to work for his party's presidential candidate, Luis Alberto Monge, who won in 1982. Nominated himself in 1985, Arias was elected President in 1986, winning 52.3% of the votes against 45.8% for the Christian Social Unity candidate. As President he intervened against the activities of U.S.-backed Contras on Costa Rican territory. Although critical of the political system in Nicaragua, Arias has concentrated on engaging Nicaragua and the other Central American states in a peace-making process. In May 1986, he met the presidents of Guatemala, El Salvador, Honduras, and Nicaragua to discuss the proposals for a peaceful solution that had been worked out by the Contadora group. They did not reach full agreement, but early in 1987 Arias succeeded in calling a new meeting, at which he submitted his own peace plan, departing in some respects from the Contadora plan. The accord approved by the five presidents in Guatemala on 7 August was based on President Arias's plan.

Arias continued to work for Central American peace during his term of office, which ended in 1990. With the Nobel prize money he founded the Arias Foundation for Peace and Human Progress, whose goal is to contribute to the construction of just and peaceful societies in Latin America, with specific emphasis on Central America and the Caribbean. Along with other projects, Arias and the Foundation staff have been active in encouraging both Panama and Haiti to abolish the military. Arias also took part in the Nobel peace laureate effort in 1993 to secure the freedom of Aung San Suu Kyi from detention by the military government of Myanmar.

ACCEPTANCE

OSCAR ARIAS SÁNCHEZ

When you decided to honour me with this prize, you decided to honour a country of peace, you decided to honour Costa Rica. When in this year, 1987, you carried out the will of Alfred E. Nobel to encourage peace efforts in the world, you decided to encourage the efforts to secure peace in Central America. I am grateful for the recognition of our search for peace. We are all grateful in Central America.

Nobody knows better than the honourable members of this Committee, that this prize is a sign to let the world know that you want to foster the Central American peace initiative. With your decision you are enhancing the possibilities of success. You are declaring how well you know the search for peace can never end, and how it is a permanent cause, always in need of true support from real friends, from people with courage to promote change in favour of peace, even against all odds.

Peace is not a matter of prizes or trophies. It is not the product of a victory or command. It has no finishing line, no final deadline, no fixed definition of achievement.

Peace is a never-ending process, the work of many decisions by many people in many countries. It is an attitude, a way of life, a way of solving problems and resolving conflicts. It cannot be forced on the smallest nation or enforced by the largest. It cannot ignore our differences or overlook our common interests. It requires us to work and live together.

Peace is not only a matter of noble words and Nobel lectures. We have ample words, glorious words, inscribed in the charters of the United Nations, the World Court, the Organization of American States and a network of international treaties and laws. We need deeds that will respect those words, honour those commitments, abide by those laws. We need to strengthen our institutions of peace like the United Nations, making certain they are fully used by the weak as well as the strong.

I pay no attention to those doubters and detractors unwilling to believe that a lasting peace can be genuinely embraced by those who march under a different ideological banner or those who are more accustomed to cannons of war than to councils of peace.

We seek in Central America not peace alone, not peace to be followed some day by political progress, but peace and democracy, together, indivisible, an end to the shedding of human blood, which is inseparable from an end to the suppression of human rights. We do not judge, much less condemn, any other nation's political or ideological system, freely chosen and never exported. We cannot require sovereign states to conform to patterns of government not of their own choosing. But we can and do insist that every government respect those universal rights of man that have meaning beyond national boundaries and ideological labels. We believe that justice and peace can only thrive together, never apart. A nation that mistreats its own citizens is more likely to mistreat its neighbours.

To receive this Nobel prize on the 10th of December is for me a marvellous coincidence. My son Oscar Felipe, here present, is eight years old today. I say to him, and through him to all the children of my country, that we shall never resort to violence, we shall never support military solutions to the problems of Central America. It is for the new generation that we must understand more than ever that peace can only be achieved through its own instruments: dialogue and understanding; tolerance and forgiveness; freedom and democracy.

I know well you share what we say to all members of the international community, and particularly to those in the East and the West, with far greater power and resources than my small nation could never hope to possess, I say to them, with the utmost urgency: let Central Americans decide the future of Central America. Leave the interpretation and implementation of our peace plan to us. Support the efforts for peace instead of the forces of war in our region. Send our people ploughshares instead of swords, pruning hooks instead of spears. If they, for their own purposes, cannot refrain from amassing the weapons of war, then, in the name of God, at least they should leave us in peace.

I say here to His Majesty and to the honourable members of the Nobel Peace Committee, to the wonderful people of Norway, that I accept this prize because I know how passionately you share our quest for peace, our eagerness for success. If, in the years to come peace prevails, and violence and war are thus avoided; a large part of that peace will be due to the faith of the people of Norway, and will be theirs forever.

ONLY PEACE CAN WRITE THE NEW HISTORY

Nobel lecture, December 11, 1987
by
OSCAR ARIAS SÁNCHEZ

Desiring peace

Peace consists, very largely, in the fact of desiring it with all one's soul. The inhabitants of my small country, Costa Rica, have realised those words by Erasmus. Mine is an unarmed people, whose children have never seen a fighter or a tank or a warship. One of my guests at this award, here with us today, is José Figueres Ferrer, the man with the vision to abolish my country's armed forces in 1948, and thus set our history on a new course.

I am a Latin American

I am not receiving this prize as Oscar Arias, any more than I am receiving it as the president of my country. While I have not the arrogance to presume to represent anyone, neither do I fear the humility which identifies me with everyone, and with their great causes.

I receive it as one of the 400 million Latin Americans who, in the return to liberty, in the exercise of democracy, are seeking the way to overcome so much misery and so much injustice. I come from that Latin America whose face is deeply marked with pain, the record of the exile, torture, imprisonment and death of many of its men and its women. I come from that Latin American region where totalitarian regimes still exist which put the whole of humanity to shame.

America's scars

The scars by which America is marked are deep. At this very time, America is seeking to return to freedom, and it is only as it approaches democracy that it can see the dreadful trail of torture, banishment and death left by dictators. The problems America has to overcome are enormous. An inheritance from an unjust past has been aggravated by the fatal deeds of tyrants to produce foreign debts, social insensitivity, economic upheavals, corruption and the many other evils of our societies. The evils are manifest, naked to the view of anyone who cares to see them.

Seeing the size of the challenge, no wonder many are prey to discouragement; or that apocalyptic prophets abound, announcing the failures of the fight against poverty, proclaiming the immediate fall of the democracies, forecasting the futility of peace-making efforts.

I do not share this defeatism. I cannot accept to be realistic means to tolerate misery, violence and hate. I do not believe that the hungry man should be treated as subversive for expressing his suffering. I shall never accept that the law can be used to justify tragedy, to keep things as they are, to make us abandon our ideas of a different world. Law is the path of liberty, and must as such open the way to progress for everyone.

Liberty performs miracles

Liberty performs miracles. To free men, everything is possible. A free and democratic America can meet the challenges confronting it. When I assumed the presidency of Costa Rica, I called for an alliance for freedom and democracy in the Americas. I said then, and I repeat today, that we should not be the allies, either politically or economically, of governments which oppress their peoples. Latin America has never known a single war between two democracies. That is sufficient reason for every man of good faith, every well-intentioned nation, to support efforts to put an end to tyranny.

America cannot wait

America's freedom, the freedom of the whole of America, cannot wait. I come from a world with huge problems, which we shall overcome in freedom. I come from a world in a hurry, because hunger cannot wait. When hope is forgotten, violence does not delay. Dogmatism is too impatient for dialogue. I come from a world where, if we are to make sure that there will be no turning back from our progress towards liberty, if we are to frustrate every oppressive intent, we have no time to lose. I come from a world which cannot wait for the guerilla and the soldier to hold their fire: young people are dying, brothers are dying, and tomorrow who can tell why. I come from a world which cannot wait to open prison gates not, as before, for free men to go in, but for those imprisoned to come out.

America's liberty and democracy have no time to lose, and we need the whole world's understanding to win freedom from dictators, to win freedom from misery.

I come from Central America

I accept this prize as one of 27 million Central Americans. Behind the democratic awakening in Central America lies over a century of merciless dictatorships and general injustice and poverty. The choice before my little America is whether to suffer another century of violence, or to achieve peace by overcoming the fear of liberty. Only peace can write the new history.

We in Central America will not lose faith. We shall set history right. How sad that they would have us believe that peace is a dream, justice utopian, shared well-being impossible! How sad that there should be people in the world who cannot understand that in the former plantations of Central America, nations are asserting themselves and striving, with every right, for better destinies for their peoples! How sad that some cannot see that Central America does not want to prolong its past, but to create a new future, with hope for the young and dignity for the old!

Realising dreams

The Central American isthmus is a region of great contrasts, but also of heartening unison. Millions of men and women share dreams of freedom and progress. In some countries, the dreams are dispelled by systematic violations of human rights; they are shattered by fratricidal struggles in town and country, and come up against the realities of poverty so extreme it stops the heart. Poets who are the pride of mankind know that millions upon millions cannot read them in their own countries, because so many of the men and women there are illiterate. There are on this narrow strip of land painters and sculptors whom we shall admire for ever, but also dictators whom we have no wish to remember because they offend most cherished human values.

Central America cannot go on dreaming, nor does it want to. History demands that dreams turn into realities. Now, when there is no time to lose. Today, when we can take our destiny in our own hands. In this region, home alike to the oldest and strongest democracy in Latin America — that of Costa Rica — and to a history of the most merciless and cruel dictatorships, democratic awakening requires a special loyalty to freedom.

Seeing that the past dictatorships were only capable of creating misery and crippling hope, how absurd to pretend to cure the evils of one extreme dictatorship by means of its opposite! No one in Central America has the right to fear freedom, no one is entitled to preach absolute truths. The evils of one dogma are the evils of any dogma. They are all the enemies of human creativity. As Pascal said: "We know a great deal to make us sceptical. We know very little to make us dogmatic".

History can only move towards liberty. History can only have justice at its heart. To march in the opposite direction to history is to be on the road to shame, poverty and oppression. Without freedom, there is no revolution. All oppression runs counter to man's spirit.

Freedom: a shared longing

Central America is at an agonising crossroad: faced with terrible poverty, some call, from mountains or from governments, for dictatorships with other ideologies, ignoring the cries for freedom of many generations. To the serious problems of general misery, as we know them in their North-South context, is added the conflict between East and West. Where poverty meets conflicting ideologies and the fear of liberty, one can see a cross of ill omen taking shape in Central America.

Let us make no mistake. The only answer for Central America, the answer to its poverty as well as to its political challenges, is freedom from misery and freedom from fear. Anyone who proposes to solve the ills of centuries in the name of dogma will only help to make the problems of the past grow bigger in the future.

There is a shared desire in the spirit of man which has for centuries sought liberty in Central America. No one must betray this spiritual union. To do so would be to condemn our little America to another hundred years of horrifying oppression, of meaningless death, of fighting for freedom.

I am from Costa Rica
I am receiving this prize as one of 2.7 million Costa Ricans. My people draw their sacred liberty from the two oceans which bound us to the East and West. To the South and to the North, Costa Rica has almost always been bounded by dictators and dictatorships. We are an unarmed people, and we are fighting to remain free from hunger. To America we are a symbol of peace, and we hope to be a symbol of development. We intend to show that peace is both the prerequisite and the fruit of progress.

Country of teachers
My country is a country of teachers. It is therefore a country of peace. We discuss our successes and failures in complete freedom. Because our country is a country of teachers, we closed the army camps, and our children go with books under their arms, not with rifles on their shoulders. We believe in dialogue, in agreement, in reaching a consensus. We reject violence. Because my country is a country of teachers, we believe in convincing our opponents, not defeating them. We prefer raising the fallen to crushing them, because we believe that no one possesses the absolute truth. Because mine is a country of teachers, we seek an economy in which men cooperate in a spirit of solidarity, not an economy in which they compete to their own extinction.

Education in my country has been compulsory and free for 118 years. Health care now extends to every citizen, and housing for the people is a basic aim of my Government.

A new economy
Just as we take pride in many of our achievements, we make no secret of our worries and problems. In hard times, we must be capable of establishing a new economy and restoring growth. We have said that we do not want an economy which is insensitive to domestic needs or to the demands of the most humble. We have said that we will not, merely for the sake of economic growth, give up our hope of creating a more egalitarian society. Our country has the lowest rate of unemployment in the Western hemisphere. We hope to be the first Latin American country to be rid of slums. We are convinced that a country free from slums will be a country free from hatred, where poor people, too, can enjoy the privilege of working for progress in freedom.

Stronger than a thousand armies
In these years of bitterness in Central America, many people in my country are afraid that, driven by minds diseased and blinded by fanaticism, the violence in the region may spread to Costa Rica. Some have given way to the fear that we would have to establish an army to keep violence away from our

borders. What senseless weakness! Such ideas are worth less than the thirty pieces of silver handed to Judas. Costa Rica's fortress, the strength which makes it invincible by force, which makes it stronger than a thousand armies, is the power of liberty, of its principles, of the great ideals of our civilisation. When one honestly lives up to one's ideas, when one is not afraid of liberty, one is invulnerable to totalitarian blows.

We know in Costa Rica that only freedom allows political projects to be realised which embrace a country's entire population. Only freedom allows people to be reconciled in tolerance. The painful paths trodden aimlessly around the world by wandering Cubans, Nicaraguans, Paraguayans, Chileans, and so many others who cannot return to their own countries, testify most cruelly to the rule of dogma. Liberty bears no labels, democracy no colours. One can tell them when one meets them, as the real experience of a people.

A peace plan

Faced with the nearness of Central America's violence, Costa Rica with all its history, and especially with its youthful idealism, obliged me to take to the region's battlefield the peace of my people, the faith in dialogue, the need for tolerance. As the people's servant, I proposed a peace plan for Central America. The plan was also founded on Simon Bolivar's[1] cry for freedom, manifested in the tenacious and brave work of the Contadora Group and the Support Group.

I am one of five presidents

I receive this award as one of the five presidents who have pledged to the world the will of their peoples to exchange a history of oppression for a future of freedom; a history of hunger for a destiny of progress; the cry of mothers and the violent death of youths for a hope, a path of peace which we wish to take together.

Hope is the strongest driving force for a people. Hope which brings about change, which produces new realities, is what opens man's road to freedom. Once hope has taken hold, courage must unite with wisdom. That is the only way of avoiding violence, the only way of maintaining the calm one needs to respond peacefully to offences.

However noble a crusade, some people will desire and promote its failure. Some few appear to accept war as the normal course of events, as the solution to problems. How ironic that powerful forces are angered by interruptions in the course of war, by efforts to eliminate the sources of hatred! How ironic that any intention to stop war in its course triggers rages and attacks, as if we were disturbing the sleep of the just or halting a necessary measure, and not a heart-rending evil! How ironic for peace-making efforts to discover that hatred is stronger for many than love; that the longing to achieve power through military victories makes so many men lose their reason, forget all shame, and betray history.

Let weapons fall silent

Five presidents in Central America have signed an accord to seek a firm and lasting peace. We want arms to fall silent and men to speak. Our sons are being killed by conventional weapons. Our youths are being killed by conventional weapons.

Fear of nuclear war, the horrors of what we have heard about the nuclear end of the world, seems to have made us uncaring about conventional war. Memories of Hiroshima are stronger than memories of Vietnam! How welcome it would be if conventional weapons were treated with the same awe as the atom bomb! How welcome it would be if the killing of many little by little, everyday, was considered just as outrageous as the killing of many all at once! Do we really live in such an irrational world that we would be more reluctant to use conventional weapons if every country had the bomb, and the fate of the world depended on a single madman? Would that make universal peace more secure? Have we any right to forget the 78 million human beings killed in the wars of this twentieth century?

The world today is divided between those who live in fear of being destroyed in nuclear war, and those who are dying day by day in wars fought with conventional weapons. This terror of the final war is so great that it has spread the most frightening insensibility towards the arms race and the use of non-nuclear weapons. We need most urgently — our intelligence requires us, our pity enjoins us — to struggle with equal intensity to ensure that neither Hiroshima nor Vietnam is repeated.

Weapons do not fire on their own. Those who have lost hope fire them. Those who are controlled by dogmas fire them. We must fight for peace undismayed, and fearlessly accept these challenges from those without hope and from the threats of fanatics.

I say to the poet

The peace plan which we five presidents signed accepts all the challenges. The path to peace is difficult, very difficult. We in Central America need everyone's help to achieve peace.

It is easier to predict the defeat of peace in Central America than its victory. That is how it was when man wanted to fly, and when he wanted to conquer space. That is how it was in the hard days of the two world wars which our century has known. That is how it was and still is as man confronts the most dreadful diseases and the task eliminating poverty and hunger in the world.

History was not written by men who predicted failure, who gave up their dreams, who abandoned their principles, who allowed their laziness to put their intelligence to sleep. If certain men at times were alone in seeking victory, they always had at their side the watchful spirit of their peoples, the faith and destiny of many generations.

Perhaps it was in difficult times for Central America, like those we are living through today, perhaps it was in premonition of the present crossroads, that

Rubén Darío, our America's greatest poet,[2] wrote these lines, convinced that history would take its course:

> Pray, generous, pious and proud;
> pray, chaste, pure, heavenly and brave;
> intercede for us, entreat for us,
> for already we are almost without sap or shoot,
> without soul, without life, without light, without Quixote,
> without feet and without wings, without Sancho and without God.

I assure the immortal poet that we shall not cease to dream, we shall not fear wisdom, we shall not flee from freedom. To the eternal poet I say that in Central America we shall not forget Quixote, we shall not renounce life, we shall not turn our backs on the spirit, and we shall never lose our faith in God.

I am one of those five men who signed an accord, a commitment which consists, very largely, in the fact of desiring peace with all one's soul.

Thank you.

ENDNOTES

1. Simon Bolivar (1783–1830), the South American revolutionary who led wars of independence in the present nations of Venezuela, Colombia, Panama, Ecuador, Peru and Bolivia.
2. Rubén Darío (1867–1916) of Nicaragua has had a tremendous influence upon both Spanish and Spanish American writers.

SELECTED BIBLIOGRAPHY

By Arias Sánchez

Dawn of a New Political Era. Address to the forty-second session of the UN General Assembly, 23 September 1987. San José: Presidencia de la República, 1987.

Grupos de Presión en Costa Rica. San Jose: Editorial Costa Rica, 1971. (A study of pressure groups.)

Let Us Go Together on the Road to Peace. Address, Harvard University, 24 September 1987. San José: Presidencia de la Republica, 1987.

Quien Gobierna en Costa Rica? ("Who Governs?") San José: EDUCA, 1976. (The subject of his doctoral thesis.)

Other Sources:

Abrams, Irwin. "Behind the Scenes: The Nobel Committee and Oscar Arias". *Antioch Review* **46**, 3 (Summer 1988).

Ameringer, Charles D. *Democracy in Nicaragua.* New York: Praeger, 1982.

Ameringer, Charles D. *Don Pepe: A Political Biography of José Figueres of Costa Rica.* Albuquerque: University of New Mexico Press, 1978.

Peace 1988

THE UNITED NATIONS PEACEKEEPING FORCES

INTRODUCTION

The Committee announced at the end of September that the 1988 prize would go to the United Nations Peacekeeping Forces, "recruited from among the young people of many nations, who, in keeping with their ideals, voluntarily take on a demanding and hazardous service in the cause of peace". Their work in reducing tensions and facilitating peace negotiations in conflict situations, the announcement stated, represents an important contribution to the realisation of the goals of the United Nations and has significantly strengthened the United Nations.

In the presence of a delegation of these UN peacekeepers on the stage behind him, flown to Oslo from the seven existing peacekeeping operations, Chairman Egil Aarvik of the Committee begins his speech of presentation asking for a moment of silence in memory of the 733 of their comrades who have died in this service since it began. He refers to the origins of this UN body in 1956 and tells of the efforts of the two types of peacekeepers, the observers of ceasefire agreements and the military units stationed between the parties in conflict.

In view of the achievements of this UN organ, Aarvik declares, the 1988 prize is to be regarded as a recognition of the whole United Nations itself: "The prize gives expression to the hope we all place in the United Nations". Aarvik then turns to UN Secretary-General Javier Pérez de Cuéllar, who is to receive the prize on behalf of the Peacekeeping Forces, and says of him, "He is himself one of the prizewinners today! With his never-tiring work and the results he has achieved as an active mediator, he should be accorded his part of the honour for the growing confidence which is shown in the United Nations".

Aarvik concludes by emphasising the Nobel Committee's desire to give recognition through this prize to the role of the young people in the Peacekeeping Forces. To those young people in the world today who may feel powerless and question whether they can indeed do anything, Aarvik would have the young prizewinners lift their UN flag and answer in the words of Nordahl Grieg, the young Norwegian poet who died in the Second World War. In his poem *To Youth*, Grieg called on them to keep their faith in this life and the future: armed with the spirit, they could bring about "true peace".

In his acceptance speech, Pérez de Cuéllar also pays tribute to the UN wearers of the blue helmets who lost their lives serving peace, and he appeals for the immediate release of the United States officer who had been kidnapped by Shi'ite pro-Palestinian guerrillas while he was serving in the UN unit in southern Lebanon.

Like Aarvik, the Secretary-General recalls the earlier peace laureates who were the architects of the Peacekeeping Forces, Ralph Bunche (1950), Lester

Pearson (1957), and Dag Hammarskjöld (1961). He points out how peacekeeping "uses soldiers as the servants of peace rather than as the instruments of war". "It introduces to the military sphere the principle of nonviolence". Again like Aarvik, he speaks optimistically of the hope and promise of the United Nations in the new international climate after the Cold War and declares that the peacekeeping operations symbolise the world community's will to peace.

Pérez de Cuéllar has to leave Oslo after the award ceremony but returns a month later to present the required lecture. After first considering the meaning of the word "peace", he refers to how the Cold War kept the United Nations from realising the hopes of its founders, although the UN did help prevent the interventions of West and East in regional conflicts from developing into more serious confrontations. Now, with the more positive policy of the Soviet Union, the UN's prospects are better than at any time in the past forty years. The challenge today is to develop the international authority of the UN in a world of more than 160 independent sovereign states. The Secretary-General then discusses the evolution of peacekeeping as an indication of how this international authority can be built up. He tells how the Security Council has usually followed the route of peaceful development instead of using the provisions in the Charter for military enforcement. The peacekeepers, "soldiers without enemies", represent "the exact opposite of the military action against aggression foreseen in Chapter VII". They are like the civilian police in nation states.

In conclusion the Secretary-General describes the requirements for the future success of peacekeeping, including the undivided support of the Security Council and adequate financing. Peacekeeping is only one UN activity, but its principles and techniques may well be applicable to the development of the collective system of international peace and security which is the long-term aim.

Pérez de Cuéllar could not anticipate how in the years following the award peacemaking missions would proliferate, grow more complex and even involve enforcement. There would be successes, but also failures, and unfortunately, the lack of adequate financing would remain a constant problem.

209

ANNOUNCEMENT

The Norwegian Nobel Committee has decided that the 1988 Nobel Peace Prize is to be awarded to the United Nations Peacekeeping Forces.

The Peacekeeping Forces of the United Nations have under extremely difficult conditions contributed to reducing tensions where an armistice has been negotiated but a peace treaty has yet to be established. In situations of this kind the UN forces represent the manifest will of the community of nations to achieve peace through negotiations, and the forces have by their presence made a decisive contribution towards the initiation of actual peace negotiations.

It is the considered opinion of the Committee that the Peacekeeping Forces through their efforts have made important contributions towards the realisation of one of the fundamental tenets of the United Nations. Thus the world organisation has come to play a more central part in world affairs and has been invested with increasing trust.

The Peacekeeping Forces are recruited from among the young people of many nations, who, in keeping with their ideals, voluntarily take on a demanding and hazardous service in the cause of peace. In the opinion of the Committee their efforts contribute in a particularly appropriate way towards the realisation of the goals of the United Nations.

PRESENTATION

Speech by EGIL AARVIK, Chairman of the Norwegian Nobel Committee.

Your Majesty, Your Royal Highnesses, Your Excellencies, Ladies and Gentlemen:

The award of the Nobel Peace Prize to the United Nations Peacekeeping Forces is unfortunately a reminder to us that peace is not a matter of course here in our world. Peace has to be actively protected — and this protection has its price. 733 young people have sacrificed their lives in the service of the particular form of peacekeeping which is under consideration here.

The Norwegian Nobel Committee asks those gathered together here today to join them in honouring the memory of those young people.

They came from different countries and had widely different backgrounds, but they were united in one thing: they were willing to devote their youth and their energy to the service of peace. They volunteered to the service, knowing that it could involve risk. It became their lot to pay the highest price a human being can pay.

We honour them for their unselfish contribution, and we join their relatives in their sorrow over their loved ones' early departure. Let us show this through a moment's silence.

We invoke peace on the memory of these young people in a spirit of thankfulness and deep respect.

For the first time in its history, the Peace Prize is to be awarded today to an organisation which, at least in part, consists of military forces. It might be reasonable to ask whether this is, in fact, in direct contradiction to the whole idea of the Peace Prize. The fact that this question has not been raised is an indication that it is universally accepted that the United Nations Peacekeeping Forces *are* in the spirit of the Peace Prize.

The description "Forces" is in itself inadequate since it conjures up the idea of a military operation in the traditional sense, while the reality is in many ways the diametric opposite. A more correct description would be "The United Nations Peacekeeping Operation" — consisting of both contingents of troops and unarmed observation corps.

These peacekeeping operations were commenced in 1956 when the UNEF (United Nations Emergency Force) was established in connection with the Suez crisis. The Security Council was unable to act because of a veto from two of the member states. Instead, use was made of the so-called "Uniting for Peace" resolution which gives the General Assembly of the United Nations the power to intervene in the event of the Security Council being unable to act in the face of a threat to world peace.

The General Assembly was summoned to a special session. In the following events, important roles were played by two prominent individuals: the former

foreign minister of Canada, Lester Pearson, and the then Secretary-General
of the United Nations, Dag Hammarskjöld. Both of these men were later
awarded the Nobel Peace Prize.

Through the influence of these two, plans were made and a resolution
passed for a peacekeeping force which was to supervise the retreat of foreign
troops from the canal zone.

The principles which were defined for this peace operation were written,
in the main, by Dag Hammarskjöld. It is an honour to his memory that the
same guidelines are, generally speaking, in use today.

The most important points in these guidelines are:

1. The involved parties must give their support and cooperation to
    the United Nations forces.
2. The primary aim is to prevent new hostilities and provide a
    background against which it is possible to work for a peaceful
    solution of the conflict.
3. The force is to make use of negotiation and persuasion instead of
    violence.
4. The force is under the command of the leadership of the United
    Nations and is not allowed to accept orders from other parts, not
    even the states who have made the troops available.
5. All member nations should contribute to the financing of the
    forces.

The peacekeeping forces have, on the basis of the resolution of 1956
and the guidelines drawn up by Dag Hammarskjöld, developed into what
present Secretary-General Pérez de Cuéllar calls "The United Nations' most
successful renewal".

Strangely enough, the peacekeeping forces as such were a new creation:
they are not named — or even envisaged — in the original United Nations
treaty. The treaty does mention the possibility of military involvement on the
part of the United Nations in the event of hostilities, but, because of the
relationship between the great powers, it has never been possible to make use
of this part of the treaty — the possible exception being the action in Korea
in 1950.

Today's peacekeeping operations are something quite different. The
troops are made available on a voluntary basis and are approved by the
Security Council. They are stationed in areas where a ceasefire has already
been established but where no formal peace treaty has been concluded,
and they are stationed in such a way that the conflicting parties, in the event
of a resumption of hostilities, would meet the United Nations troops first.
Actual fighting can thus be avoided, peace and quiet maintained, and it is
possible to develop an atmosphere which makes active peace work possible.
The very presence of the United Nations troops can have a positive effect. The
soldiers very often make friends among the local population, they can offer
help and aid in many ways, and are a conciliating element in otherwise
explosive situations.

In this connection it is interesting to note a parallel with one of the ideas Alfred Nobel worked on — following a model from the French duelling etiquette. The seconds in such a conflict could intervene between the combatants with the aim of achieving a delay in the duel so that tempers could be cooled and the whole business possibly solved by other means.

It is perhaps reasonable that there were powerful political objections to this model, but the point remains: the United Nations Peacekeeping Forces today have just such an "interventionist" role. Because the United Nations is, in this way, on speaking terms with both parts, negotiations which are at a standstill can perhaps be reopened, and in many situations it is possible that armed fighting can be avoided.

The English brigadier, Michael Harbottle, who took part in the United Nations Peacekeeping Forces in Cyprus at the end of the 1960's, has written a book on his experiences there. The book is called *The Impartial Soldier*, and in it he relates an episode which illustrates what the United Nations peacekeeping operations mean better than any official report.

The Finnish contingent under the command of Colonel Uolevi Koskenpalo was involved in the episode. A message was received to the effect that the Turks had begun to dig trenches in a suspicious manner; the Greeks had observed this, under the leadership of a general, they had decided to take the affair into their own hands. Colonel Koskenpalo had, however, placed his three platoons in precisely the right strategic position, so that the Greeks met the Finnish United Nations troops first as intended. The Greek general disliked being hindered in this way and began to protest loudly. In fact he screamed at the Finn — an obvious mistake. In contrast to the Greek, Colonel Koskenpalo was a well built man with a chest and shoulders of Nordic dimensions. He advanced slowly and from a height of well over six feet looked down at the Greek and said in a moderately loud voice, "Don't shout, general. I am a colonel in the Finnish army and don't like being shouted at."

The reaction was surprising. The general naturally didn't believe his ears, but the shouting stopped immediately and in a little while he retreated together with his forces. This gave the Finn the opportunity to both inform and placate the Greek high command and to persuade the Turks to stop the provocative trench digging.

In this way a violent episode was avoided. There have been many similar episodes where the United Nations Peacekeeping Forces have intervened. It is a question of a strictly peaceful behaviour combined with authority. The Finnish colonel was able to act as an efficient peace medium because he had the authority of the United Nations and the force of his well-trained Finnish United Nations soldiers behind him.

What has been said about the United Nations Peacekeeping Forces is equally true of the United Nations observers. Their duties are to ensure that the Security Council's ceasefire demands are kept. They mark the ceasefire line, establish observation posts and report to the Secretary-General if there are violations of the ceasefire.

This is an important role in critical situations. Reports from the observation corps will be non-partisan and accurate, in contrast to reports from the involved parties themselves. This gives them an obvious value both to the involved parties and to the outside world generally.

It is often emphasised that the United Nations' peacekeeping operations are only carried out at the invitation of the countries involved. The troops and observation corps are guests in the area, and they have a special responsibility to behave in a way which is in agreement with international law and ordinary politeness. Experience to now indicates that the peacekeeping forces have been a correct solution to the problem.

To the present there have been — or are — 13 peacekeeping operations. fifty-three countries have contributed with personnel, and the maximum force has been a total of 50,000 men. If one counts all the soldiers who have been involved in these operations, the total is something like 500,000 men.

The Norwegian Nobel Committee sees this mobilisation of troops from countries all over the world as a tangible expression of the world community's will to solve conflicts by peaceful means. The technological development of weapons systems has resulted in the peaceful resolution of conflicts becoming the only realistic possibility. Nuclear weapons have made the concept of wielding total power an absurdity. In conflict situations it is therefore vitally necessary that there are openings where real negotiations can be initiated. In the opinion of the Nobel Committee the United Nations peacekeeping operations contribute precisely to this.

The Committee believes also that the peacekeeping operations and the way they are carried out contribute to making the ideas which were the very reason for the establishment of the United Nations a reality. This year's Peace Prize should therefore also be regarded as a recognition of the whole organisation, the United Nations. The prize gives expression to the hope we all place in the United Nations.

Secretary-General Pérez de Cuéllar, who is directly responsible for the peacekeeping operations, and who is therefore present today to receive the prize, is here not only as the formal recipient, receiving the prize on behalf of others. He is himself one of the prizewinners today! With his never-tiring work and the results he has achieved as an active mediator he should be accorded his part of the honour for the growing confidence which is shown in the United Nations.

Confidence in the United Nations has otherwise been a variable factor. The United Nations has for many been seen as a body without power or effectiveness, a forum for bilateral insults, a theatre stage at the side of the reality of world politics. One has been able to have negative opinions of the United Nations without thereby colliding with the accepted state of affairs. But there is one overpowering argument in favour of the United Nations: the organisation has survived, and now defends more and more both its right to exist and its capacity to survive.

It has been pointed out, quite correctly, that the United Nations can only be what the member states make it. They can paralyse the United Nations by ignoring its resolutions, by vetoing, by sabotaging its economy. But they can also make the United Nations an active instrument in the fight for peace, a focus for international law and human rights, and a forum for the development of inter-racial understanding.

The signs today indicate that it is the latter alternative which is in the course of realising itself. Perhaps the very idea of the United Nations is now coming into its own? After what we have been through: Cold War, unsuccessful negotiations, growing fear of a universal atomic death, it is perhaps not so surprising that one again looks to the decisions that were made when the United Nations treaty was signed. On the ruins of the Second World War the survivors decided that conflicts should thereafter be solved by peaceful means. Barbarism should be replaced by friendly relations between nations. Freedom and human rights should be respected without reference to race, sex, language or religion. And the United Nations were to be the means by which the aims of the United Nations Treaty were to be realised.

This year's Peace Prize is a recognition of and homage to one organ of the United Nations. But it ought to be understood as a serious comment on the fact that we must, united and with our whole hearts, invest in the United Nations. It becomes clearer and clearer that what has to be done to secure the future for new generations has to be done together. Our determination has to be channelled into the United Nations. This is the best hope for the future of the world — indeed its only hope!

The belief and the hope which are placed in the United Nations have to be the hope and belief of the younger generations. In the ideals of the United Nations they can search for their own ideals, and it is they who are to form the world of the future.

In the selection of this year's Peace Prize laureate the Nobel Committee attached therefore great importance to the role of young people in the United Nations Peacekeeping Forces. It is precisely the contribution of the young which makes the realisation of the United Nations' aims possible in a positive way.

For obvious reasons it is precisely the young who today feel the crippling powerlessness in their meeting with the powers who steer the development of our world. It is easy to lose one's foothold, it is difficult to retain one's optimism — at times it is unclear whether there is any point in attempting to do anything at all.

To all the young people who feel their situation in this way, I would direct a question, the question which the young Norwegian poet Nordahl Grieg took up in his poem *To Youth*:

> Well may you ask, in despondent alarm:
> What is my weapon? What is my arm?

And thus it is that the young prizewinners can today raise their United Nations flag and answer with the words of this poem by one of our own young fallen:

> *This* is the sword you must bear in your fight —
> Faith in this life and man's God-given right.
> For the future of all, seek it and choose it;
> Die, if you must, gird it on and use it.
> Silent the path of the arrow by night;
> Halt *with the spirit* its death-dealing flight.
> Then, only then, will all warfare cease.
> Man's dignity only can give us true peace.

THE UNITED NATIONS PEACEKEEPING FORCES

The United Nations Peacekeeping Forces are employed by the World Organisation to maintain or re-establish peace in an area of armed conflict. The UN may engage in conflicts between states as well as in struggles within states. The UN acts as an impartial third party in order to prepare the ground for a settlement of the issues that have provoked armed conflict. If it proves impossible to achieve a peaceful settlement, the presence of UN forces may contribute to reducing the level of conflict.

The UN Peacekeeping Forces may only be employed when both parties to a conflict accept their presence. Accordingly, they may also be used by the warring parties to avoid having a conflict escalate and in the event also to have a struggle called off.

The Peacekeeping Forces are subordinate to the leadership of the United Nations. They are normally deployed as a consequence of a Security Council decision, however, on occasion, the initiative has been taken by the General Assembly. Operational control belongs to the Secretary-General and his secretariat.

We distinguish between two kinds of peacekeeping operations — unarmed observer groups and lightly armed military forces. The latter are only allowed to employ their weapons for self-defense. Altogether, 14 UN operations have been carried out. They are evenly divided between observer groups and military forces. The observer groups are concerned with gathering information for the UN about actual conditions prevailing in an area, e.g., as to whether both parties adhere to an armistice agreement. The military forces are entrusted with more extended tasks, such as keeping the parties to a conflict apart and maintaining order in an area.

UN interventions have been in particular demand in the Middle East, both as regards observer groups and military forces. The UN first took on the task of sending observers to monitor the armistice between Israel and the Arab states in 1948. Observer group activity was resumed after the wars of 1956, 1967, and 1973. After the 1956 war the first armed UN force was established to create a buffer between Israeli and Egyptian forces in the Sinai. Ten nations contributed soldiers. Another force was established after the war between Egypt and Israel in 1967 to monitor the armistice agreement between the parties. This took place during a period of extremely high tension both locally and between the great powers. In 1974, a smaller UN force was set up on the Golan Heights to maintain the boundary line between Syrian and Israeli forces. The most extensive UN operation in the Middle East is represented by the formation of UNIFIL subsequent upon the Israeli invasion of Lebanon in 1978. Its tasks included watching over the Israeli withdrawal, maintaining conditions of peace and security, and helping the Lebanese government re-establish its authority. Such tasks have taxed the capabilities of UNIFIL to the utmost, but the UN forces have made an important contribution by reducing the level of conflict in the area. However, this achievement has not come without significant cost. UN casualties now amount to more than 200.

The UN played an important role during the struggles that erupted when the Belgian colony of the Congo achieved independence in 1960. As anarchy and chaos reigned in the area, a UN force numbering almost 20,000 was set up to help the Congolese government maintain peace and order. It ended up being above all engaged in bringing a raging civil war to an end and preventing the province of Katanga from seceding. It was while carrying out the UN mission in the Congo that Secretary-General Dag Hammarskjöld was killed in an air crash.

Among other important tasks may be mentioned monitoring the border between India and Pakistan, and maintaining the peacekeeping force that was established on Cyprus on account of the civil war that broke out between the Greek and Turkish populations on the island. The UN force has succeeded in creating a buffer zone between the two ethnic groups.

The UN has in these and other areas played a significant role in reducing the level of conflict even though the fundamental causes of the struggles frequently remain.

After the Peace Prize award in 1988, UN peacekeeping entered the most active period in its history, taking on tasks which involved new functions and went beyond the traditional principles of mutual consent of the parties, impartiality, and the non-use of force. Article VII of the UN Charter was invoked in certain missions, involving measures of enforcement, and as the missions became more complex, defining what constituted peacekeeping became more difficult. "Multi-dimensional" peacekeeping has involved such non-military functions as supervising elections, monitoring human rights, and engaging in police work and civilian administration. In the early 1990s peacekeepers were delivering humanitarian aid under fire, monitoring no-fly zones and trying to protect "safe areas". By 1996 there was a return to more traditional peacekeeping and the period of expansion appeared to be over.

Up to 1988, in the 43 years since the United Nations was established only 13 peacekeeping operations were launched; the next 13 followed in 43 months, more than a half dozen more in the succeeding years. In the initial period only the Congo operation mentioned above did not follow the traditional lines. In using considerable military force in combination with civilian elements, it was a precursor of more recent peacekeeping operations.

The "second generation" of peacekeeping is considered to have begun in 1988 with the Good Offices Mission in Afghanistan and Pakistan, with observers monitoring the Soviet withdrawal from Afghanistan, and with the Iran-Iraq Military Observer Group. In 1989 missions were sent to monitor the Central American peace accord and to observe the Nicaraguan election and to observe the Cuban withdrawal from Angola. In the same year a mission was sent to assist the former South African colony of Namibia to make the transition to independence and hold democratic elections. Not unlike in the Congo, it included both military and civilian detachments, but the military did not engage in fighting. The Namibian mission is considered one of the most successful of the peacekeeping operations.

The next two years saw the establishment of the mission for the Verification of Elections in Haiti, the Observer Mission in El Salvador, the Iraq-Kuwait Observer Mission (after the Gulf War), the Mission for the Referendum in Western Sahara, and the Angola Verification Mission. In 1991 the UN Transitional Authority in Cambodia began an ambitious undertaking with a contingent as large as in the Congo operation and combining both military and civilian forces, with the task of restoring peace and beginning the reconstruction of a war-torn country. There were many successes, but a complete peace settlement is still to be reached.

In 1991 the UN Protection Force (UNPROFOR) was established in former Yugoslavia, and in 1992 United Nations Operation in Somalia (UNOSOM) began, both large-scale missions conducted in the midst of fratricidal conflicts where there was no peace to keep, and both involved enforcement along with humanitarian assistance. In Somalia armed intervention against one of the parties in conflict led to the killing of UN soldiers and an unsuccessful manhunt for the warlord held responsible. In Bosnia the effort to remain impartial left the peacekeepers remaining as onlookers while the Bosnian Serbs were committing acts of genocide. When the Security Council authorised them to call in air strikes "in self-defense", the Bosnian Serbs took peacekeepers as hostages.

Although more than 100,000 lives in Somalia were saved, the mission was considered a disaster, and its failure delayed timely response of the UN to the massacres in Rwanda. In the United States, whose role is crucial, the deaths of its soldiers turned public opinion against peacekeeping and intensified public critism of the UN. In Bosnia the United States finally led a NATO military action and a multilateral diplomatic effort which produced a peace agreement between the warring factions. A NATO military contingent replaced UNPROFOR, authorised to use armed force to keep the rival armies apart and provide security for the reconstruction and rebuilding.

In December 1995 UNPROFOR was formally ended. Although it had succeeded in assisting refugees and distributing food in the most difficult of situations and had helped reduce the number of deaths from 130,000 in 1992 to fewer than 3,000 in 1994, UNPROFOR had been much criticised for not using greater force, for not doing, in fact, what the peacekeepers in Somalia had been blamed for doing. What many critics fail to recognise is that a peacekeeping mission can only carry out what the Security Council has mandated it to do. Regarding Bosnia, there was little agreement among the Council members to take strong military action. Nor would the resources have been available for this if it had been ordered. The UN member states sent less than a fourth of the number of troops for which the Secretary-General originally asked.

The difficulties encountered in Somalia and Bosnia discouraged the sending of peacekeeping missions to regions already locked in conflict, where the line between peacekeeping and peace-enforcing would not be clear. Traditional peacekeeping remains in good repute and peacekeepers have shown that they can effectively serve as peacebuilders, as in Namibia and Cambodia. This was recognised in the provision of the Bosnian peace agreement for the UN to contribute an international contingent of civilian police. A new type of peacekeeping has been demonstrated by the Preventive Deployment Force in Macedonia, a successor state of former Yugoslavia, designed to prevent conflicts from spreading there by its presence.

By 1995 there had been a total of 18 separate peacekeeping operations, to which 84 countries had contributed personnel. Since 1948 over 750,000 had served, of whom more than 1,400 had given their lives. In the heyday of peacekeeping in 1993, there were over 78,000 soldiers, military observers and civilian police officers in the field. In 1995 there were more than 58,000, but early in 1996 this number had been reduced to about 26,3000, deployed in 16 missions, and the 1995 budget of about $3 billion had been cut by half for 1996. Both budgetary constraints and political considerations were bringing about personnel reductions in current projects and dictating the planning of fewer, smaller and less costly missions. Expectations were that the total number of personnel could shrink to less than fifteen thousand as existing missions were reduced in size, replaced by regional organisations, or not renewed.

While the highest hopes for peacekeeping expressed at the award ceremony in 1988 have not been realised, there can be no question but that this mechanism, when properly used, has made a significant contribution to the peace of the world. Now that the UN has learned the limitations of peacekeeping and is likely to plan for more modest and more tightly controlled projects in the future, success will depend in a large measure upon the willingness of member nations to provide adequate financing.

ACCEPTANCE

JAVIER PÉREZ DE CUÉLLAR
(Translation)

Your Majesty, Your Royal Highnesses, Mr Chairman, Ladies and Gentlemen,

I should like to thank you, Mr Chairman, and the other members of the Norwegian Nobel Committee, for the award which I have received today on behalf of the United Nations peacekeeping operations. I should also like to pay homage to the memory of Alfred Nobel, that visionary Scandinavian. His commitment to the cause of peace lives on in the prize which he so generously endowed.

The award of the Nobel Peace Prize to the United Nations peacekeeping operations gives recognition to an idea of striking originality and power and pays brilliant tribute to those who have made it a reality.

The great experiment you are honouring here today has been shaped by many people. I recall in particular its original architects, Ralph Bunche, Dag Hammarskjöld and Lester Pearson, all three of them Nobel Laureates. Their remarkable work has been built upon by their successors who set up and directed further peacekeeping operations.

You are also honouring the soldiers of peace, some half a million young men and women from fifty-eight countries. Seven hundred and thirty-three "Blue Helmets" have given their lives in the service of peace. One of them, Lieutenant Colonel William Higgins, is still in the hands of his kidnappers. I take this opportunity to appeal once again for his immediate release.[1] We cannot forget these brave soldiers. Nor can we forget the civilians of the United Nations Secretariat, and especially the Field Operations Service, who have supported their military colleagues with dedication and courage in fifteen peacekeeping operations all over the world.

The technique which has come to be called peacekeeping uses soldiers as the servants of peace rather than as the instruments of war. It introduces to the military sphere the principle of nonviolence. It provides an honourable alternative to conflict and a means of reducing strife and tension, so that a solution can be sought through negotiation. Never before in history have military forces been employed internationally *not* to wage war, *not* to establish domination and *not* to serve the interests of any power or group of powers, but rather to prevent conflict between peoples.

We are now at a time of extraordinary hope and promise for the United Nations, after a long period when the spectre, and too often the grim reality of war have darkened our planet, there is a new mood of understanding and common sense, a new determination to move away from international conflict and devote ourselves instead to the immense task of building a better world. Recently, we have seen several conflicts give way to negotiation and conciliation.

These developments have not been fortuitous. They are the result of diplomatic activity by the United Nations sustained over the years and intensified recently. Indeed, the prospects of realising the vision expressed in the Charter of the United Nations seem better today than at any time since the organisation was founded.

In the past forty years we have experienced perhaps the most revolutionary period in all of human history. The instruments of war have been developed to the point where war itself has become a futile anachronism, an anachronism so expensive and terrifying that even the richest and most powerful countries can no longer afford to contemplate it. We have redrawn the political map of the world so that for the first time in history the international community is not dominated by competing empires, but consists of more than 160 independent sovereign states. Thus collective responsibility for peace can be evolved in a truly representative international system. At the same time, the technological revolution of the past forty years, which has radically changed the way people live, work and communicate, presents enormous opportunities as well as grave risks. We must now reflect upon these changes and start to assimilate them.

With a better international climate, it now seems possible to further develop modes and techniques to control conflict and settle disputes. We can, and must, achieve what we have dreamed of for so long, that is to make the rule of law standard rather than the exception in world affairs. Our technological capacity and the undoubted basic fact of interdependence, make this even more urgent. With a reliable system of collective responsibility we can face the vast economic and social challenges of our time and alleviate the massive poverty and suffering which are a disgrace to the human condition. Without it, we run the risk of a steady deterioration of the conditions of life on this planet.

In our striving for a world at peace with itself, and governed by the rule of law, I believe that peacekeeping operations play a vital and significant role. In some ways they are analogous to the role of the civil police in the development of peaceful, law-abiding nation states. The technique of peacekeeping, which has already proved itself in fifteen operations all over the world, can help us to cross the line from a world of international conflict and violence to a world in which respect for international law and authority overcomes belligerence and ensures justice.

Peacekeeping operations symbolise the world community's will to peace and represent the impartial, practical expression of that will. The award of the Nobel Peace Prize to these operations illuminates the hope and strengthens the promise of this extraordinary concept.

NOBEL LECTURE*

January 9, 1989
by
Secretary-General Javier Pérez de Cuéllar

Mr. Chairman, Excellencies, Ladies and Gentlemen,

I should like first of all, to once again thank the Norwegian Nobel Committee for the award they have made to the United Nations Peacekeeping Operations. Their decision has been acclaimed all over the world. I take this opportunity also to express once again my deep gratitude to the countries which have contributed troops or provided logistical support to these operations. It is to their willing cooperation that we owe the success of this great experiment in conflict control.

Peace — the word evokes the simplest and most cherished dream of humanity. Peace is, and has always been, the ultimate human aspiration. And yet our history overwhelmingly shows that while we speak incessantly of peace, our actions tell a very different story.

Peace is any easy word to say in any language. As Secretary-General of the United Nations I hear it so frequently from so many different mouths and different sources, that it sometimes seems to me to be a general incantation more or less deprived of practical meaning. What do we really mean by peace?

Human nature being what it is, peace must inevitably be a relative condition. The essence of life is struggle and competition, and to that extent perfect peace is an almost meaningless abstraction. Struggle and competition are stimulating, but when they degenerate into conflict they are usually both destructive and disruptive. The aim of political institutions like the United Nations is to draw the line between struggle and conflict and to make it possible for nations to stay on the right side of that line. Peacekeeping operations are one very practical means of doing this. What we are trying to create in the United Nations is a world where nations recognise at the same time the ultimate futility of war and the collective responsibility which men and women everywhere share for ensuring a decent future.

All human experience seems to show that in international, as in national, affairs, the rule of law is an essential ultimate objective for any society which wishes to survive in reasonable conditions. We now recognise that all humanity — the whole population of this planet — has in many respects become, through the revolutionary force of technological and other changes, a single society. The evolution of, and respect for, international law and international authority may well be decisive in determining whether this global society is going to survive in reasonable conditions.

We have come a long way in the forty-three years since World War II. With the creation and ratification of the United Nations Charter it seemed that governments had, at last, learned the lessons of two world wars. However, in the forty years of ideological strife, tumultous change, and evolution which followed, the initial enthusiasm for the Charter largely evaporated. Even the *possibility* of an orderly international future began to be questioned. The Cold War paralysed the United Nations, which was founded on the assumption that the great powers would be unanimous in dealing with matters of international peace and security. Regional conflicts defied the authority of the world organisation. The arms race proceeded at full speed at all levels.

In spite of these discouraging developments, the basic will to peace of the world community survived. A third world war — which at times seemed imminent — was avoided. The UN played an important role in preventing regional conflicts from escalating into an armed confrontation between East and West. Improvisations, including new techniques of peacemaking and peacekeeping and a large expansion of the role of the Secretary-General, to some extent filled the gap caused by the absence of great power unanimity. In this process, a practical reassessment of the realities of international peace and security has gradually emerged. Sixteen peacekeeping operations and countless good offices missions by successive Secretaries-General have been the backbone of this effort.

In the last eighteen months a new and mild international climate has relaxed the rigors of the Cold War and calmed the storm of regional conflict. The prospect of realising the dreams of 1945 seems better than at anytime in forty years. At last we have an opportunity to assess our situation, to consider the revolutionary changes that have taken place to cooperate in making plans for a better future.

This opportunity has not come a moment too soon. Modern warfare has become a lethal and unacceptable anachronism. Even the most powerful states are finding that preparations for modern warfare are prohibitively expensive. An improvement in the way the existing system of international stability and security operates is urgently needed, and may now at last be within the bounds of political reality.

But, there is another compelling challenge to the community of nations — a challenge which will not respect nor wait upon the disputes and disagreements of nations. We are now encountering a new generation of global problems which can only be faced effectively through an unprecedented degree of international cooperation. Our capacity to face these problems will determine the nature and conditions of life on this planet in the next century. Clearly this task requires outstanding leadership and an extraordinary concentration of resources and political energy. We shall have to study our existing international mechanisms and decide in what way they need to be strengthened and coordinated.

In dealing with both sets of issues — peace and stability, and global problems — the key question will be the extent to which collective responsibility and international authority can be exercised and respected. We now have a world of more than 160 independent sovereign states. This is a new situation which clearly demands an acceptable, but effective, degree of international authority in matters of common concern. The nature and evolution of this authority will be the key to building a better world and dealing with the global threats we now face.

Forty-three years ago the international organisation was primarily preoccupied with international peace and security. The evolution of thinking and practice on this essential question may give some clues as to the basis upon which international authority may rest in the future.

As regards international peace and security the United Nations Charter sets out a process which, in its first stage, is based on the renunciation of force in international relations and on the peaceful settlement of disputes. If these principles are rejected, the Charter provides for collective enforcement action by the world community through the Security Council. Such action ranges from various forms of sanctions and embargoes to the use of military force by the Security Council.

In the political and military conditions of the post-war world, forceful international action has not proved to be a practical proposition. Sanctions and embargoes have rarely been agreed on, and military enforcement action never, apart from the exceptional case of Korea. Instead the Security Council and the Secretary-General have pioneered a different route — the route of consensus, conciliation, good offices, diplomatic pressure and non-forceful, cooperative peacekeeping.

This last concept — peacekeeping — was honoured this year with the award of the Nobel Peace Prize. This was a recognition not only of the architects and the soldiers of peacekeeping, but also of an extremely important idea. The evolution of peacekeeping may provide a useful practical indication of how international authority, and respect for it, can be built up.

Before considering the evolution of peacekeeping, however, I would like to say a word about its opposite, enforcement. Chapter VII of the Charter, the enforcement chapter, was a recognition by the authors of the Charter that the failure of the international community to deal with the aggressions of the 1930s had inevitably led to World War II. They were determined that the international community should not make this mistake again.

In the period since World War II aggressors on this scale have, mercifully, not emerged. The measures of Chapter VII have thus not been invoked in order to take forceful action against aggression. The Security Council, in its wisdom, has never seen fit or been able to agree on the full-scale use of Chapter VII. Instead, international disputes and threats to the peace have been, for the most part, dealt with by non-forceful means. That should not mean that Chapter VII should be forgotten. It is all well and good to evolve a design for international peace and security based not on forceful techniques, but on cooperation and persuasion. But we cannot say for certain that the world will never again be threatened by irrational aggressors. The capacity to react forcefully, and in time, to such a contingency must therefore be maintained, while we pursue the option of peacemaking and peacekeeping as the normal approach to international disputes or threats to the peace.

The essence of peacekeeping is the use of soldiers as a catalyst for peace rather than as the instruments of war. It is in fact the exact opposite of the military action against aggression foreseen in Chapter VII of the charter. Although the arms race continues, it would seem that the majority of nations have, in practice, opted for the rule of international authority and law in their relations with each other. The only sanction for this authority is usually persuasion, the moral force of international authority and diplomatic pressure. In addition, international authority can be symbolised in conflict areas by non-fighting soldiers, the UN's peacekeepers.

These are soldiers without enemies. Their duty is to remain above the conflict. They may only use their weapons in the last resort for self-defense. Their strength is that, representing the will of the international community, they provide an honourable alternative to war and a useful pretext for peace. Their presence is often the essential prerequisite for negotiating a settlement. They have, or should have, a direct connection with the process of peacemaking.

The peacekeeping and peacemaking route has been pioneered even as governments also follow the course of armaments and military alliances. I have a feeling that self-styled experts and realists, who are not always farsighted, have tended to regard the UN's peacekeeping and peacemaking efforts rather patronizingly as something of a sideshow. Certainly, some major powers, including the Soviet Union, were for many years highly sceptical of — and even actively opposed to — UN peacekeeping operations.

Recent changes in Soviet policy on peacekeeping, as well as on other important matters, mean that for the first time there is virtually a unanimous international constituency for promoting the concept of international authority through consensus and joint action, by the non-forceful techniques of peacemaking and peacekeeping.

What are the practical prospects of making this approach to international peace and stability effective? It is perhaps worth recalling how, in nation states, the evolution of civilian police as the guardians of public safety and the symbols of the law helped many states to cross the line from lawless violence and tyranny to civil authority and respect for the law in the common interest of all citizens. When they were first introduced, the police were often resented or not taken seriously. They were the butt of many jokes and demonstrations. When however, they gained the support both of the governmental establishment and of the vast majority of the populace, they became a trusted and indispensable institution. They were an institution which did not depend on physical force but on the support of the authorities and the people and on the majesty of the law.

Some of the factors which allowed the emergence of the police as guardians of the law and protectors of public safety may have begun to be present in the international world of today. There is a widespread weariness and disgust with violence and a heightened consciousness that the use of force seldom solves, and usually exacerbates, problems. Our powers of destruction have increased to the point where it is madness to use them. The necessity of the rule of law in our crowded, interdependent planet is becoming increasingly evident. It is clear that if we fail to act together on many matters, we may lose the capacity to act at all. At the superpower level we are seeing the first practical steps of disarmament — a recognition of the undoubted fact that war is no longer a practical instrument of national policy.

These factors would seem to indicate that the way to peace and security might in future generally be based on consensus and cooperation rather than on the use of force. Peacekeeping operations would be an important visible symbol and monitor of such a system, although, as I have said, we must also preserve some collective capacity to deal with aggression.

The basic prerequisites for the success of the peacekeeping technique are now present to a far greater extent than before. Successful peacekeeping requires a strong and supportive international consensus, starting in the Security Council. I must add that this support must include the necessary financial and logistical support. The cost of peacekeeping is usually infinitesimal by comparison with the cost of war, destruction and disruption. Nonetheless, the sums involved are considerable by diplomatic standards, if not by military standards. The present uncertain situation about financing is deplorable. It puts an intolerable burden on the countries which provide the troops, and is also harmful to the essential principle of collective responsibility. It sends a feeble and wavering message, when what is required is confidence and strong support. Collective governmental responsibility for the financing of peacekeeping operations is an essential basic principle. However, if governments decide that the financial burden is too heavy for them to bear alone, other means of financing may have to be considered. In some cases, those who benefit financially from the results of a peacemaking and peacekeeping operation might be asked to share in the costs. A reserve fund for peacekeeping emergencies has also been suggested. A more far-reaching idea has been floated, embracing the concept of using some of the money spent on war to pay for peace through an appropriate international levy on all overseas arms sales. This money could be used to build up such a fund. As long as, regrettably, the arms trade continues, we would at least be robbing war to pay for peace. It is an interesting coincidence that the figure of 1.5 billion dollars, often mentioned as the possible bill for peacekeeping in 1989, is almost exactly one percent of the official arms exports for 1987 — 164 billion dollars.

A peacekeeping operation must have a workable and realistic mandate fully supported by the international community. It must also have the cooperation, however grudging, of the governments and authorities in the area of conflict, and their understanding that the operation serves their long-term interests, no matter what their short-term political difficulties may be.

A peacekeeping operation needs disciplined and broadly representative contingents and an effective integrated command. The operation must be guided at all times by the Secretary-General and kept on course with the objectives of the Security Council.

The nonviolent nature of peacekeeping must be understood by the soldiers and respected by the parties to the conflict. A peacekeeping force that uses its weapons for purposes other than strict self-defense quickly becomes part of the conflict and therefore part of the problem. It loses its essential quality of being above the conflict.

These essential conditions seem to be present to a far greater extent than any time in the past forty years. Indeed we have come a very long way since 1948, when Secretary-General Trygve Lie's suggestion of "a small guard force" for Palestine was dismissed without serious discussion.

The situation in the Security Council is particularly encouraging. For the first time the permanent members seem to be becoming a collegial body working together with the non-permanent members and with the Secretary-General to evolve common approaches and solutions for problems of international peace and security. This development opens up new possibilities of a more general nature in arms control and disarmament and in the settlement of international disputes, as well as in the development and use for the technique of peacekeeping.

Here the change in the Soviet attitude is particularly encouraging. New Soviet proposals, both as regards the future development of peacekeeping and the wider use of such operations, indicate that a major obstacle to progress has been removed. The Soviet proposals aim at seeing "the positive experience and practice of United Nations peacekeeping operations consolidated and further developed and put on a more solid legal and financial basis" so that they can be used "more extensively for the implementation of Security Council decisions as well as for the prevention of emerging armed conflicts".

This new consensus behind peacekeeping comes at a time when important operations are imminent — in Namibia and Western Sahara,[2] for example. These operations should provide a practical testing ground for strengthening the foundations of this important technique.

The long-term aim remains what it has always been — to evolve a collective system of international peace and security, reliable and strong enough that governments in trouble or under threat will choose to bring their problems to the United Nations rather than trying to go it alone in unilateral efforts which usually end in disaster. To achieve this goal the member states of the United Nations should make deliberate and practical efforts to foster the growth of collective responsibility, international confidence, operational capacity, and respect for the decisions and operations of the United Nations. Such an effort could give the phrase "international peace and security" a reality which it has so far lacked.

In a larger perspective, we must work towards a time when war will cease to be an acceptable option of national policy or a possible means of settling disputes, and when a reliable and respected international system will take its place. In this perspective the development of international peacekeeping has an essential place. Just as the concept of civil police was essential to the development of the rule of law within nation states.

When we talk of peacekeeping we are, at the present time, referring to one area of international activity. But the principles and techniques involved in peacekeeping may be applicable and relevant to other areas and other problems: the principles of impartiality and objectivity; the symbolic representation of international authority; the process of securing compliance through cooperation; the providing of pretexts for conforming to international decisions; the capacity for fact-finding; the monitoring of the implementation of agreements; the developing of a capacity for pre-empting disasters or preventing conflicts. These are all essential elements of the peacekeeping technique which need further development. They may also prove to be an important basis for dealing with the global problems which now present an urgent challenge to the international community.

I hope that the attention now being given to peacekeeping, which is symbolised by the award of the Nobel Peace Prize, will not only strengthen our capacity to conduct the affairs of nations in a more peaceful and just manner. I hope it will also stimulate a wider effort to consider the new means and the new institutions which we shall need if we are to ensure our common future.

ENDNOTES

1. Lieutenant William Higgins was abducted in February 1988 near Tyre and, despite the pleas by the Secretary-General and others, was killed by his captors.
2. In April 1989 the United Nations Transitional Assistance Group (UNTAG) began operations in Namibia. It was not until 1991, however, that the United Nations Mission for Referendum in Western Sahara (MINURSO) was established.

SELECTED BIBLIOGRAPHY

Daniel, Donald C. F. and Bradd C. Hayes, eds. *Beyond Traditional Peacekeeping*. New York: St. Martin's Press, 1995. (Excellent essays on past, present and future of peacekeeping, with case studies and helpful appendices.)

Diehl, Paul F. *International Peacekeeping*. Baltimore, Md.: Johns Hopkins University Press, 1994. (History and analysis from the period of the League of Nations, with an epilogue on Somalia, Bosnia and Cambodia.)

Fetherston, A. B. *Towards a Theory of United Nations Peacekeepers*. New York: St. Martin's, 1995. (Includes history to 1993 and case studies.)

Harbottle, Michael. *The Impartial Soldier*. London: Oxford University Press, 1970. (The first of his many publications on the peacekeepers.)

Heininger, Janet E. *Peacekeeping in Transition: The United Nations in Cambodia, 1991–1993*. New York: Twentieth Century Fund Press, 1994. (A key example of peacekeeping combined with peace-building.)

Hirsch, John L. and Robert B. Oakley. *Somalia and Operation Restore Hope: Reflections on Peacekeeping and Peacemaking*. Herndon, Virginia: U.S. Institute of Peace Press, 1995. (A detailed study, covering both achievements and mistakes.)

International Peacekeeping. 1994– . (Invaluable newsletter reporting and analysing developments with emphasis on legal and policy issues.)

Urquhart, Brian. *A Life in Peace and War*. New York: W. W. Norton, 1971. (Valuable memoirs by former UN peacekeeping administrator and biographer of Ralph Bunche and Dag Hammarskjöld, with whom he worked closely.)

Peace 1989

XIVth DALAI LAMA, TENZIN GYATSO

INTRODUCTION

In announcing in early October its award of the 1989 prize to Tenzin Gyatso, the XIVth Dalai Lama of Tibet, the Norwegian Nobel Committee emphasised his constant opposition of the use of violence in his struggle for the liberation of Tibet from Chinese occupation and his "constructive and forward-looking proposals for the solution of international conflicts, human rights issues, and global environmental problems". Some commentators had suggested that the Committee intended the prize to be a show of support for the student movement which the Chinese government had suppressed on Tiananmen Square the previous June, but the announcement made no mention of this, nor did Committee Chairman Egil Aarvik in his presentation speech.

In presenting the award, Aarvik tells the dramatic life story of the laureate and describes his efforts to win Tibet's freedom from China by following the principle of nonviolence. This principle the Dalai Lama would apply "not only to Tibet", Aarvik declares, "but to each and every conflict". He is a successor of Mahatma Gandhi, and the Committee regards this prize "as in part a tribute to the memory of Mahatma Gandhi".

In accepting it, the Dalai Lama modestly declares that he is only "a simple monk from Tibet... no one special". He sees the prize rather as "a recognition of the true value of altruism, love, compassion and nonviolence, which I practise in accordance with the teachings of the Buddha and the great sages of India and Tibet".

He accepts on behalf of "the oppressed everywhere", and he echoes the Committee in calling it a tribute to Gandhi, the founder of nonviolent action for change, "whose life taught and inspired me". He accepts on behalf of the suffering Tibetans and declares, "The prize reaffirms our conviction that with truth, courage and determination as our weapons, Tibet will be liberated".

He refers to the brave students on Tiananmen Square, who "showed the Chinese leadership and the world the human face of that great nation" and speaks of his own efforts to reach a peace settlement with China. After touching briefly upon themes he will develop in his lectures, he ends on an optimistic note about the coming "kinder, happier 21st century".

On the next day the Dalai Lama makes an unusual entrance to the university hall to give his Nobel lecture, stopping at each row to greet those sitting on the aisle. He is introduced by Gunnar Stålsett, the Committee member who is also the Secretary-General of the Lutheran World Federation in Geneva. Stålsett calls the Dalai Lama "one of the great spiritual leaders of our time ... who combines rationality, humanism and religious traditions as foundations for moral responses to the great challenges of the 20th century".

The Dalai Lama tells the audience that the speech he has prepared has been circulated and that "yesterday I tried my best to be more formal, but today

I feel more free, so I will speak informally", not in Tibetan, with a translator, but "directly with my broken English". A young monk stands by his side to supply an occasional word or phrase when needed. Both speeches are printed below. The prepared but undelivered address is officially considered to be his Nobel lecture. The impromptu speech, which he presents without notes, is available in Tibetan publications, edited from a recording. Though given in the early afternoon, it is entitled, "The Nobel Evening Address".

In his official Nobel lecture, the Dalai Lama speaks of the common problems which human beings face as part of the "global family" and then discusses the special problems of the Tibetan people. He explains his Five-Point Plan for the restoration of peace and human rights in Tibet and tells of his dream to develop the entire Tibetan plateau into a sanctuary of peace and environmental protection, a zone of Ahimsa (the ethical principle of noninjury to both men and animals developed by Gandhi in his movement of nonviolence). The Dalai Lama finds encouragement in the proposal of President Mikhail Gorbachev of the Soviet Union [Nobel Peace Prize, 1990] for the demilitarisation of the Soviet-Chinese borders.

In his more spontaneous speech the Dalai Lama intends to cover three topics, speaking as a human being, a Buddhist monk, and a Tibetan. He begins in saying that he wants to talk of the purpose of life. On a seeming impulse, he reaches down from the podium to the floral arrangement decorating the stage and withdraws a single flower, holding it up as the answer to the question of life's purpose, holding it there for some time without a word, leaving the audience to consider how the blooming flower in its fullness helps us see what all creation is meant to do.

Then he explains that everyone wants happiness, which in its truest form can come from a sense of inner peace, achieved through cultivating altruism, love and compassion. He speaks at length explaining compassion and nonviolence, which he feels are part of human nature. True compassion is the sense of responsibility and closeness we feel toward another being, knowing that this other person, just like ourselves, wants to be happy and avoid suffering and has every right to pursue these ends. True compassion is the basis of the altruism and forgiveness which can bring humanity together.

Little time is left to discuss Buddhism, which he calls "not a religion but a science of mind", or the Tibetan problem, which is, however, covered in the formal address. Here he emphasises the seriousness of the present situation for Tibet and closes, expressing his deeply felt gratitude for the warm support he has received from this audience.

ANNOUNCEMENT

The Norwegian Nobel Committee has decided to award the 1989 Nobel Peace Prize to the XIVth Dalai Lama, Tenzin Gyatso, the religious and political leader of the Tibetan people.

The Committee wants to emphasise the fact that the Dalai Lama in his struggle for the liberation of Tibet has consistently opposed the use of violence. He has instead advocated peaceful solutions based upon tolerance and mutual respect in order to preserve the historical and cultural heritage of his people.

The Dalai Lama has developed his philosophy of peace from a great reverence for all things living and upon the concept of universal responsiblity embracing all mankind as well as nature. In the opinion of the Committee the Dalai Lama has come forward with constructive and forward-looking proposals for the solution of international conflicts, human rights issues, and global environmental problems.

PRESENTATION

Speech by EGIL AARVIK, Chairman of the Norwegian Nobel Committee.

The Nobel Peace Prize is one of six awards bearing the name Alfred Nobel that are presented today. Five of these awards are made in Stockholm, and the Norwegian Nobel Committee would like to take this opportunity to congratulate the laureates who will be honoured in the Swedish capital today. This year's ceremony is an occasion of special gratification to us Norwegians, as one of the recipients is a Norwegian, Professor Trygve Haavelmo, the winner of this year's Nobel Prize for Economics. We would like to congratulate him on this honour.

This year's Nobel Peace Prize has been awarded to H.H. The Dalai Lama, first and foremost for his consistent resistance to the use of violence in his people's struggle to regain their liberty.

Ever since 1959 the Dalai Lama, together with some one hundred thousand of his countrymen, has lived in an organised community in exile in India. This is by no means the first community of exiles in the world, but it is assuredly the first and only one that has not set up any militant liberation movement. This policy of nonviolence is all the more remarkable when it is considered in relation to the sufferings inflicted on the Tibetan people during the occupation of their country. The Dalai Lama's response has been to propose a peaceful solution which would go a long way to satisfying Chinese interests. It would be difficult to cite any historical example of a minority's struggle to secure its rights, in which a more conciliatory attitude to the adversary has been adopted than in the case of the Dalai Lama. It would be natural to compare him with Mahatma Gandhi, one of this century's greatest protagonists of peace, and the Dalai Lama likes to consider himself one of Gandhi's successors. People have occasionally wondered why Gandhi himself was never awarded the Nobel Peace Prize, and the present Nobel Committee can with impunity share this surprise, while regarding this year's award of the prize as in part a tribute to the memory of Mahatma Gandhi. This year's laureate will also be able to celebrate a significant jubilee, as it is now fifty years since he was solemnly installed as H.H. the Fourteenth Dalai Lama of the Tibetan people, when he was four years old. Pursuing the process of selection that resulted in the choice of him in particular would involve trespassing what, to a Westerner, is *terra incognita*, where belief, thought and action exist in a dimension of existence of which we are ignorant or maybe have merely forgotten.

According to Buddhist tradition every new Dalai Lama is a reincarnation of his predecessor, and when the thirteenth died in 1933 a search was immediately instigated to find his reincarnation; oracles and learned lamas were consulted and certain signs observed. Strange cloud formations drifted across the heavens; the deceased, placed in the so-called Buddha position facing south, was found two days later facing east. This indicated that a search should be carried out to the east, and a delegation accordingly set forth, first to one of Tibet's sacred lakes, where the future could be revealed in the surface of the water. In this case, a monastery was indicated, as well as a house with turquoise-coloured tiles.

The delegation continued on its way, and found first the monastery and then the house, in the village of Takster in Eastern Tibet. It was the home of a crofter and his family, and they were asked if they had any children. They had a two-year-old son called Tenzin Gyatso. A number of inexplicable acts carried out by this boy convinced the delegation that they were at their journey's end, and that the Fourteenth Dalai Lama had been found.

Like so much else in the realm of religion this is not something we are asked to comprehend without reason: we encounter phenomena that belong to a reality different from our own, and to which we should respond not with an attempt at rational explanation, but with reverent wonder.

Throughout its history Tibet has been a closed country, with little contact with the outside world. This is also true of modern times, and maybe explains why its leaders failed to attach due importance to formal *de jure* recognition of their country as an autonomous state. This, too, may be one of the reasons why the outside world did not feel any obligation to support Tibet, when the country in 1950 and the years that followed was gradually occupied by the Chinese, who — in direct opposition to the Tibetans' own interpretation — claimed that Tibet has always been a part of China. In occupying the country the Chinese have, according to the conclusion reached by the International Commission of Jurists, been guilty of "the most pernicious crime that any individual or nation can be accused of, viz., a wilful attempt to annihilate an entire people".

Meanwhile Tenzin Gyatso had by now reached the age of sixteen, and in the critical situation that now arose, he was charged with the task of playing the role of political leader to his people. Up till then the country had been ruled on his behalf by regents. He would have to assume the authority that the title of Dalai Lama involved, a boy of sixteen, without political experience, and with no education beyond his study of Buddhist lore, which he had absorbed throughout his upbringing. In his autobiography *My Life and My People* he has given us a vivid account of his rigorous apprenticeship at the hands of Tibetan lamas, and he declares that what he learnt was to prove no mean preparation for his allotted career, not least the political part of his work. It was on this basis he now developed the policy of nonviolence with which he decided to confront the Chinese invaders. As a Buddhist monk it was his duty never to harm any living creature, but instead to show compassion to all life. It is maybe not to be wondered at that people so closely involved in what they call the world of reality should consider his philosophy somewhat remote from ordinary considerations of military strategy.

The policy of nonviolence was also, of course, based on pragmatic considerations: a small nation of some six million souls, with no armed forces to speak of, faced one of the world's military superpowers. In a situation of this kind the nonviolence approach was, in the opinion of the Dalai Lama, the only practical one.

In accordance with this he made several attempts during the 1950s to negotiate with the Chinese. His aim was to arrive at a solution of the conflict that would be acceptable to both parties to the dispute, based on mutual respect and tolerance. To achieve this he staked all his authority as Dalai Lama to prevent any use of violence on the part of the Tibetans; and his authority proved decisive, for as the Dalai Lama he is, according to the Buddhist faith, more than a leader in the traditional sense: he symbolises the whole nation. His very person is imbued with some of the attributes of a deity, which doubtless explains why his people, despite gross indignities and acute provocation, have to such a marked degree obeyed his wishes and abstained from the use of violence.

From his exile in India he now waged his unarmed struggle for his people with untiring patience. He has every justification for calling his autobiography *My Life and My People*, because the life of the Tibetans is in truth *his* life.

But political support from the outside world remained conspicuous by its absence, apart from a few rather toothless UN resolutions that were adopted in 1961 and 1965. Throughout the 60s and 70s, the Dalai Lama was regarded as a pathetic figure from a distant past: his beautiful and well-meaning philosophy of peace was unfortunately out of place in this world.

But in the course of the 1980s things have taken a dramatic turn. There are several reasons for this. What has happened — and is still happening — in Tibet has become more generally known, and the community of nations has started to feel a sense of joint responsibility for the future of the Tibetan people. That their trials and tribulations have failed to break the spirit of the Tibetans is another reason; on the contrary, their feeling of national pride and identity and their determination to survive have been enhanced, and these are expressed in massive demonstrations. Here, as in other parts of the world, it is becoming increasingly obvious that problems cannot be solved by the use of brutal military power to crush peaceful demonstrations. In Tibet, as elsewhere, conflicts must be resolved politically through the medium of genuine negotiation.

The Dalai Lama's negotiating policy has received the support of a number of national assemblies and international bodies, such as the United States Senate, the West German Bundestag, the Parliament of Europe, the United States Congress, eighty-six members of the Australian Parliament and the Swiss National Assembly. Nor should we forget that the Dalai Lama has been the recipient of a number of international awards and honours in recognition of his work and in support of his cause. It now seems in fact as if things are beginning to move in the right direction, and what has been achieved in this respect may be entirely ascribed to the Dalai Lama's consistent policy of nonviolence.

For perfectly understandable reasons the policy of nonviolence is often regarded as something negative, as a failure to formulate a well-considered strategy, as a lack of initiative and a tendency to evade the issue and adopt a passive attitude. But this is not so: the policy of nonviolence is to a very high degree a well thought-out combat strategy. It demands singleminded and purposeful action, but one that eschews the use of force. Those who adopt this strategy are by no means shirking the issue: they manifest a moral courage which, when all is said and done, exceeds that of men who resort to arms. It is courage of this kind, together with an incredible measure of self-discipline, that has characterised the attitude of the Dalai Lama. His policy of nonviolence too, has been carefully considered and determined. As he himself put it in April of last year, after a peaceful demonstration in Lhasa has been fired on by troops: "As I have explained on many occasions, nonviolence is for us the only way. Quite patently, in our case violence would be tantamount to suicide. For this reason, whether we like it or not, nonviolence is the only approach, and the right one. We only need more patience and determination".

In 1987 the Dalai Lama submitted a peace plan for Tibet, the gist of which was that Tibet should be given the status of a "peace zone" on a par with what had been proposed for Nepal, a proposal which the Chinese in fact have supported. The plan also envisaged a halt to Chinese immigration to Tibet. This has proceeded on such a scale that there is a risk of the Tibetans becoming a minority in their own country. Not least interesting is the fact that the plan also contains measures for the conservation of Tibet's unique natural environment. Wholesale logging operations in the forests on the slopes of the Himalayas have resulted in catastrophic soil erosion, and are one of the causes of the flood disasters suffered by India and Bangladesh. The peace plan failed to initiate any negotiations with the Chinese, even though the discrepancies between the two sides were not particularly profound.

The Dalai Lama's willingness to compromise was expressed still more clearly in his address to the European Parliament on June 15th last year, where he stated his readiness to abandon claims for full Tibetan independence. He acknowledged that China, as an Asian superpower, had strategic interests in Tibet, and was prepared to accept a Chinese military presence, at any rate until such time as a regional peace plan could be adopted. He also expressed his willingness to leave foreign policy and defence in the hands of the Chinese. In return the Tibetans should be granted the right to full internal autonomy. In his efforts to promote peace the Dalai Lama has shown that what he aims to achieve is not a power base at the expense of others. He claims no more for his people than what everybody — no doubt the Chinese themselves — recognises as elementary human rights. In a world in which suspicion and aggression have all too long characterised relations between peoples and nations, and where the only realistic policy has been reliance on the use of power, a new confession of faith is emerging, namely that the least realistic of all solutions to conflict is the consistent use of force. Modern weapons have in fact excluded such solutions.

The world has shrunk. Increasingly peoples and nations have grown dependent on one another. No one can any longer act entirely in his own interest. It is therefore imperative that we should accept mutual responsibility for all political, economic, *and* ecological problems.

In view of this, fewer and fewer people would venture to dismiss the Dalai Lama's philosophy as utopian: on the contrary, one would be increasingly justified in asserting that his gospel of nonviolence is the truly realistic one, with most promise for the future. And this applies not only to Tibet but to each and every conflict. The future hopes of oppressed millions are today linked to the unarmed battalions, for they will win the peace: the justice of their demands, moreover, is now so clear and the normal strength of their struggle so indomitable that they can only temporarily be halted by force of arms.

In awarding the Peace Prize to H.H. the Dalai Lama we affirm our unstinting support for his work for peace, and for the unarmed masses on the march in many lands for liberty, peace and human dignity.

THE XIVTH DALAI LAMA, TENZIN GYATSO

His Holiness the XIVth Dalai Lama, Tenzin Gyatso, is the spirtual and temporal leader of the Tibetan people. He was born on July 6th, 1935, in a small village called Takster in North Eastern Tibet. Born to a peasant family, His Holiness was recognised at the age of two, in accordance with Tibetan tradition, as the reincarnation of his predecessor the 13th Dalai Lama. The Dalai Lamas are the manifestations of the Bodhisattva of Compassion, who chose to reincarnate to serve the people. Dalai Lama means Ocean of Wisdom. Tibetans normally refer to His Holiness as Yeshin Norbu, the Wish-fulfilling Gem, or simply Kundun, meaning The Presence.

Education in Tibet
He began his education at the age of six and completed the Geshe Lharampa Degree (Doctorate of Buddhist Philosophy) when he was 25. At 24, he took the preliminary examination at each of the three monastic universities: Drepung, Sera and Ganden. The final examination was held in the Jokhang, Lhasa, during the annual Monlam Festival of Prayer, held in the first month of every year. In the morning he was examined by 30 scholars on logic. In the afternoon, he debated with 15 scholars on the subject of the Middle Path, and in the evening, 35 scholars tested his knowledge of the canon of monastic discipline and the study of metaphysics. His Holiness passed the examinations with honours, conducted before a vast audience of monk scholars.

Leadership responsibilities
In 1950, at 16, His Holiness was called upon to assume full political power — Head of State and Government — when Tibet was threatened by the might of China. In 1954 he went to Peking to talk with Mao Tse-Tung and other Chinese leaders, including Chou En-Lai and Deng Xiaoping. In 1956, while visiting India to attend the 2500th Buddha Jayanti, he had a series of meetings with Prime Minister Nehru and Premier Chou about deteriorating conditions in Tibet. In 1959 he was forced into exile in India after the Chinese military occupation of Tibet. Since 1960 he has resided in Dharamsala, aptly known as "Little Lhasa", the seat of the Tibetan Government-in-Exile.

In the early years of exile, His Holiness appealed to the United Nations on the question of Tibet, resulting in three resolutions adopted by the General Assembly in 1959, 1961 and 1965. In 1963, His Holiness promulgated a draft constitution for Tibet which assures a democratic form of government. In the last two decades His Holiness has set up educational, cultural and religious institutions which have made major contributions towards the preservation of the Tibetan identity and its rich heritage. He has given many teachings and initiations, including the rare Kalachakra Initiation, which he has conducted more than any of his predecessors.

His Holiness continues to present new initiatives to resolve the Tibetan issues. At the Congressional Human Rights Caucus in 1987 he proposed a Five-Point Peace Plan as a first step towards resolving the future status of Tibet. This plan calls for the designation of Tibet as a zone of peace, an end to the massive transfer of ethnic Chinese into Tibet, restoration of fundamental human rights and democratic freedoms and the abandonment of China's use of Tibet for nuclear weapons production and the dumping of nuclear waste, as well as urging "earnest negotiations" on the future of Tibet and relations between the Tibetan and Chinese people. In Strasbourg, France, on June 15, 1988, he elaborated on this Five-Point Peace Plan and proposed the creation of a self-governing democratic Tibet, "in association with the People's Republic of China". In his address the Dalai Lama said that this represented "the most realistic means by which to re-establish Tibet's separate identity and restore the fundamental rights of the Tibetan people while accommodating China's own interests". His Holiness emphasised that "whatever the outcome of the negotiations with the Chinese may be, the Tibetan people themselves must be the ultimate deciding authority".

Contact with the west
Unlike his predecessors, His Holiness has met and talked with many Westerners and has visited the United States, Canada, Western Europe, the United Kingdom, the Soviet Union, Mongolia, Greece, Japan, Thailand, Malaysia, Singapore, Indonesia, Nepal, Costa Rica, Mexico, the Vatican, China and Australia. He has met with religious leaders from all these countries.

His Holiness met with the late Pope Paul VI at the Vatican in 1973, and with His Holiness Pope John Paul II in 1980, 1982, 1986 and 1988. At a press conference in Rome His Holiness the Dalai Lama outlined his hopes for the meeting with John Paul II: "We live in a period of great crisis, a period of troubling world developments. It is not possible to find peace in the soul without security and harmony between the people. For this reason, I look forward with faith and hope to my meeting with the Holy Father; to an exchange of ideas and feelings, and to his suggestions, so as to open the door to a progressive pacification between people".

In 1981, His Holiness talked with the Archbishop of Canterbury, Dr Robert Runcie, and with other leaders of the Anglican Church in London. He also met with leaders of the Roman Catholic and Jewish communities and spoke at an interfaith service in his honour by the World Congress of Faiths. His talk focused on the commonality of faiths and the need for unity among different religions: "I always believe that it is much better to have a variety of religions, a variety of philosophies, rather than one single religion or philosophy. This is necessary because of the different mental dispositions of each human being. Each religion has certain unique ideas or techniques, and learning about them can only enrich one's own faith".

Recognition by the west

Since his first visit to the West in the early 1970s, His Holiness' reputation as a scholar and man of peace has grown steadily. In recent years, a number of western universities and institutions have conferred Peace Awards and honorary Doctorate Degrees upon His Holiness in recognition of his distinguished writings in Buddhist philosophy and of his distinguished leadership in the service of freedom and peace.

Universal responsibility

During his travels abroad, His Holiness has spoken strongly for better understanding and respect among the different faiths of the world. Towards this end, His Holiness has made numerous appearances in interfaith services, imparting the message of universal responsibility, love, compassion and kindness. "The need for simple human-to-human relationships is becoming increasingly urgent ... Today the world is smaller and more interdependent. One nation's problems can no longer be solved by itself completely. Thus, without a sense of universal responsibility, our very survival becomes threatened. Basically, universal responsibility is feeling for other people's suffering just as we feel our own. It is the realisation that even our enemy is entirely motivated by the quest for happiness. We must recognise that all beings want the same thing that we want. This is the way to achieve a true understanding, unfettered by artificial consideration".

In 1996, in his annual statement in March on the 37th anniversary of the Tibetan national uprising of 1959, the Dalai Lama noted a general hardening of the Chinese government policy and an intensification of the repression in Tibet. He remained convinced, however, that there would be a change for the better as a new generation took power in China. Meanwhile, he asked the international community to undertake a policy of "responsible and principled engagement" with the Chinese leadership. He declared that he had always opposed any effort to isolate and contain China, and he would continue to seek negotiations with China for a mutually acceptable solution for Tibet.

The year 1996 was a typical one for the Dalai Lama, and he pursued both his spiritual and political functions. In April the Tibetan exile community in India voted for members of the Twelfth Assembly of the Tibetan People's Deputies, an event which he welcomed as another sign that the experiment with democracy he had initiated was progressing well. In that same month he was in Denmark, speaking before a parliamentary committee considering the question of Tibet.

In June he was to be back in India, performing a religious ceremony at an ancient monstery. In July there were to be meetings in England where he would give religious teachings. Later that month he would return to the United States for his fifteenth visit, the first since September 1995, when he had met with President Bill Clinton, Vice-President Al Gore and House Speaker Newt Gingrich. His program in the Mid-West and on the West Coast was to include a dialogue with representatives of the Christian community;

an address to a university audience; participation in an international conference on "Socially Engaged Buddhism and Christianity"; and three days of Buddhist teaching and initiation in Los Angeles, California, at the specific request of the Chinese community there. This would be his first time ever giving his teachings exclusively to the Chinese Buddhist Community, although many Chinese Buddhists throughout the world revere the Dalai Lama as their spiritual leader. His next stop would be Sydney, Australia, for a ten-day visit presenting his teachings.

ACCEPTANCE

HIS HOLINESS TENZIN GYATSO, THE XIVTH DALAI LAMA OF TIBET

Your Majesty, Members of the Nobel Committee, Brothers and Sisters:

I am very happy to be here with you today to receive the Nobel Prize for Peace. I feel honoured, humbled and deeply moved that you should give this important prize to a simple monk from Tibet. I am no one special. But, I believe the prize is a recognition of the true values of altruism, love, compassion and nonviolence which I try to practise, in accordance with the teachings of the Buddha and the great sages of India and Tibet.

I accept the prize with profound gratitude on behalf of the oppressed everywhere and for all those who struggle for freedom and work for world peace. I accept it as a tribute to the man who founded the modern tradition of nonviolent action for change — Mahatma Gandhi — whose life taught and inspired me. And, of course, I accept it on behalf of the six million Tibetan people, my brave countrymen and women inside Tibet, who have suffered and continue to suffer so much. They confront a calculated and systematic strategy aimed at the destruction of their national and cultural identities. The prize reaffirms our conviction that with truth, courage and determination as our weapons, Tibet will be liberated.

No matter what part of the world we come from, we are all basically the same human beings. We all seek happiness and try to avoid suffering. We have the same basic human needs and concerns. All of us human beings want freedom and the right to determine our own destiny as individuals and as peoples. That is human nature. The great changes that are taking place everywhere in the world, from Eastern Europe to Africa, are a clear indication of this.

In China the popular movement for democracy was crushed by brutal force in June this year. But I do not believe the demonstrations were in vain, because the spirit of freedom was rekindled among the Chinese people and China cannot escape the impact of this spirit of freedom sweeping many parts of the world. The brave students and their supporters showed the Chinese leadership and the world the human face of that great nation.

Last week a number of Tibetans were once again sentenced to prison terms of up to nineteen years at a mass show trial, possibly intended to frighten the population before today's event. Their only "crime" was the expression of the widespread desire of Tibetans for the restoration of their beloved country's independence.

The suffering of our people during the past forty years of occupation is well documented. Ours has been a long struggle. We know our cause is just. Because violence can only breed more violence and suffering, our struggle must remain nonviolent and free of hatred. We are trying to end the suffering of our people, not to inflict suffering upon others.

It is with this in mind that I proposed negotiations between Tibet and China on numerous occasions. In 1987, I made specific proposals in a five-point plan for the restoration of peace and human rights in Tibet. This included the conversion of the entire Tibetan plateau into a Zone of Ahimsa, a sanctuary of peace and nonviolence where human beings and nature can live in peace and harmony.

Last year, I elaborated on that plan in Strasbourg, at the European Parliament. I believe the ideas I expressed on those occasions are both realistic and reasonable, although they have been criticised by some of my people as being too conciliatory. Unfortunately, China's leaders have not responded positively to the suggestions we have made, which included important concessions. If this continues we will be compelled to reconsider our position.

Any relationship between Tibet and China will have to be based on the principle of equality, respect, trust and mutual benefit. It will also have to be based on the principle which the wise rulers of Tibet and of China laid down in a treaty as early as 823 A.D., carved on the pillar which still stands today in front of the Jo-khang, Tibet's holiest shrine, in Lhasa, that "Tibetans will live happily in the great land of Tibet, and the Chinese will live happily in the great land of China".

As a Buddhist monk, my concern extends to all members of the human family and, indeed, to all sentient beings who suffer. I believe all suffering is caused by ignorance. People inflict pain on others in the selfish pursuit of their happiness or satisfaction. Yet true happiness comes from a sense of inner peace and contentment, which in turn must be achieved through the cultivation of altruism, of love and compassion and elimination of ignorance, selfishness and greed.

The problems we face today, violent conflicts, destruction of nature, poverty, hunger, and so on, are human-created problems which can be resolved through human effort, understanding and the development of a sense of brotherhood and sisterhood. We need to cultivate a universal responsibility for one another and the planet we share. Although I have found my own Buddhist religion helpful in generating love and compassion, even for those we consider our enemies, I am convinced that everyone can develop a good heart and a sense of universal responsibility with or without religion.

With the ever-growing impact of science on our lives, religion and spirituality have a greater role to play by reminding us of our humanity. There is no contradiction between the two. Each gives us valuable insights into the other. Both science and the teachings of the Buddha tell us of the fundamental unity of all things. This understanding is crucial if we are to take positive and decisive action on the pressing global concern with the environment.

I believe all religions pursue the same goals, that of cultivating human goodness and bringing happiness to all human beings. Though the means might appear different the ends are the same.

As we enter the final decade of this century I am optimistic that the ancient values that have sustained mankind are today reaffirming themselves to prepare us for a kinder, happier twenty-first century.

I pray for all of us, oppressor and friend, that together we succeed in building a better world through human understanding and love, and that in doing so we may reduce the pain and suffering of all sentient beings.

Thank you.

THE INFORMAL LECTURE

December 11, 1989
by _____
HIS HOLINESS TENZIN GYATSO

Brothers and Sisters:

It is a great honour to come to this place and to share some of my thoughts with you. Although I have written a speech, it has already been circulated. You know, some of my friends told me it is better to speak in Tibetan and have it translated into English; some say it is better to read my English statement; and some say it is better to speak directly with my broken English. I don't know. Yesterday, I tried my best to be formal but today I feel more free, so I will speak informally. In any case, the main points of my speech are on paper for you to see.

I think it is advisable to summarise some of the points that I will consider. I usually discuss three main topics. First, as a human being, as a citizen of the world, every human being has a responsibility for the planet. Secondly, as a Buddhist monk, I have a special connection with the spiritual world. I try to contribute something in that field. Thirdly, as a Tibetan I have a responsibility to the fate of the Tibetan nation. On behalf of these unfortunate people, I will speak briefly about their concerns.

So now, firstly, what is the purpose of life for a human being? I believe that happiness is the purpose of life. Whether or not there is a purpose to the existence of the universe or galaxies, I don't know. In any case, the fact is that we are here on this planet with other human beings. Then, since every human being wants happiness and does not want suffering, it is clear that this desire does not come from training, or from some ideology. It is something natural. Therefore, I consider that the attainment of happiness, peace, and joy is the purpose of life. Therefore, it is very important to investigate what are happiness and satisfaction and what are their causes.

I think that there is a mental factor as well as a physical factor. Both are very important. If we compare these two things, the mental factor is more important, superior to the physical factor. This we can know through our daily life. Since the mental factor is more important, we have to give serious thought to inner qualities.

Then, I believe compassion and love are necessary in order for us to obtain happiness or tranquility. These mental factors are key. I think they are the basic source. What is compassion? From the Buddhist viewpoint there are different varieties of compassion. The basic meaning of compassion is not just a feeling of closeness, or just a feeling of pity. Rather, I think that with genuine compassion we not only feel the pains and suffering of others but we also have a feeling of determination to overcome that suffering. One aspect of compassion is some kind of determination and responsibility. Therefore, compassion brings us tranquility and also inner strength. Inner strength is the ultimate source of success.

When we face some problem, a lot depends on the personal attitude towards that problem or tragedy. In some cases, when one faces the difficulty, one loses one's hope and becomes discouraged and then ends up depressed. On the other hand, if one has a certain mental attitude, then tragedy and suffering bring one more energy, more determination.

Usually, I tell our generation we are born during the darkest period in our long history. There is a big challenge. It is very unfortunate. But if there is a challenge then there is an opportunity to face it, an opportunity to demonstrate our will and our determination. So from that viewpoint I think that our generation is fortunate. These things depend on inner qualities, inner strength. Compassion is very gentle, very peaceful, and soft in nature, not harsh. You cannot destroy it easily as it is very powerful. Therefore, compassion is very important and useful.

Then, again, if we look at human nature, love and compassion are the foundation of human existence. According to some scientists, the foetus has feeling in the mother's womb and is affected by the mother's mental state. Then the few weeks after birth are crucial for the enlarging of the brain of the child. During that period, the mother's physical touch is the greatest factor for the healthy development of the brain. This shows that the physical needs some affection to develop properly.

When we are born, our first action is sucking milk from the mother. Of course, the child may not know about compassion and love, but the natural feeling is one of closeness toward the object that gives the milk. If the mother is angry or has ill feeling, the milk may not come fully. This shows that from our first day as human beings the effect of compassion is crucial.

If unpleasant things happen in our daily life, we immediately pay attention to them but do not notice other pleasant things. We experience these as normal or usual. This shows that compassion and affection are part of human nature.

Compassion or love has different levels; some are more mixed than others with desire or attachment. For example, parents' attitudes toward their children contain a mixture of desire and attachment with compassion. The love and compassion between husband and wife — especially at the beginning of marriage when they don't know the deep nature of each other — are on a superficial level. As soon as the attitude of one partner changes, the attitude of the other becomes opposite to what it was. That kind of love and compassion is more of the nature of attachment. Attachment means some kind of feeling of closeness projected by oneself. In reality, the other side may be very negative, but due to one's own mental attachment and projection, it appears as something nice. Furthermore, attachment causes one to exaggerate a small good quality and make it appear 100% beautiful or

100% positive. As soon as the mental attitudes change, that picture completely changes. Therefore, that kind of love and compassion is, rather, attachment.

Another kind of love and compassion is not based on something appearing beautiful or nice, but based on the fact that the other person, just like oneself, wants happiness and does not want suffering and indeed has every right to be happy and to overcome suffering. On such a basis, we feel a sense of responsibility, a sense of closeness toward that being. That is true compassion. That is because the compassion is based on reason, not just on emotional feeling. As a consequence, it does not matter what the other's attitude is, whether negative or positive. What matters is that it is a human being, a sentient being that has the experience of pain and pleasure. There is no reason not to feel compassion so long as it is a sentient being.

The kinds of compassion at the first level are mixed, interrelated. Some people have the view that some individuals have a very negative, cruel attitude towards others. These kinds of individuals appear to have no compassion in their minds. But I feel that these people do have the seed of compassion. The reason for this is that even these people very much appreciate it when someone else shows them affection. A capacity to appreciate other people's affection means that in their deep mind there is the seed of compassion.

Compassion and love are not man-made. Ideology is man-made, but these things are produced by nature. It is important to recognise natural qualities, especially when we face a problem and fail to find a solution. For example, I feel that the Chinese leaders face a problem which is in part due to their own ideology, their own system. But when they try to solve that problem through their ideology, then they fail to tackle that problem. Sometimes even in religion, we create a problem. If we try to solve that problem using religious methods, it is quite certain that we will not succeed. So I feel that when we face those kind of problems, it is important to return to our basic human quality. Then I think we will find that solutions come easier. Therefore, I usually say that the best way to solve human problems is with human understanding.

It is very important to recognise the basic nature of humanity and the value of human qualities. Whether one is educated or uneducated, rich or poor, or belongs to this nation or that nation, this religion or that religion, the ideology or that ideology, is secondary and doesn't matter. When we return to this basis, all people are the same. Then we can truly say the words *brother*, *sister*, then they are not just nice words — they have some meaning. That kind of motivation automatically builds the practice of kindness. This gives us inner strength.

What is my purpose in life, what is my responsibility? Whether I like it or not, I am on this planet, and it is far better to do something for humanity. So you see that compassion is the seed or basis. If we take care to foster compassion, we will see that it brings out the other good human qualities. The topic of compassion is not at all religious business; it is very important to know that it is human business, that it is a question of human survival, that it is not a question of human luxury. I might say that religion is a kind of luxury. If you have religion, that is good. But it is clear that even without religion we can manage. However, without these basic human qualities we cannot survive. It is a question of our own peace and mental stability.

Next, let us talk about the human being as a social animal. Even if we do not like other people, we have to live together. Natural law is such that even bees and other animals have to live together in cooperation. I am attracted to bees because I like honey — it is really delicious. Their product is something that we cannot produce, very beautiful, isn't it? I exploit them too much, I think. Even these insects have certain responsibility, they work together very nicely. They have no constitution, they have no law, no police, nothing, but they work together effectively. This is because of nature. Similarly, each part of a flower is not arranged by humans but by nature. The force of nature is something remarkable. We human beings, we have constitutions, we have law, we have a police force, we have religion, we have many things. But in actual practice, I think that we are behind those small insects.

Sometimes civilisation brings good progress, but we become too involved with this progress and neglect or forget about our basic nature. Every development in human society should take place on the basis of the foundation of the human nature. If we lose that basic foundation, there is no point in such developments taking place.

In cooperation, working together, the key thing is the sense of responsibility. But this cannot be developed by force as has been attempted in Eastern Europe and in China. There a tremendous effort has to be made to develop in the mind of every individual human being a sense of responsibility, a concern for the common interest rather than the individual interest. They aim their education, their ideology, their efforts to brainwash, at this. But their means are abstract, and the sense of responsibility cannot develop. The genuine sense of responsibility will develop only through compassion and altruism.

The modern economy has no national boundaries. When we talk about ecology, the environment, when we are concerned about the ozone layer, one individual, one society, one country cannot solve these problems. We must work together. Humanity needs more genuine cooperation. The foundation for the development of good relations with one another is altruism, compassion and forgiveness. For small arguments to remain limited, in the human circle the best method is forgiveness. Altruism and forgiveness are the basis for bringing humanity together. Then no conflict, no matter how serious, will go beyond the bounds of what is truly human.

I will tell you something. I love friends, I want more friends. I love smiles. That is a fact. How to develop smiles? There is a variety of smiles. Some smiles are sarcastic. Some smiles are artificial — diplomatic smiles. These smiles do not produce satisfaction, but rather fear or suspicion. But a genuine smile gives us hope, freshness. If we want a genuine smile, then first we must produce the basis for a smile to come. On every level of human life, compassion is the key thing.

Now, on the question of violence and nonviolence. There are many different levels of violence and nonviolence. On the basis of external action, it is difficult to distinguish whether an action is violent or nonviolent. Basically, it depends on the motivation behind the action. If the motivation is negative, even though the external appearance may be very smooth and gentle, in a deeper sense the action is very violent. On the contrary, harsh actions and words done with a sincere, positive motivation are essentially nonviolent. In other words, violence is a destructive power. Nonviolence is constructive.

When the days become longer and there is more sunshine, the grass becomes fresh and, consequently, we feel very happy. On the other hand, in autumn, one leaf falls down and another leaf falls down. These beautiful plants become as if dead and we do not feel very happy. Why? I think it is because deep down our human nature likes construction, and does not like destruction. Naturally, every action which is destructive is against human nature. Constructiveness is the human way. Therefore, I think that in terms of basic human feeling, violence is not good. Nonviolence is the only way.

Practically speaking, through violence we may achieve something, but at the expense of someone else's welfare. That way, although we may solve one problem, we simultaneously sow a new problem. The best way to solve problems is through human understanding, mutual respect. On one side make some concessions; on the other side take serious consideration about the problem. There may not be complete satisfaction, but something happens. At least future danger is avoided. Nonviolence is very safe.

Before my first visit to Europe in 1973, I had felt the importance of compassion, altruism. On many occasions I expressed the importance of the sense of universal responsibility. Sometimes during this period, some people felt that the Dalai Lama's idea was a bit unrealistic. Unfortunately, in the Western world Gandhian nonviolence is seen as passive resistance more suitable to the East. The Westerners are very active, demanding immediate results, even in the course of daily life. But today the actual situation teaches nonviolence to people. The movement for freedom is nonviolent. These recent events reconfirm to me that nonviolence is much closer to human nature.

Again, if there are sound reasons or bases for the points you demand, then there is no need to use violence. On the other hand, when there is no sound reason that concessions should be made to you but mainly your own desire, then reason cannot work and you have to rely on force. Thus, using force is not a sign of strength but rather a sign of weakness. Even in daily human contact, if we talk seriously, using reasons, there is no need to feel anger. We can argue the points. When we fail to prove with reason, then anger comes. When reason ends, then anger begins. Therefore, anger is a sign of weakness. In this, the second part of my talk, I speak as a Buddhist monk. As a result of more contact with people from other traditions, as time passes I have formed my conviction that all religions can work together despite fundamental differences in philosophy. Every religion aims at serving humanity. Therefore, it is possible for the various religions to work together to serve humanity and contribute to world peace. So, during these last few years, at every opportunity I try to develop closer relations with other religions.

Buddhism does not accept a theory of God, or a Creator. According to Buddhism, one's own actions are the creator, ultimately. Some people say that, from a certain angle, Buddhism is not a religion but rather a science of mind. Religion has much involvement with faith. Sometimes it seems that there is quite a distance between a way of thinking based on faith and one entirely based on experiment, remaining sceptical. Unless you find something through investigation, you do not want to accept it as fact. From one viewpoint, Buddhism is a religion; from another viewpoint, Buddhism is a science of mind and not a religion. Buddhism can be a bridge between these two sides. Therefore, with this conviction I try to have closer ties with scientists, mainly in the fields of cosmology, psychology, neurobiology, physics. In these fields there are insights to share, and to a certain extent we can work together.

Thirdly, I will speak on the Tibetan problem. One of the crucial, serious situations is the Chinese population transfer into Tibet. If the present situation continues for another ten or fifteen years, the Tibetans will be an insignificant minority in their own land, a situation similar to that in Inner Mongolia. There the native population is around three million and the Chinese population is around ten million. In East Turkestan, the Chinese population is increasing daily. In Tibet, the native population is six million, whereas the Chinese population is already around seven and one-half million. This is really a serious matter.

In order to develop a closer understanding and harmony between the Chinese and Tibetans — the Chinese call it the unity of the motherland — the first thing necessary to provide the basis for the development of mutual respect is demilitarisation, first to limit the number of Chinese soldiers and eventually to remove them altogether. This is crucial. Also, for the purposes of peace in that region, peace and genuine friendship between India and China, the two most populated nations, it is very essential to reduce military forces on both sides of the Himalayan range. For this reason, one point that I have made is that eventually Tibet should be a zone of ahimsa, a zone of nonviolence.

Already there are clear indications of nuclear dumping in Tibet and of factories where nuclear weapons are produced. This is a serious matter. Also, there is deforestation, which is very dangerous for the environment. Respect for human rights is also necessary. These are the points I expressed in my Five-Point Peace Plan. These are crucial matters.

We are passing through a most difficult period. I am very encouraged by your warm expression and by the Nobel Peace Prize. I thank you from the depth of my heart.

NOBEL LECTURE

December 11, 1989
by
HIS HOLINESS TENZIN GYATSO, THE XIVTH DALAI LAMA OF TIBET

Brothers and Sisters:

It is an honour and pleasure to be among you today. I am really happy to see so many old friends who have come from different corners of the world, and to make new friends, whom I hope to meet again in the future. When I meet people in different parts of the world, I am always reminded that we are all basically alike: we are all human beings. Maybe we have different clothes, our skin is of a different colour, or we speak different languages. That is on the surface. But basically, we are the same human beings. That is what binds us to each other. That is what makes it possible for us to understand each other and to develop friendship and closeness.

Thinking over what I might say today, I decided to share with you some of my thoughts concerning the common problems all of us face as members of the human family. Because we all share this small planet earth, we have to learn to live in harmony and peace with each other and with nature. That is not just a dream, but a necessity. We are dependent on each other in so many ways, that we can no longer live in isolated communities and ignore what is happening outside those communities, and we must share the good fortune that we enjoy. I speak to you as just another human being; as a simple monk. If you find what I say useful, then I hope you will try to practise it.

I also wish to share with you today my feelings concerning the plight and aspirations of the people of Tibet. The Nobel Prize is a prize they well deserve for their courage and unfailing determination during the past forty years of foreign occupation. As a free spokesman for my captive countrymen and -women, I feel it is my duty to speak out on their behalf. I speak not with a feeling of anger or hatred towards those who are responsible for the immense suffering of our people and the destruction of our land, homes and culture. They too are human beings who struggle to find happiness and deserve our compassion. I speak to inform you of the sad situation in my country today and of the aspirations of my people, because in our struggle for freedom, truth is the only weapon we possess.

The realisation that we are all basically the same human beings, who seek happiness and try to avoid suffering, is very helpful in developing a sense of brotherhood and sisterhood; a warm feeling of love and compassion for others. This, in turn, is essential if we are to survive in this ever shrinking world we live in. For if we each selfishly pursue only what we believe to be in our own interest, without caring about the needs of others, we not only may end up harming others but also ourselves. This fact has become very clear during the course of this century. We know that to wage a nuclear war today, for example, would be a form of suicide; or that by polluting the air or the oceans, in order to achieve some short-term benefit, we are destroying the very basis for our survival. As interdependents, therefore, we have no other choice than to develop what I call a sense of universal responsibility.

Today, we are truly a global family. What happens in one part of the world may affect us all. This, of course, is not only true of the negative things that happen, but is equally valid for the positive developments. We not only know what happens elsewhere, thanks to the the extraordinary modern communications technology. We are also directly affected by events that occur far away. We feel a sense of sadness when children are starving in Eastern Africa. Similarly, we feel a sense of joy when a family is reunited after decades of separation by the Berlin Wall. Our crops and livestock are contaminated and our health and livelihood threatened when a nuclear accident happens miles away in another country. Our own security is enhanced when peace breaks out between warring parties in other continents.

But war or peace; the destruction or the protection of nature; the violation or promotion of human rights and democratic freedoms; poverty or material well-being; the lack of moral and spiritual values or their existence and development; and the breakdown or development of human understanding, are not isolated phenomena that can be analysed and tackled independently of one another. In fact, they are very much interrelated at all levels and need to be approached with that understanding.

Peace, in the sense of the absence of war, is of little value to someone who is dying of hunger or cold. It will not remove the pain of torture inflicted on a prisoner of conscience. It does not comfort those who have lost their loved ones in floods caused by senseless deforestation in a neighbouring country. Peace can only last where human rights are respected, where the people are fed, and where individuals and nations are free. True peace with oneself and with the world around us can only be achieved throught the development of mental peace. The other phenomena mentioned above are similarly interrelated. Thus, for example, we see that a clean environment, wealth or democracy mean little in the face of war, especially nuclear war, and that material development is not sufficient to ensure human happiness.

Material progress is of course important for human advancement. In Tibet, we paid much too little attention to technological and economic development, and today we realise that this was a mistake. At the same time, material development without spiritual development can also cause serious problems. In some countries too much attention is paid to external things and very little importance is given to inner development. I believe both are important and must be developed side by side so as to achieve a good balance between them. Tibetans are always described by foreign visitors as being a happy, jovial people. This is part of our national character, formed by cultural and religious values that stress the importance of mental peace through the generation of love and kindness to all other living sentient beings, both human and animal. Inner peace is the key: if you have inner peace, the external problems do not affect your deep sense of peace and tranquility. In that state of mind you can deal with situations with calmness and reason, while keeping your inner happiness. That is very important. Without this inner peace, no matter how comfortable your life is materially, you may still be worried, disturbed or unhappy because of circumstances.

Clearly, it is of great importance, therefore, to understand the interrelationship among these and other phenomena, and to approach and attempt to solve problems in a balanced way that takes these different aspects into consideration. Of course it is not easy. But it is of little benefit to try to solve one problem if doing so creates an equally serious new one. So really we have no alternative: we must develop a sense of universal responsibility not only in the geographic sense, but also in respect to the different issues that confront our planet.

Responsibility does not only lie with the leaders of our countries or with those who have been appointed or elected to do a particular job. It lies with each one of us individually. Peace, for example, starts with each one of us. When we have inner peace, we can be at peace with those around us. When our community is in a state of peace, it can share that peace with neighbouring communities, and so on. When we feel love and kindness towards others, it not only makes others feel loved and cared for, but it helps us also to develop inner happiness and peace. And there are ways in which we can consciously work to develop feelings of love and kindness. For some of us, the most effective way to do so is through religious practice. For others it may be non-religious practices. What is important is that we each make a sincere effort to take our responsibility for each other and for the natural environment we live in seriously.

I am very encouraged by the developments which are taking place around us. After the young people of many countries, particularly in northern Europe, have repeatedly called for an end to the dangerous destruction of the environment which was being conducted in the name of economic development, the world's political leaders are now starting to take meaningful steps to address this problem. The report to the United Nations Secretary-General by the World Commission on the Environment and Development (the Brundtland Report) was an important step in educating governments on the urgency of the issue. Serious efforts to bring peace to war-torn zones and to implement the right to self-determination of some people have resulted in the withdrawal of Soviet troops from Afghanistan and the establishment of independent Namibia. Through persistent nonviolent popular efforts dramatic changes, bringing many countries closer to real democracy, have occurred in many places, from Manila in the Philippines to Berlin in East Germany. With the Cold War era apparently drawing to a close, people everywhere live with renewed hope. Sadly, the courageous efforts of the Chinese people to bring similar change to their country was brutally crushed last June. But their efforts too are a source of hope. The military might has not extinguished the desire for freedom and the determination of the Chinese people to achieve it. I particularly admire the fact that these young people who have been taught that "power grows from the barrel of the gun", chose, instead, to use nonviolence as their weapon.

What these positive changes indicate, is that reason, courage, determination, and the inextinguishable desire for freedom can ultimately win. In the struggle between forces of war, violence and oppression on the one hand, and peace, reason and freedom on the other, the latter are gaining the upper hand. This realisation fills us Tibetans with hope that some day we too will once again be free.

The awarding of the Nobel Prize to me, a simple monk from faraway Tibet, here in Norway, also fills us Tibetans with hope. It means, despite the fact that we have not drawn attention to our plight by means of violence, we have not been forgotten. It also means that the values we cherish, in particular our respect for all forms of life and the belief in the power of truth, are today recognised and encouraged. It is also a tribute to my mentor, Mahatma Gandhi, whose example is an inspiration to so many of us. This year's award is an indication that this sense of universal responsibility is developing. I am deeply touched by the sincere concern shown by so many people in this part of the world for the suffering of the people of Tibet. That is a source of hope not only for us Tibetans, but for all oppressed people.

As you know, Tibet has, for forty years, been under foreign occupation. Today, more than a quarter of a million Chinese troops are stationed in Tibet. Some sources estimate the occupation army to be twice this strength. During this time, Tibetans have been deprived of their most basic human rights, including the right to life, movement, speech, worship, only to mention a few. More than one sixth of Tibet's population of six million died as a direct result of the Chinese invasion and occupation. Even before the Cultural Revolution started, many of Tibet's monasteries, temples and historic buildings were destroyed. Almost everything that remained was destroyed during the Cultural Revolution. I do not wish to dwell on this point, which is well documented. What is important to realise, however, is that despite the limited freedom granted after 1979, to rebuild parts of some monasteries and other such tokens of liberalisation, the fundamental human rights of the Tibetan people are still today being systematically violated. In recent months this bad situation has become even worse.

If it were not for our community in exile, so generously sheltered and supported by the government and people of India and helped by organisations and individuals from many parts of the world, our nation would today be little more than a shattered remnant of a people. Our culture, religion and national identity would have been effectively eliminated. As it is, we have built schools and monasteries in exile and have created democratic institutions to serve our people and preserve the seeds of our civilisation. With this experience, we intend to implement full democracy in a future free Tibet. Thus, as we develop our community in exile on modern lines, we also cherish and preserve our own identity and culture and bring hope to millions of our countrymen and -women in Tibet.

The issue of most urgent concern at this time, is the massive influx of Chinese settlers into Tibet. Although in the first decades of occupation a considerable number of Chinese were transferred into the eastern parts of Tibet — in the Tibetan provinces of Amdo (Chinghai) and Kham (most of which has been annexed by neighboring Chinese provinces) — since 1983 an unprecedented number of Chinese have been encouraged by their government to migrate to all parts of Tibet, including central and western Tibet (which the People's Republic of China refers to as the so-called Tibet Autonomous Region). Tibetans are rapidly being reduced to an insignificant minority in their own country. This development, which threatens the very survival of the Tibetan nation, its culture and spiritual heritage, can still be stopped and reversed. But this must be done now, before it is too late.

The new cycle of protest and violent repression, which started in Tibet in September of 1987 and culminated in the imposition of martial law in the capital, Lhasa, in March of this year, was in large part a reaction to this tremendous Chinese influx. Information reaching us in exile indicates that the protest marches and other peaceful forms of protest are continuing in Lhasa and a number of other places in Tibet, despite the severe punishment and inhumane treatment given to Tibetans detained for expressing their grievances. The number of Tibetans killed by security forces during the protest in March and of those who died in detention afterwards is not known but is believed to be more than two hundred. Thousands have been detained or arrested and imprisoned, and torture is commonplace.

It was against the background of this worsening situation and in order to prevent further bloodshed, that I proposed what is generally referred to as the Five-Point Peace Plan for the restoration of peace and human rights in Tibet. I elaborated on the plan in a speech in Strasbourg last year. I believe the plan provides a reasonable and realistic framework for negotiations with the People's Republic of China. So far, however, China's leaders have been unwilling to respond constructively. The brutal suppression of the Chinese democracy movement in June of this year, however, reinforced my view that any settlement of the Tibetan question will only be meaningful if it is supported by adequate international guarantees.

The Five-Point Peace Plan addresses the principal and interrelated issues, which I referred to in the first part of this lecture. It calls for (1) Transformation of the whole of Tibet, including the eastern provinces of Kham and Amdo, into a zone of Ahimsa (nonviolence); (2) Abandonment of China's population transfer policy; (3) Respect for the Tibetan people's fundamental rights and democratic freedoms; (4) Restoration and protection of Tibet's natural environment; and (5) Commencement of earnest negotiations on the future status of Tibet and of relations between the Tibetan and Chinese people. In the Strasbourg address I proposed that Tibet become a fully self-governing democratic political entity.

I would like to take this opportunity to explain the Zone of Ahimsa or peace sanctuary concept, which is the central element of the Five-Point Peace Plan. I am convinced that it is of great importance not only for Tibet, but for peace and stability in Asia.

It is my dream that the entire Tibetan plateau should become a free refuge where humanity and nature can live in peace and in harmonious balance. It would be a place where people from all over the world could come to seek the true meaning of peace within themselves, away from the tensions and pressures of much of the rest of the world. Tibet could indeed become a creative center for the promotion and development of peace.

The following are key elements of the proposed Zone of Ahimsa:

— the entire Tibetan plateau would be demilitarised;
— the manufacture, testing, and stockpiling of nuclear weapons and other armaments on the Tibetan plateau would be prohibited;
— the Tibetan plateau would be transformed into the world's largest natural park or biosphere. Strict laws would be enforced to protect wildlife and plant life; the exploitation of natural resources would be carefully regulated so as not to damage relevant ecosystems; and a policy of sustainable development would be adopted in populated areas;
— the manufacture and use of nuclear power and other technologies which produce hazardous waste would be prohibited;
— national resources and policy would be directed towards the active promotion of peace and environmental protection. Organisations dedicated to the furtherance of peace and to the protection of all forms of life would find a hospitable home in Tibet;
— the establishment of international and regional organisations for the promotion and protection of human rights would be encouraged in Tibet.

Tibet's height and size (the size of the European Community), as well as its unique history and profound spiritual heritage makes it ideally suited to fulfill the role of a sanctuary of peace in the strategic heart of Asia. It would also be in keeping with Tibet's historical role as a peaceful Buddhist nation and buffer region separating the Asian continent's great and often rival powers.

In order to reduce existing tensions in Asia, the President of the Soviet Union, Mr. Gorbachev, proposed the demilitarisation of Soviet-Chinese borders and their transformation into "a frontier of peace and good-neighborliness". The Nepal government had earlier proposed that the Himalayan country of Nepal, bordering on Tibet, should become a zone of peace, although that proposal did not include demilitarisation of the country.

For the stability and peace of Asia, it is essential to create peace zones to separate the continent's biggest powers and potential adversaries. President Gorbachev's proposal, which also included a complete Soviet troop withdrawal from Mongolia, would help to reduce tension and the potential for confrontation between the Soviet Union and China. A true peace zone must, clearly, also be created to separate the world's two most populous states, China and India.

The establishment of the Zone of Ahimsa would require the withdrawal of troops and military installations from Tibet, which would enable India and Nepal also to withdraw troops and military installations from the Himalayan regions bordering Tibet. This would have to be achieved by international agreements. It would be in the best interest of all states in Asia, particularly China and India, as it would enhance their security, while reducing the economic burden of maintaining high troop concentrations in remote areas. Tibet would not be the first strategic area to be demilitarised. Parts of the Sinai peninsula, the Egyptian territory separating Israel and Egypt, have been demilitarised for some time. Of course, Costa Rica is the best example of an entirely demilitarised country.

Tibet would also not be the first area to be turned into a natural preserve or biosphere. Many parks have been created throughout the world. Some very strategic areas have been turned into natural "peace parks". Two examples are the La Amistad Park, on the Costa Rica–Panama border and the Si A Paz project on the Costa Rica–Nicaragua border.

When I visited Costa Rica earlier this year, I saw how a country can develop successfully without an army, to become a stable democracy committed to peace and the protection of the natural environment. This confirmed my belief that my vision of Tibet in the future is a realistic plan, not merely a dream.

Let me end with a personal note of thanks to all of you and our friends who are not here today. The concern and support which you have expressed for the plight of the Tibetans have touched us all greatly, and continue to give us courage to struggle for freedom and justice: not through the use of arms, but with the powerful weapons of truth and determination. I know that I speak on behalf of all the people of Tibet when I thank you and ask you not to forget Tibet at this critical time in our country's history. We too hope to contribute to the development of a more peaceful, more humane and more beautiful world. A future free Tibet will seek to help those in need throughout the world, to protect nature, and to promote peace. I believe that our Tibetan ability to combine spiritual qualities with a realistic and practical attitude enables us to make a special contribution, in however modest a way. This is my hope and prayer.

In conclusion, let me share with you a short prayer which gives me great inspiration and determination:

> For as long as space endures,
> And for as long as living beings remain,
> Until then may I, too, abide
> To dispel the misery of the world.

Thank you.

SELECTED BIBLIOGRAPHY

By the Dalai Lama:

Freedom in Exile. The Autobiography of the Dalai Lama. New York: Harper Collins, 1990. (The fullest account, written in English.)

My Land and My People. Memoirs of the Dalai Lama of Tibet. New York: McGraw-Hill, 1962, Reprinted, New York: Potala Corp., 1983, 1985. (His first account, translated from Tibetan, written with David Howarth, English writer, after escaping to India.)

Ocean of Wisdom. Guidelines for Living. Santa Fe, N.M.: Clear Light Publ., 1989. Reprinted, San Francisco: Harper & Row, 1990. (Includes Nobel acceptance speech.)

A Policy of Kindness. An Anthology of Writings by and about the Dalai Lama. Sidney Piburn, ed., Ithaca, NY: Snow Lion Press, 1990. (Includes the official Nobel lecture and the informal lecture.)

Other Sources:

Avedon, John F. *In Exile from the Land of Snows.* New York: Knopf, 1984. (Tibet, before and after the invasion, focusing on lives of individuals, based largely on interviews, including many with the Dalai Lama.)

Piburn, Sidney, ed., *The Nobel Peace Prize and the Dalai Lama.* Ithaca, NY: Snow Lion Publ., 1990. (The Nobel speeches and statements.)

Peace 1990

MIKHAIL SERGEYEVICH GORBACHEV

INTRODUCTION

The Committee declared in the October announcement that the winner of the 1990 prize was Mikhail Sergeyevich Gorbachev, President of the Soviet Union, for his decisive contributions to the peace process which was bringing dramatic changes in the relationships between East and West.

Gidske Anderson, Committee Chair, in her speech of presentation, declares that the award is quite in keeping with Alfred Nobel's wishes for promoting "fraternity between nations", disarmament and peace negotiations. She tells of the life of the laureate, who has himself said that the story of his family is the history of the Soviet Union. Yet he has been "capable of breaking the mould of the society from which he sprang" with the policies of *perestroika* ("restructuring") and *glasnost* ("openness").

However, Anderson says the award is not for the Soviet Union's internal affairs, rather it is for Gorbachev's "leading role in international politics". At the same time the prize may also be seen as a "helping hand in an hour of need" for the Soviet people in their bold struggle to overcome the problems of their society.

Since Gorbachev could not come to Oslo for the award ceremony on 10 December, his message of acceptance is read by his representative, Andrej Kovaljov, First Deputy Foreign Minister of the Soviet Union. Here, Gorbachev declares that this year, 1990, is a turning point in history, and he promises to do everything in his power "to ensure that future developments in Europe and the world as a whole are based on openness, mutual trust, international law and universal values".

Gorbachev himself delivers his lecture in June 1991 in the spacious Oslo city hall, to which the award ceremony was moved in December in expectation of his appearance, and where it is to continue to be held in the future. He tells of the irrevocable decision he made when taking office in 1985. The country was in a state of stagnation internally, and internationally there was the rigid East-West confrontation. "I realised", he says, "that we could no longer live as before and that I would not want to remain in that office unless I got support in undertaking major reforms".

In the balance of the lecture he tells of the changes made both domestically and internationally by this "restructuring" during his more than five years as head of the Soviet government. Often he speaks of *perestroika* and "new thinking" in the same breath. In international affairs he spells out some of the events which represent the turning point to which he has alluded to in his acceptance message: the Cold War over, the Iron Curtain gone, Germany united, the USSR and the United States moved from confrontation to interaction and toward partnership, enabling a beginning to be made in arms control.

He paints a picture of the new world order he envisions in the future. The world needs *perestroika*, he declares.

In the Soviet Union itself there have been many changes, although Gorbachev warns that there is no intention to disregard tradition and to copy the West. A mixed market economy is being introduced, and the effort is being made to transform the Soviet Union into a genuine free and voluntary federation, with recognition of freedom of secession. The transition is painful, however, and there are many problems and obstacles.

Nevertheless, Gorbachev declares, "I am an optimist". He concludes by thanking the Committee for acknowledging his commitment to *perestroika*, which he feels has not been well understood. Yet he himself has not understood that what the Committee was acknowledging in granting him the Peace Prize was not his efforts to restructure Soviet society, but primarily his role in bringing to an end the Cold War.

ANNOUNCEMENT

The Norwegian Nobel Committee has decided to award the 1990 Nobel Peace Prize to Mikhail Sergeyevich Gorbachev, President of the Soviet Union, for his leading role in the peace process which today characterises important parts of the international community.

During the last few years dramatic changes have taken place in the relationship between East and West. Confrontation has been replaced by negotiations. Old European nation states have regained their freedom. The arms race is slowing down and we see a definite and active process in the direction of arms control and disarmament. Several regional conflicts have been solved or have at least come closer to a solution. The UN is beginning to play the role which was originally planned for it in an international community governed by law.

These historic changes spring from several factors, but in 1990 the Nobel Committee wants to honour Mikhail Gorbachev for his many and decisive contributions. The greater openness he has brought about in Soviet society has also helped promote international trust.

In the opinion of the Committee this peace process, which Gorbachev has contributed so significantly to, opens up new possibilities for the world community to solve its pressing problems across ideological, religious, historical and cultural dividing lines.

PRESENTATION

Speech by GIDSKE ANDERSON, Chairperson of the Norwegian Nobel Committee

Your Royal Highnesses, Your Excellencies, Ladies and Gentlemen,

This year's Nobel Peace Prize has been awarded to the President of the Soviet Union, Mikhail Sergeyevich Gorbachev.

The Norwegian Nobel Committee has made this award in recognition of the leading role he has played in the radical changes that have taken place in East-West relations. President Gorbachev has undoubtedly cooperated with other persons and other nations. But we recognise quite clearly that his manifold personal contributions and his efforts on behalf of the Soviet Union have proved decisive. For this reason the Nobel Committee has in 1990 decided to honour him.

We are experiencing dramatic changes in a world that is still rent with conflict. Nevertheless, we also have clear evidence that a peace process has started. East and West, the two mighty power blocs, have managed to abandon their life-threatening confrontation and have, instead, embarked on the long and patient road to cooperation on the basis of negotiation. The task now is to create a peaceful framework for the far-reaching transformation which will inevitably continue to take place in our part of the world.

We have already seen the fruits of this new climate between East and West.

Ancient European nations, such as Poland, Czechoslovakia, Hungary, and now East Germany too, have regained their freedom and have, for better or for worse, assumed responsibility for their own national destiny. Even though this process of détente still has its problems and is yet not terminated in all parts of our continent of Europe, it is nevertheless possible today, maybe for the first time in many hundreds of years, to envisage a Europe of the people and, we hope, also a Europe at peace.

This is due not least to the fact that the armaments race is ebbing out in our part of the globe.

In mistrust and fear this race has been going on for close on half a century. The result has been a terrifying waste of intellectual and material resources on both sides of the Iron Curtain.

Here too, we now at last see a change.

Comprehensive negotiations, bilateral as well as multilateral, accompanied by concrete and realistic compromise, have led to a process involving substantial reductions in standing armies and death-dealing armaments. Within the last few months disarmament agreements have been reached which are without parallel in our part of the world, in this or indeed in previous centuries.

In making this year's award of the Peace Prize, the Nobel Committee wishes to emphasise the tremendous potential which is now available for a more secure world, and for a more responsible and rational use of our resources.

The way in which confrontation has been replaced by cooperation has also had its consequences in other parts of the world. Several regional conflicts have been resolved, or at least come closer to a solution. The uncompromising attitude of the Cold War has given way to a pattern of negotiation, in which the interests and responsibility of the regional communities themselves have replaced old ideological considerations, or the all-too-often ruthless laws of the balance of power.

These changes have given the United Nations a new lease of life: for the first time since its creation after the Second World War this organisation has been able to play the role for which it was originally intended. It can now start to exercise its supremely important responsibility for the creation of an international community based on the rule of law and the establishment of peace between nations.

The award this year of the Peace Prize to the President of the Soviet Union, Mikhail Gorbachev, is an historic event not least because some of the previous awards made by our Committee — for example to the great champion of human rights Andrei Sakharov in 1975, and to the trade union leader Lech Wałesa in 1983 — were received with cool hostility in the Soviet Union and in Poland at the time, involving the rejection, in these countries, of all that the Norwegian Nobel Committee stood for. On these grounds too the award constitutes a landmark. The Norwegian Nobel Committee considers that there is thus a historical link between today's event and December 10th, 1975, and 1983, which augurs well for the future.

The Norwegian Nobel Committee is an independent organisation answerable neither to the Government nor to the National Assembly (the Storting) of our country. The five members of the Committee are only answerable to their own consciences, and their decisions are based on the personal political judgment and sound common sense of each one. The guidelines governing our work are nevertheless clearly set out: these are to be found in Alfred Nobel's testament, written nearly a hundred years ago.

The award this year is very much in line with Alfred Nobel's own wishes and desires. Nobel wanted the prize to be awarded to someone who had worked to promote "fraternity between nations". That was the expression generally used in his day to denote the substitution of international cooperation for conflict. Nobel also wished his prize to be given to someone who had actively promoted a reduction in "standing armies" and worked for the "holding of peace congresses", what we today would call disarmament and negotiation.

Seldom has our Committee felt more in tune with Alfred Nobel's wishes than this year.

It is with a special sense of satisfaction that we award the Peace Prize to President Gorbachev. Each one of us, maybe in our different ways, has experienced the tension and threat of war that have cast a dark shadow over all the post-war years. The new-found openness and willingness to cooperate shown by the Soviet Union, and its readiness to accept realistic compromise, have created fresh hope under his leadership.

We fully realise that the Soviet Union is undergoing a dramatic period of transformation within its own borders: dictatorship is to be replaced by greater democracy, centralisation by the right of each republic for self-determination, a command economy by a freer market. This transformation is inevitably a painful process, involving great sacrifice. But we should like the many peoples of the Soviet Union to know that the respect and expectation of the outside world for their great country have never been as profound as today. There has been nothing comparable since the "Great Patriotic War", which this country and our Western Allies fought together against the barbarism of National Socialism. At that time the road that led from world war to Cold War proved disappointingly short. It is our hope that we are now celebrating the end of the Cold War.

Mikhail Sergeyevich Gorbachev was born in 1931 in a small village just outside Stavropol, north of the Caucasus Mountains, in a region that forms part of the Russian Republic, adjoining the ancient non-Russian countries of Georgia, Armenia and Azerbaijan, with their profound Christian and Muslim roots. Our laureate is in fact a native of the southern Soviet Union.

He comes of peasant stock, and was born 14 years after the great revolution which shook not only the Russian Empire but the entire world. He was born during the dramatic collectivisation of Soviet agriculture, and grew up on a collective farm, where his father worked at a tractor station.

He was an eight-year-old schoolboy when the last world war broke out, and only 10 years old when Germany attacked the Soviet Union. His schooling was both sporadic and limited by wartime conditions: he was forced to work as a replacement for soldiers fighting at the front. When peace came he was 14 years old, and was able to continue his education, but, in common with most young people of his age, worked during his summer holidays. He was soon involved in the Communist Party's youth organisation, and was rapidly promoted. As a matter of course he joined the Communist party at the age of 21.

Two years before, he had left his native village in the Northern Caucasus, and made his way to the capital to embark on the study of law at the University of Moscow. Here he not only met Raisa Titorenko, who subsequently became his wife, but was also active in the Communist Party student movement, with responsibility for ideology and propaganda among fellow students in his faculty. He took a degree in law and then returned to Stavropol, where he was employed full-time in the Communist youth movement. By the age of 25 he was in fact a member of the establishment, with agricultural questions as his chief concern. In 1967, he took a second degree, this time in agriculture, and was rapidly promoted in the local party hierarchy.

By the 1970s this year's laureate was active politically on the national scene: his breakthrough came in 1978, when at the age of 47, he was given joint responsibility for the entire agricultural set-up of the Soviet Union in the Communist Party's Secretariat in Moscow, which meant permanent residence in the capital. Seven years later he was elected leader of the Soviet Union's Communist Party, the most influential post in the country. This was in 1985, by which time he was 54 years old. He is now a figure of international prominence. While still retaining the position of Party Secretary, he is also elected President of the Soviet Union by a reformed parliament.

Although Mikhail Gorbachev is a man of quite outstanding talent and ability, he insisted recently that the story of his own family is actually history itself or in other words the history of the Soviet Union. Gorbachev is in fact a child of the revolution and the world war, of Lenin's, Stalin's, Khrushchev's and Breshnev's Soviet Union. And like most people in this world he is a product of the society in which he grew up.

Today, this Soviet society is a historical experiment which is being shaken to its foundations, and this is so not least because Mikhail Gorbachev was also capable of breaking the mould of the society from which he sprang. Or as he personally expressed it in the televised interview, in which he spoke of the *perestroika* which he symbolises: "We came to the conclusion that we could no longer continue to live the way we were. We needed major changes in every department of life".

Our laureate has in fact been a Communist all his life; and he still is to this day, even though this might shock us, as he declared in an interview he recently gave in the USA. We are not really so shocked. But this is neither the time nor the place to discuss the Soviet Union's *internal* affairs. The Norwegian Nobel Committee has given President Gorbachev the Peace Prize for his leading role in international politics.

Our Committee has nonetheless observed one aspect of life in the Soviet Union — the much greater openness President Gorbachev has introduced. This has to a very large extent helped to promote international confidence. Greater openness has in many ways ensured a basis for the comprehensive agreements on disarmament and cooperation between East and West that we are witnessing today.

An entire world is today watching the Soviet Union's dramatic and heroic struggle to overcome the awesome economic, social and political problems which shake the country. The Norwegian Nobel Committee, not least, is also watching.

It is our wish that the award of the Peace Prize to its President, Mikhail Sergeyevich Gorbachev, will be recognised as a helping hand in an hour of need, as a greeting to all the peoples of the Soviet Union, as a sign that the outside world is watching their struggle with a sense of fellow feeling, and with a sense of participating in the historical events that are taking place.

It has been suggested that the award of this year's prize to the President of the Soviet Union by the Nobel Committee was somewhat bold. Our boldness is, however, nothing like the boldness shown by Mikhail Gorbachev when he embarked on the course which has today led to the receipt of the Nobel Peace Prize, or the boldness shown by the many peoples of the Soviet Union too in rewriting history.

MIKHAIL SERGEYEVICH GORBACHEV

1931   : March 2, born, Privolnoye, Krasnogvardeisky District, Stavropol territory in the North Caucasus, to a peasant family in a small village, his father an agricultural mechanic on a collective farm.

1942   : German army occupies the Privolnoye area.

1945   : Begins work as assistant to combine harvest operator.

1949   : Awarded Order of Red Banner of Labour.

1950   : Enrolled in Faculty of Law, Moscow University.

1952   : After having been a member of Komsomol (Communist Youth Organisation), now joined the Communist Party of the Soviet Union (CPSU).

1955   : Marries Raisa Maximovna Titorenko, philosophy student. Receives degree in law.

1955–60   : Appointed First Secretary, Komsomol Territorial Committee, then moves up to higher posts, finally becoming top Komsomol official in Stavropol.

1956   : Daughter Irina born.

1961   : Delegate from Stavropol to 22nd Communist Party Congress in Moscow.

1962   : Appointed to key position in Stavropol Communist Party, responsible for personnel in administration, farms and industry.

1964–67   : Studies for second degree at Stavropol Agricultural Institute.

1970   : Appointed First Secretary for Stavropol territory, governing an area of 2.4 million people.

1971–   : Member CPSU Central Committee.

1978   : Moves to Moscow as Secretary of Agriculture in Central Committee.

1980   : Becomes youngest full member of Politburo.

1985   : March, Elected by Central Committee as General Secretary of CPSU.

1989   : Elected by new parliament as Executive President of Soviet Union.

1991   : August, abortive coup of hardliners, resigns as General Secretary of CPSU, dissolves Central Committee.

1991   : December 25, resigns as President when Soviet Union disintegrates.

1992–   : Head of Foundation for Social, Economic and Political Research, think-tank founded after August coup.

ACCEPTANCE*

MIKHAIL SERGEYEVICH GORBACHEV
(Translation)

Your Majesty, Esteemed Chairman of the Norwegian Nobel Committee, Ladies and gentlemen,

I have been requested by the President of the USSR, Mikhail Gorbachev, to present his address to the Norwegian Nobel Committee and to all those present today at this award ceremony:

To the Chairman of the Norwegian Nobel Committee, Mrs. Gidske Anderson: Esteemed Mrs. Anderson,

I am deeply and personally moved by the decision of the Nobel Committee to award me the 1990 Nobel Peace Prize.

The prestige and authority of the Nobel Peace Prize are universally recognised. The prize has been awarded ever since the beginning of this century. The disasters and tragedies of this period, which have not managed to subdue man's optimism and unflagging belief in human reason, have given the Peace Prize the unique aura associated with it today.

Immanuel Kant prophesied that mankind would one day be faced with a dilemma: either to be joined in a true union of nations or to perish in a war of annihilation ending in the extinction of the human race.[1] Now, as we move from the second to the third millennium, the clock has struck the moment of truth.

In this respect, the year 1990 represents a turning point. It marks the end of the unnatural division of Europe. Germany has been reunited. We have begun resolutely to tear down the material foundations of a military, political and ideological confrontation. But there are some very grave threats that have not been eliminated: the potential for conflict and the primitive instincts which allow it, aggressive intentions, and totalitarian traditions.

I would like to assure you that the leadership of the USSR is doing and will continue to do everything in its power to ensure that future developments in Europe and the world as a whole are based on openness, mutual trust, international law and universal values.

The recent meeting in Paris of heads of state and government from the European nations, the United States and Canada, embodying all the best elements in international movements such as the Helsinki Process, has established the framework for a Europe based on the rule of law, stability, good relations

*Read by Andrej Kovaljov.

between neighbouring countries and humane attitudes.[2] It is my hope that such a Europe will be understood and accepted by nations and governments in other parts of the world as an example of universal security and genuine cooperation.

I do not regard the 1990 Nobel Peace Prize as an award to me personally, but as a recognition of what we call *perestroika* and innovative political thinking, which is of vital significance for human destinies all over the world.

The Nobel Peace Prize for 1990 confirms that *perestroika* and innovative political thinking no longer belong only to us, the people of the Soviet Union. They are the property of the whole of mankind and are an inseparable part of its destiny and of a safe, peaceful future. We are deeply grateful to Norway and other members of the international community who have shown such understanding and who, through their conduct in international issues and in their relations with the Soviet Union, have shown their solidarity as we proceed with our *perestroika* and their sympathy as we struggle to resolve our problems. If we all took this as our point of departure, mankind would have no cause to regret the loss of a unique opportunity for reason and the logic of peace to prevail over that of war and alienation.

Once more, I would like to express my appreciation for this very great honour. I intend to do everything in my power to live up to the expectations and hopes of my countrymen and all those who support the Nobel Committee's choice.

With my sincere wishes for peace and prosperity,

Mikhail Gorbachev
President of the USSR

This was the address by the winner of the Nobel Peace Prize for 1990, which I, as his personal representative, have had the honour of making on his behalf.

Thank you for your attention.

NOBEL LECTURE

June 5, 1991
by
MIKHAIL GORBACHEV

Mr. Chairman, Ladies and gentlemen,

This moment is no less emotional for me than the one when I first learned about the decision of the Nobel Committee. For on similar occasions great men addressed humankind — men famous for their courage in working to bring together morality and politics. Among them were my compatriots.

The award of the Nobel Peace Prize makes one think once again about a seemingly simple and clear question: What is peace?

Preparing for my address I found in an old Russian encyclopaedia a definition of "peace" as a "commune" — the traditional cell of Russian peasant life. I saw in that definition the people's profound understanding of peace as harmony, concord, mutual help, and cooperation.

This understanding is embodied in the canons of world religions and in the works of philosophers from antiquity to our time. The names of many of them have been mentioned here before. Let me add another one to them. Peace "propagates wealth and justice, which constitute the prosperity of nations;" a peace which is "just a respite from wars ... is not worthy of the name;" peace implies "general counsel". This was written almost 200 years ago by Vasiliy Fyodorovich Malinovskiy — the dean of the Tsarskoye Selo Lyceum at which the great Pushkin was educated.

Since then, of course, history has added a great deal to the specific content of the concept of peace. In this nuclear age it also means a condition for the survival of the human race. But the essence, as understood both by the popular wisdom and by intellectual leaders, is the same.

Today, peace means the ascent from simple coexistence to cooperation and common creativity among countries and nations.

Peace is movement towards globality and universality of civilisation. Never before has the idea that peace is indivisible been so true as it is now.

Peace is not unity in similarity but unity in diversity, in the comparison and conciliation of differences.

And, ideally, peace means the absence of violence. It is an ethical value. And here we have to recall Rajiv Gandhi, who died so tragically a few days ago.

I consider the decision of your Committee as a recognition of the great international importance of the changes now under way in the Soviet Union, and as an expression of confidence in our policy of new thinking, which is based on the conviction that at the end of the twentieth century force and arms will have to give way as a major instrument in world politics.

I see the decision to award me the Nobel Peace Prize also as an act of solidarity with the monumental undertaking which has already placed enormous demands on the Soviet people in terms of efforts, costs, hardships, willpower, and character. And solidarity is a universal value which is becoming indispensable for progress and for the survival of humankind.

But a modern state has to be worthy of solidarity, in other words, it should pursue, in both domestic and international affairs, policies that bring together the interests of its people and those of the world community. This task, however obvious, is not a simple one. Life is much richer and more complex than even the most perfect plans to make it better. It ultimately takes vengeance for attempts to impose abstract schemes, even with the best of intentions. *Perestroika* has made us understand this about our past, and the actual experience of recent years has taught us to reckon with the most general laws of civilisation.

This, however, came later. But back in March–April 1985 we found ourselves facing a crucial, and I confess, agonising choice. When I agreed to assume the office of the General Secretary of the Communist Party of the Soviet Union Central Committee, in effect the highest State office at that time, I realised that we could no longer live as before and that I would not want to remain in that office unless I got support in undertaking major reforms. It was clear to me that we had a long way to go. But of course, I could not imagine how immense were our problems and difficulties. I believe no one at that time could foresee or predict them.

Those who were then governing the country knew what was really happening to it and what we later called "*zastoi*", roughly translated as "stagnation". They saw that our society was marking time, that it was running the risk of falling hopelessly behind the technologically advanced part of the world. Total domination of centrally-managed state property, the pervasive authoritarian-bureaucratic system, ideology's grip on politics, monopoly in social thought and sciences, militarised industries that siphoned off our best, including the best intellectual resources, the unbearable burden of military expenditures that suffocated civilian industries and undermined the social achievements of the period since the Revolution which were real and of which we used to be proud — such was the actual situation in the country.

As a result, one of the richest countries in the world, endowed with immense overall potential, was already sliding downwards. Our society was declining, both economically and intellectually.

And yet, to a casual observer the country seemed to present a picture of relative well-being, stability and order. The misinformed society under the spell of propaganda was hardly aware of what was going on and what the immediate future had in store for it. The slightest manifestations of protest were suppressed. Most people considered them heretical, slanderous and counter-revolutionary.

Such was the situation in the spring of 1985, and there was a great temptation to leave things as they were, to make only cosmetic changes. This, however, meant continuing to deceive ourselves and the people.

This was the domestic aspect of the dilemma then before us. As for the foreign policy aspect, there was the East-West confrontation, a rigid division into friends and foes, the two hostile camps with a corresponding set of Cold War attributes. Both the East and the West were constrained by the logic of military confrontation, wearing themselves down more and more by the arms race.

The mere thought of dismantling the existing structures did not come easily. However, the realisation that we faced inevitable disaster, both domestically and internationally, gave us the strength to make a historic choice, which I have never since regretted.

Perestroika, which once again is returning our people to commonsense, has enabled us to open up to the world, and has restored a normal relationship between the country's internal development and its foreign policy. But all this takes a lot of hard work. To a people which believed that its government's policies had always been true to the cause of peace, we proposed what was in many ways a *different policy*, which would genuinely serve the cause of peace, while differing from the prevailing view of what it meant and particularly from the established stereotypes as to how one should protect it. We proposed new thinking in foreign policy.

Thus, we embarked on a path of major changes which may turn out to be the most significant in the twentieth century, for our country and for its peoples. But we also did this for the entire world.

I began my book about *perestroika* and the new thinking with the following words: "We want to be understood". After a while I felt that it was already happening. But now I would like once again to repeat those words here, from this world rostrum. Because to understand us really — to understand so as to believe us — proved to be not at all easy, owing to the immensity of the changes under way in our country. Their magnitude and character are such as to require indepth analysis. Applying conventional wisdom to *perestroika* is unproductive. It is also futile and dangerous to set conditions, to say: We'll understand and believe you, as soon as you, the Soviet Union, come completely to resemble "us", the West.

No one is in a position to describe in detail what *perestroika* will finally produce. But it would certainly be a self-delusion to expect that *perestroika* will produce "a copy" of anything.

Of course, learning from the experience of others is something we have been doing and will continue to do. But this does not mean that we will come to be exactly like others. Our State will preserve its own identity within the international community. A country like ours, with its uniquely close-knit ethnic composition, cultural diversity and tragic past, the greatness of its historic endeavors and the exploits of its peoples — such a country will find its own path to the civilisation of the twenty-first century and its own place in it. *Perestroika* has to be conceived solely in this context, otherwise it will fail and will be rejected. After all, it is impossible to "shed" the country's thousand-year history — a history, which, we still have to subject to serious analysis in order to find the truth that we shall take into the future.

We want to be an integral part of modern civilisation, to live in harmony with mankind's universal values, abide by the norms of international law, follow the "rules of the game" in our economic relations with the outside world. We want to share with all other peoples the burden of responsibility for the future of our common house.

A period of transition to a new quality in all spheres of society's life is accompanied by painful phenomena. When we were initiating *perestroika* we failed to properly assess and foresee everything. Our society turned out to be hard to move off the ground, not ready for major changes which affect people's vital interests and make them leave behind everything to which they had become accustomed over many years. In the beginning we imprudently generated great expectations, without taking into account the fact that it takes time for people to realise that all have to live and work differently, to stop expecting that new life would be given from above.

Perestroika has now entered its most dramatic phase. Following the transformation of the philosophy of *perestroika* into real policy, which began literally to explode the old way of life, difficulties began to mount. Many took fright and wanted to return to the past. It was not only those who used to hold the levers of power in the administration, the army and various government agencies and who had to make room, but also many people whose interests and way of life was put to a severe test and who, during the preceding decades, had forgotten how to take the initiative and to be independent, enterprising and self-reliant.

Hence the discontent, the outbursts of protest and the exorbitant, though understandable, demands which, if satisfied right away, would lead to complete chaos. Hence, the rising political passions and, instead of a constructive opposition which is only normal in a democratic system, one that is often destructive and unreasonable, not to mention the extremist forces which are especially cruel and inhuman in areas of inter-ethnic conflict.

During the last six years we have discarded and destroyed much that stood in the way of a renewal and transformation of our society. But when society was given freedom it could not recognise itself, for it had lived too long, as it were, "beyond the looking glass". Contradictions and vices rose to the surface, and even blood has been shed, although we have been able to avoid a bloodbath. The logic of reform has clashed with the logic of rejection, and with the logic of impatience which breeds intolerance.

In this situation, which is one of great opportunity and of major risks, at a high point of *perestroika*'s crisis, our task is to stay the course while also addressing current everyday problems — which are literally tearing this policy apart — and to do it in such a way as to prevent a social and political explosion.

Now about my position. As to the fundamental choice, I have long ago made a final and irrevocable decision. Nothing and no one, no pressure, either from the right or from the left, will make me abandon the positions of *perestroika* and new thinking. I do not intend to change my views or convictions. My choice is a final one.

It is my profound conviction that the problems arising in the course of our transformations can be solved solely by constitutional means. That is why I make every effort to keep this process within the confines of democracy and reforms.

This applies also to the problem of self-determination of nations, which is a challenging one for us. We are looking for mechanisms to solve that problem within the framework of a constitutional process; we recognise the peoples' legitimate choice, with the understanding that if a people really decides, through a fair referendum, to withdraw from the Soviet Union, a certain agreed transition period will then be needed.

Steering a peaceful course is not easy in a country where generation after generation of people were led to believe that those who have power or force could throw those who dissent or disagree out of politics or even in jail. For centuries all the country's problems used to be finally resolved by violent means. All this has left an almost indelible mark on our entire "political culture", if the term is at all appropriate in this case.

Our democracy is being born in pain. A political culture is emerging — one that presupposes debate and pluralism, but also legal order and, if democracy is to work, strong government authority based on one law for all. This process is gaining strength. Being resolute in the pursuit of *perestroika*, a subject of much debate these days, must be measured by the commitment to democratic change. Being resolute does not mean a return to repression, diktat or the suppression of rights and freedoms. I will never agree to having our society split once again into Reds and Whites, into those who claim to speak and act "on behalf of the people" and those who are "enemies of the people". Being resolute today means to act within the framework of political and social pluralism and the rule of law to provide conditions for continued reform and prevent a breakdown of the state and economic collapse, prevent the elements of chaos from becoming catastrophic.

All this requires taking certain tactical steps, to search for various ways of addressing both short- and long-term tasks. Such efforts and political and economic steps, agreements based on reasonable compromise, are there for everyone to see. I am convinced that the One-Plus-Nine Statement will go down in history as one such step, as a great opportunity.[3] Not all parts of our decisions are readily accepted or correctly understood. For the most part, our decisions are unpopular; they arouse waves of criticism. But life has many more surprises in store for us, just as we will sometimes surprise it. Jumping to conclusions after every step taken by the Soviet leadership, after every decree by the President, trying to figure out whether he is moving left or right, backward or forward, would be an exercise in futility and would not lead to understanding.

We will seek answers to the questions we face only by moving forward, only by continuing and even radicalising reforms, by consistently democratising our society. But we will proceed prudently, carefully weighing each step we take.

There is already a consensus in our society that we have to move towards a mixed market economy. There are still differences as to how to do it and how fast we should move. Some are in favor of rushing through a transitional period as fast as possible, no matter what. Although this may smack of adventurism we should not overlook the fact that such views enjoy support. People are tired and are easily swayed by populism. So it would be just as dangerous to move too slowly, to keep people waiting in suspense. For them, life today is difficult, a life of considerable hardship.

Work on a new Union Treaty has entered its final stage. Its adoption will open a new chapter in the history of our multinational state.

After a time of rampant separatism and euphoria, when almost every village proclaimed sovereignty, a centripetal force is beginning to gather momentum, based on a more sensible view of existing realities and the risks involved. And this is what counts most now. There is a growing will to achieve consensus, and a growing understanding that we have a State, a country, a common life. This is what must be preserved first of all. Only then can we afford to start figuring out which party or club to join and what God to worship.

The stormy and contradictory process of *perestroika*, particularly in the past two years, has made us face squarely the problem of criteria to measure the effectiveness of State leadership. In the new environment of a multi-party system, freedom of thought, rediscovered ethnic identity and sovereignty of the republics, the interests of society must absolutely be put above those of various parties or groups, or any other sectoral, parochial or private interests, even though they also have the right to exist and to be represented in the political process and in public life, and, of course, they must be taken into account in the policies of the State.

Ladies and gentlemen, *international politics* is another area where a great deal depends on the correct interpretation of what is now happening in the Soviet Union. This is true today, and it will remain so in the future.

We are now approaching what might be the crucial point when the world community and, above all, the States with the greatest potential to influence world developments will have to decide on their stance with regard to the Soviet Union, and to act on that basis.

The more I reflect on the current world developments, the more I become convinced that the world needs *perestroika* no less than the Soviet Union needs it. Fortunately, the present generation of policy-makers, for the most part, are becoming increasingly aware of this interrelationship, and also of the fact that now that *perestroika* has entered its critical phase the Soviet Union is entitled to expect large-scale support to assure its success.

Recently, we have been seriously rethinking the substance and the role of our economic cooperation with other countries, above all major Western nations. We realise, of course, that we have to carry out measures that would enable us really to open up to the world economy and become its organic part. But at the same time we come to the conclusion that there is a need for a kind of *synchronisation of our actions* towards that end with those of the Group of Seven and of the European Community.[4] In other words, we are thinking of a *fundamentally new phase* in our international cooperation.

In these months much is being decided and will be decided in our country to create the prerequisites for overcoming the systemic crisis and gradually recovering to a normal life.

The multitude of specific tasks to be addressed in this context may be summarised within *three main areas:*

— Stabilising the democratic process on the basis of a broad social consensus and a new constitutional structure of our Union as a genuine, free, and voluntary federation.
— Intensifying economic reform to establish a mixed market economy based on a new system of property relations.
— Taking vigorous steps to open the country up to the world economy through ruble convertibility and acceptance of civilised "rules of the game" adopted in the world market, and through membership in the World Bank and the International Monetary Fund.

These three areas are closely interrelated.

Therefore, there is a need for discussion in the Group of Seven and in the European Community. We need a joint program of action to be implemented over a number of years.

If we fail to reach an understanding regarding a new phase of cooperation, we will have to look for other ways, for time is of the essence. But if we are to move to that new phase, those who participate in and even shape world politics also must continue to change, to review their philosophic perception of the changing realities of the world and of its imperatives. Otherwise, there is no point in drawing up a joint program of practical action.

The Soviet leadership, both in the center and in the republics, as well as a large part of the Soviet public, understand this need, although in some parts of our society not everyone is receptive to such ideas. There are some flag-wavers who claim a monopoly of patriotism and think that it means "not getting entangled" with the outside world. Next to them are those who would like to reserve the course altogether. That kind of patriotism is nothing but a self-serving pursuit of one's own interests.

Clearly, as the Soviet Union proceeds with *perestroika*, its contribution to building a new world will become more constructive and significant. What we have done on the basis of new thinking has made it possible to channel international cooperation along new, peaceful lines. Over these years we have come a long way in the general political cooperation with the West. It stood a difficult test at a time of momentous change in Eastern Europe and of the search for a solution to the German problem. It has withstood the crushing stress of the crisis in the Persian Gulf. There is no doubt that this cooperation, which all of us need, will become more effective and indispensable if our economies become more integrated and start working more or less in synchronised rhythm.

To me, it is self-evident that if Soviet *perestroika* succeeds, there will be a real chance of building a new world order. And if *perestroika* fails, the prospect of entering a new peaceful period in history will vanish, at least for the foreseeable future.

I believe that the movement that we have launched towards that goal has fairly good prospects of success. After all, mankind has already benefited greatly in recent years, and this has created a certain positive momentum.

The Cold War is over. The risk of a global nuclear war has practically disappeared. The Iron Curtain is gone. Germany has united, which is a momentous milestone in the history of Europe. There is not a single country on our continent which would not regard itself as fully sovereign and independent.

The USSR and the USA, the two nuclear superpowers, have moved from confrontation to interaction and, in some important cases, partnership. This has had a decisive effect on the entire international climate. This should be preserved and filled with new substance. The climate of Soviet-US trust should be protected, for it is a common asset of the world community. Any revision of the direction and potential of the Soviet-US relationship would have grave consequences for the entire global process.

The ideas of the Helsinki Final Act have begun to acquire real significance, they are being transformed into real policies and have found a more specific and topical expression in the Charter of Paris for a New Europe.[5] Institutional forms of European security are beginning to take shape.

Real disarmament has begun. Its first phase is nearing completion, and following the signing, I hope shortly, of the START Treaty,[6] the time will come to give practical consideration to the ideas which have already been put forward for the future. There seems, however, to be a need to develop a general concept for this new phase, which would embrace all negotiations concerning the principal components of the problem of disarmament and new ideas reflecting the changes in Europe, the Middle East, Africa and Asia, a concept that would incorporate recent major initiatives of President Bush and President Mitterand.[7] We are now thinking about it.

Armed forces and military budgets are being reduced. Foreign troops are leaving the territories of other countries. Their strength is diminishing and their composition is becoming more defense-oriented. First steps have been taken in the conversion of military industries, and what seemed inconceivable is happening: recent Cold War adversaries are establishing cooperation in this area. Their military officials exchange visits, show each other military facilities that only recently used to be top secret and together consider ways to achieve demilitarisation.

The information environment has changed beyond recognition throughout Europe and in most of the world, and with it, the scale and intensity and the psychological atmosphere of communication among people of various countries.

De-ideologising relations among States, which we proclaimed as one of the principles of the new thinking, has brought down many prejudices, biased attitudes and suspicions and has cleared and improved the international atmosphere. I have to note, however, that this process has been more intensive and frank on our part than on the part of the West.

I dare say that the European process has already acquired elements of irreversibility, or at least that conflicts of a scale and nature that were typical of Europe for many centuries and particularly in the twentieth century have been ruled out.

Should it gain the necessary momentum, every nation and every country will have at their disposal in the foreseeable future the potential of a community of unprecedented strength, encompassing the entire upper tier of the globe, provided they make their own contribution.

In such a context, in the process of creating a new Europe, in which erstwhile "curtains" and "walls" will be forever relegated to the past and borders between States will lose their "divisive" purpose, self-determination of sovereign nations will be realised in a completely different way.

However, our vision of the European space from the Atlantic to the Urals is not that of a closed system. Since it includes the Soviet Union, which reaches to the shores of the Pacific, and the transatlantic USA and Canada with inseparable links to the Old World, it goes beyond its nominal geographical boundaries.

The idea is not at all to consolidate a part of our civilisation on, so to say, a European platform versus the rest of the world. Suspicions of that kind do exist. But, on the contrary, the idea is to develop and build upon the momentum of integration in Europe, embodied politically in the Charter of Paris for the whole of Europe. This should be done in the context of common movement towards a new and peaceful period in world history, towards new interrelationship and integrity of mankind. As my friend Giulio Andreotti[8] so aptly remarked recently in Moscow, "East-West rapprochement alone is not enough for progress of the entire world towards peace. However, agreement between them is a great contribution to the common cause". Asia, Africa, Latin America, the Near and Middle East, all of them, are to play a great role in this common cause whose prospects are difficult to forecast today.

The new integrity of the world, in our view, can be built only on the principles of the freedom of choice and balance of interests. Every State, and now also a number of existing or emerging regional interstate groups, have their own interests. They are all equal and deserve respect.

We consider it dangerously outdated when suspicions are aroused by, for instance, improved Soviet-Chinese or Soviet-German, German-French, Soviet-US or US-Indian relations, etc. In our times, good relations benefit all. Any worsening of relations anywhere is a common loss.

Progress towards the civilisation of the 21st century will certainly not be simple or easy. One cannot get rid overnight of the heavy legacy of the past or the dangers created in the post-war years. We are experiencing a turning point in international affairs and are only at the beginning of a new, and I hope mostly peaceful, lengthy period in the history of civilisation.

With less East-West confrontation, or even none at all, old contradictions resurface, which seemed of secondary importance compared to the threat of nuclear war. The melting ice of the Cold War reveals old conflicts and claims, and entirely new problems accumulate rapidly.

We can already see many obstacles and dangers on the road to a lasting peace, including:

— Increased nationalism, separatism, and disintegrational processes in a number of countries and regions;
— The growing gap in the level and quality of socio-economic development between "rich" and "poor" countries; dire consequences of the poverty of hundreds of millions of people, to whom informational transparency makes it possible to see how people live in developed countries. Hence, the unprecedented passions and brutality and even fanaticism of mass protests. Poverty is also the breeding ground for the spread of terrorism and the emergence and persistence of dictatorial regimes with their unpredictable behavior in relations among States;
— The dangerously rapid accumulation of the "costs" of previous forms of progress, such as the threat of environmental catastrophe and of the depletion of energy and primary resources, uncontrollable overpopulation, pandemics, drug abuse, and so on;
— The gap between basically peaceful policies and selfish economies bent on achieving a kind of "technological hegemony". Unless those two vectors are brought together, civilisation will tend to break down into incompatible sectors;
— Further improvements in modern weaponry, even if under the pretext of strengthening security. This may result not only in a new spiral of the arms race and a perilous overabundance of arms in many States, but also in a final divorce between the process of disarmament and development, and, what is more, in an erosion of the foundations and criteria of the emerging new world politics.

How can the world community cope with all this? All these tasks are enormously complex. They cannot be postponed. Tomorrow may be too late.

I am convinced that in order to solve these problems there is no other way but to seek and implement entirely new forms of interaction. We are simply doomed to such interaction, or we shall be unable to consolidate positive trends which have emerged and are gaining strength, and which we simply must not sacrifice.

However, to accomplish this all members of the world community should resolutely discard old stereotypes and motivations nurtured by the Cold War, and give up the habit of seeking each other's weak spots and exploiting them in their own interests. We have to respect the peculiarities and differences which will always exist, even when human rights and freedoms are observed throughout the world. I keep repeating that with the end of confrontation differences can be made a source of healthy competition, an important factor for progress. This is an incentive to study each other, to engage in exchanges, a prerequisite for the growth of mutual trust.

For knowledge and trust are the foundations of a new world order. Hence the necessity, in my view, to learn to forecast the course of events in various regions of the globe, by pooling the efforts of scientists, philosophers and humanitarian thinkers within the UN framework. Policies, even the most prudent and precise, are made by man. We need maximum insurance to guarantee that decisions taken by members of the world community should not affect the security, sovereignty and vital interests of its other members or damage the natural evironment and the moral climate of the world.

I am an optimist and I believe that together we shall be able now to make the right historical choice so as not to miss the great chance at the turn of centuries and millenia and make the current extremely difficult transition to a peaceful world order. A balance of interests rather than a balance of power, a search for compromise and concord rather than a search for advantages at other people's expense, and respect for equality rather than claims to leadership — such are the elements which can provide the groundwork for world progress and which should be readily acceptable for reasonable people informed by the experience of the twentieth century.

The future prospect of truly peaceful global politics lies in the creation through joint efforts of a single international democratic space in which States shall be guided by the priority of human rights and welfare for their own citizens and the promotion of the same rights and similar welfare elsewhere. This is an imperative of the growing integrity of the modern world and of the interdependence of its components.

I have been suspected of utopian thinking more than once, and particularly when five years ago I proposed the elimination of nuclear weapons by the year 2000 and joint efforts to create a system of international security. It may well be that by that date it will not have happened. But look, merely five years have passed and have we not actually and noticeably moved in that direction? Have we not been able to cross the threshold of mistrust, though mistrust has not completely disappeared? Has not the political thinking in the world changed substantially? Does not most of the world community already regard weapons of mass destruction as unacceptable for achieving political objectives?

Ladies and gentlemen, two weeks from today it will be exactly fifty years since the beginning of the Nazi invasion of my country. And in another six months we shall mark fifty years since Pearl Harbor, after which the war turned into a global tragedy.[9] Memories of it still hurt. But they also urge us to value the chance given to the present generations.